THIS DATE
IN

BALTIMORE

ORIOLES

&

ST. LOUIS BROWNS
HISTORY

THIS DATE
IN

BALTIMORE
ORIOLES
&
ST. LOUIS BROWNS
HISTORY

John C. Hawkins

SB

A SCARBOROUGH BOOK
STEIN AND DAY / *Publishers* / New York

First published in 1983
Copyright © 1982 by John C. Hawkins
All rights reserved
Designed by Louis A. Ditizio
Printed in the United States of America
STEIN AND DAY/*Publishers*
Scarborough House
Briarcliff Manor, N.Y. 10510

Library of Congress Cataloging in Publication Data

Hawkins, John C.
   This date in Baltimore Orioles/St. Louis Browns history.

   "A day-by-day listing of the events in the history
of the Browns and Orioles baseball teams."
   "A Scarborough book."
   1. Baltimore Orioles (Baseball team)—History.
2. St. Louis Browns (Baseball team)—History.   I. Title.
GV875.B2H38   1983   796.357'64'097526   81-40805
ISBN 0-8128-6131-0 (pbk.)   AACR2

This book is lovingly dedicated to
the two leading ladies in my life:

Dottie, the best wife a man could ever ask
for and the best friend anyone could ever
hope for;

Mary Julia, a daughter who fills each day
with love, laughter, joy, and hope for even
brighter days.

ACKNOWLEDGMENTS

The author of any book always feels a great debt of gratitude to numerous individuals who aid him along the way. To all, I offer a sincere thank you. In addition, a special word of thanks goes to—

David McIntosh, an intern with the Baltimore Orioles who proved helpful in obtaining research materials and photographs;

fellow author Bill Borst, whose book, *Last in the American League,* was a valuable research tool and recommended reading for everyone;

the Society for American Baseball Research, of which I am a member, and the valuable information provided by its members in its journals;

Stein and Day Publishers, and editor Benton Arnovitz, for their patience in letting this project be completed under trying circumstances;

my nephews, Geoffrey and Bill Hawkins, two devoted Orioles fans who constantly gave encouragement.

CONTENTS

Photos between pages 130 and 131

THIS DATE

IN

HISTORY

INTRODUCTION

Anytime you undertake to combine the sagas of two disparate sports teams like the Browns and Orioles you run the risk of alienating fans of both. After all, the hot-running Orioles probably don't like to be reminded of their humble origins. And by the same token, the Brownie cultists most likely view the modern Orioles as too efficient and machine-like and not at all like their lovable bumblers.

The fact remains that in this era of emphasis on roots and history, you can no longer view the two as separate entities. For out of that long history of hapless Brown baseball has grown a powerhouse that rivals the always-hated Yankees. Today's Orioles are simply evening the score for years and years of Yankee dominance. Indeed, the Oriole record during the decade of the Seventies goes a long way toward soothing the pain of the great 1922 Brown drive that came up short.

So dear reader, whether you are an Oriole or Brown fan, I hope you come away from this book with a new perspective about your team and a renewed interest in baseball history. For the Browns, today's Orioles represent a long-deserved triumph over the forces of evil; for the O's, the Browns are a reminder that baseball runs in cycles, and that those who go up also must endure those years when they go down.

For both, take the pledge now that the Birds will always be your ball club, whether up in first or down in last. Go Birds!

CALENDAR SECTION

The following chronological table lists Browns/Orioles players of the past and present by their birthdates. Following each name is a symbol indicating the position the individual played: P = pitcher, C = catcher, 1B = first base, 2B = second base, 3B = third base, SS = shortstop, IF = infield, OF = outfield, DH = designated hitter, PH = pinch-hitter, and MGR = manager. Following these symbols are the years each played with the Browns or Orioles or both. For the 1954 season the franchise moved from St. Louis to Baltimore, where it has remained since.

Just as important, highlights of Browns and Orioles history are also recorded here by date.

JANUARY

January 1

1874 — Ned Garvin (P 1901)

1876 — Joe Martin (OF–2B–3B 1903)

1904 — Ethan Allen (OF 1937-38)

1931 — Foster Castleman (SS–3B–2B–OF 1958)

January 2

1892 — George Boehler (P 1920-21)

1907 — Ted Gullic (OF–3B–1B 1930, 1933)

      Red Kress (SS–3B–OF–1B 1927-32, 1938-39)

1951 — Royle Stillman (SS–OF–1B–DH 1975-76)

January 3

1902 — Jim McLaughlin (3B 1932)

1950 — Jim Dwyer (OF–DH–1B 1981-present)

3

January 4

1877 — Bob Spade (P 1910)

1903 — Alex Metzler (OF 1930)

January 5

1901 — Luke Sewell (C 1942, MGR 1941-46)

1914 — Joe Grace (OF-C 1938-41, 1946)

1918 — Jack Kramer (P 1939-41, 1943-47)

1924 — Freddie Marsh (3B-SS-2B 1951-52, 1955-56)

January 6

1903 — George Grant (P 1923-25)

1912 — Hal Warnock (OF 1935)

1915 — Tom Ferrick (P 1946, 1949-50)

1934 — Lenny Green (OF 1957-59, 1964)

1978 — The Orioles release reserve catcher Ken Rudolph after he appears in just 11 games during the 1977 season.

January 7

1890 — Grover Baichley (P 1914)

1905 — Frank Grube (C 1934-35, 1941)

1950 — Ross Grimsley (P 1974-77, present)

January 8

1927 — Jim Busby (OF-3B 1957-58, 1960-61)

1933 — Willie Tasby (OF 1958-60)

January 9

1887 — Harry Hoch (P 1914-15)

1895 — Bill Lee (OF-3B 1915-16)

1935 — Fred Valentine (OF 1959, 1963, 1968)

January 10

1888 — Del Pratt (2B-SS-1B-OF-3B 1912-17)

1898 — Ed Stauffer (P 1925)

4

January 11

1899 — Alvin (General) Crowder (P 1927-30)

1911 — Roy Hughes (2B-3B-SS 1938-39)

1922 — Neil Berry (3B-2B-SS 1953-54)

1928 — Carl Powis (OF 1957)

January 12

1945 — Paul Gilliford (P 1967)

January 13

1888 — Luther Bonin (PH 1913)

1901 — Fred Schulte (OF-1B 1927-32)

January 14

1891 — John Shovlin (2B-SS 1919-20)

1963 — In a key off-season deal, the Birds send pitcher Hoyt Wilhelm, shortstop Ron Hansen, third baseman Pete Ward, and outfielder Dave Nicholson to the White Sox for shortstop Luis Aparicio and outfielder/third baseman Al Smith. The trade benefits both clubs. but the acquisition of Aparicio eventually pays off in the Orioles' first pennant in 1966 as Little Looie proves a key performer.

January 15

1882 — Ed Kinsella (P 1910)

1885 — Grover Lowdermilk (P 1915, 1917-19)

1949 — Bobby Grich (2B-SS-1B-3B 1970-76)

January 16

1880 — Jim Murray (OF 1911)

1885 — Joe Kutina (P-1B-OF 1911-12)

1886 — Ollie Moulton (2B 1911)

1899 — George (Showboat) Fisher (OF 1932)

1911 — Hank McDonald (P 1933)

Dizzy Dean (P 1947)

January 17

1889 — Pete Johns (1B-OF-SS-3B-2B 1918)

January 17 (continued)

1915 — Luman Harris (MGR 1961)

1925 — Hank Schmulbach (PR 1943)

Jehosie Heard (P 1954)

1933 — J. W. Porter (OF-3B 1952)

1935 — Dick Brown (C 1963-65)

1937 — The Browns obtain shortstop Bill Knickerbocker, outfielder Joe Vosmik, and pitcher Oral Hildebrand from Cleveland for shortstop Lyn Lary, outfielder Moose Solters, and pitcher Ivy Andrews. The Tribe gets the better of the deal as Solters belts 20 homers and Lary hits .290.

1979 — Pitcher Nelson Briles no longer makes an impression and is released by the O's.

January 18

1932 — Mike Fornieles (P 1956-57)

1941 — Mickey McGuire (SS-2B 1962, 1967)

1954 — Scott McGregor (P 1976-present)

January 19

1906 — Rip Radcliff (OF-1B 1940-41)

1972 — The Orioles sell reliever Fred Beene to the Yankees.

January 20

1888 — Bill James (P 1914-15)

1891 — Earl Smith (OF-3B 1917-21)

1905 — Ike Danning (C 1928)

1907 — Herm Holshauser (P 1930)

1933 — Gene Stephens (OF 1960-61)

1945 — Dave Boswell (P 1971)

1969 — The Birds deal outfielder Ron Stone to the Phillies for catcher Clay Dalrymple. Dalrymple serves as a valuable reserve catcher for the next three seasons.

1977 — The Orioles obtain outfielders Elliott Maddox and Rick Bladt from the

Yankees for outfielder Paul Blair. Ever the pro, Blair gives the Bronx Bombers top utility play in their '77 and '78 championship seasons.

January 21

1873 — Francis Donahue (P 1902-3)

1876 — Irv Waldron (OF 1901)

1892 — Bernie Boland (P 1921)

1899 — Ollie Voigt (P 1924)

1918 — In a blockbuster deal, the Browns send second baseman Del Pratt, pitcher Eddie Plank, and $15,000 to the Yankees for catcher Les Nunamaker, second baseman Joe Gedeon, third baseman Fritz Maisel, and pitchers Urban Shocker and Nick Cullop. Plank elects to retire and never reports to New York. Gedeon becomes a mainstay at second and Shocker develops into one of the league's premier hurlers.

1923 — Sam Mele (OF 1954)

1946 — Johnny Oates (C 1970, 1972)

1947 — Bob Reynolds (P 1972-75)

January 22

1877 — Tom Jones (1B-2B-OF 1904-9)

1925 — Bobby Young (2B 1951-55)

1942 — Dave Leonhard (P 1967-72)

January 23

1887 — Mack Allison (P 1911-13)

1896 — Billy Mullen (3B 1920-21, 1928)

1928 — Chico Carrasquel (SS-2B-3B-1B 1959)

January 24

1916 — Clem Dreisewerd (P 1948)

1917 — Walter Judnich (OF-1B 1940-42, 1946-47)

1953 — Tim Stoddard (P 1978-present)

1961 — The Birds obtain outfielders Russ Snyder and Whitey Herzog and a player to be named from Kansas City for catcher Clint Courtney, first baseman Bob Boyd, infielder Wayne Causey, outfielder Al Pilarcik, and pitcher Jim Archer. On April 15, 1961, Courtney is returned to Baltimore to complete the deal.

January 25

1876 — Fred Glade (P 1904-7)

1891 — George Lyons (P 1924)

1896 — Ray Schmandt (1B 1915)

1945 — Wally Bunker (P 1963-68)

January 26

1877 — Ben Koehler (OF-2B-1B-SS-3B 1905-6)

1884 — Edward Spencer (C 1905-8)

1904 — George Blaeholder (P 1925, 1927-35)

1927 — Bob Nieman (OF 1951-52, 1956-59)

January 27

1896 — Milt Gaston (P 1925-27)

1909 — Former Red Sox catcher Lou Criger sends an open telegram to the Boston fans expressing his great disappointment over his trade to St. Louis.

1947 — John Lowenstein (OF-DH-1B-3B 1979-present)

January 28

1906 — Lyn Lary (SS-2B 1935-36, 1940)

1916 — Bob Muncrief (P 1937, 1939, 1941-47)

1922 — Hank (Bow Wow) Arft (1B 1948-52)

1982 — The Orioles trade third baseman Doug DeCinces and reliever Jeff Schneider to the Angels for outfielder Dan Ford. The club discounts speculation that DeCinces's union activities played a role in the deal. Instead, team officials note the need for a hard-hitting outfielder and the move of Cal Ripken, Jr., to third base.

January 29

1904 — Ray Hayworth (C 1944)

1919 — Hank Edwards (OF 1953)

January 30

1889 — Henry Shanley (SS 1912)

1923 — Walt Dropo (1B-3B 1959-61)

1943 — Dave Johnson (2B-SS-3B 1965-72)

1979 — Baltimore re-signs flyhawk Al Bumbry to avoid losing him through free agency.

January 31

1891 — Tim Hendryx (OF 1918)

1896 — William (Pinky) Hargrave (C 1925-26)

1897 — Charlie Robertson (P 1926)

1914 — Mel Mazzera (OF 1935, 1937-39)

1918 — Sid Peterson (P 1943)

FEBRUARY

February 1

1903 — Carl Reynolds (OF 1933)

1921 — Dave Madison (P 1952)

1944 — Paul Blair (OF-3B-DH-1B 1964-76)

1961 — The O's purchase outfielder Chuck Essegian from the Dodgers' AAA Spokane team.

1973 — Baltimore sells outfielder Don Buford to the Fukuoka Lions in Japan.

February 2

1884 — Ray Demmitt (OF 1910, 1917-19)

1885 — Bill Abstein (1B 1910)

1892 — Dave Davenport (P 1916-19)

1901 — Otto Miller (SS-3B 1927)

1937 — Don Buford (OF-2B-3B 1968-72)

February 3

1918 — Sid Schacht (P 1950-51)

1922 — Jim Dyck (OF-3B 1951-53, 1955-56)

1925 — Harry Byrd (P 1955)

February 4

1889 — Horace Leverette (P 1920)

February 5

1923 — Chuck Diering (OF-3B-SS 1954-56)

1954 — The Birds acquire infielder Connie Berry and outfielder Sam Mele from the White Sox for second baseman John Lipon and outfielder Johnny Groth. Chicago gets the better of the deal as Groth takes over center field for the Chisox.

February 6

1872 — Lou Criger (C 1909, 1912)

1880 — Frank La Porte (2B-OF-3B 1911-12)

1926 — Dale Long (1B-OF 1951)

The Brownies acquire catcher Wally Schang from the Yankees for pitcher George Mogridge and cash. Although 37, Schang takes over the Browns' catching job for the next three seasons.

February 7

1913 — Mel Almada (OF 1938-39)

1928 — Al Smith (OF 1963)

1951 — Benny Ayala (OF-DH 1979-present)

February 8

1911 — Don Heffner (2B-SS-1B 1938-43)

1921 — Walter (Hoot) Evers (OF 1955-56)

1927 — The Browns trade outfielder Cedric Durst and pitcher Joe Giard to the Yankees for pitcher Sad Sam Jones. In his only season with St. Louis, Jones wins just eight and loses 14.

1940 — St. Louis purchases pitcher Eldon Auker from the Red Sox. Auker becomes the ace of the staff for the next three seasons, winning a total of 44 games.

February 9

1897 — Adrian Lynch (P 1920)

1903 — Roy Mahaffey (P 1936)

1925 — Vic Wertz (OF 1952-54)

1928 — Erv Palica (P 1955-56)

February 10

1899 — Bill Whaley (OF 1923)

1933 — Billy (Digger) O'Dell (P 1954, 1956-59)

1982 — The O's obtain pitcher Paul Moskau from Cincinnati for a player to be named. He fails to impress the Birds and is cut during spring training.

February 11

1882 — Ray Boyd (P 1910)

February 12

1889 — Ned Crompton (OF 1909)

1895 — Tom Rogers (P 1917-19)

1939 — Jerry Walker (P 1957-60)

1942 — Pat Dobson (P 1971-72)

1951 — Don Stanhouse (P 1978-79, present)

1976 — The Orioles release designated hitter Tommy Davis after three productive seasons. He then signs with the New York Yankees, who in turn release him before the season opens.

February 13

1876 — Fritz Buelow (C 1907)

1885 — Howard Vahrenhorst (PH 1904)

1888 — Eddie Foster (3B-2B 1922-23)

1909 — George Bell (P 1939)

1926 — Bob Habenicht (P 1953)

1927 — Jim Brideweser (SS-2B-3B 1954, 1957)

February 14

1952 — St. Louis trades catcher Matt Batts, first baseman Ben Taylor, outfielder Cliff Mapes, and pitcher Dick Littlefield to the Tigers for first baseman Dick Kryhoski and pitchers Gene Bearden and Bob Cain. The Brownies get the better of the deal as Kryhoski becomes the starting first sacker and Cain and Bearden join the starting rotation.

1959 — The Birds purchase first baseman/outfielder Whitey Lockman from San Francisco.

February 15

1886 — Ed Kusel (P 1909)

1898 — Bobby La Motte (SS-3B 1925-26)

1904 — Oscar Estrada (P 1929)

1938 — Chuck Estrada (P 1960-64)

The Brownies obtain infielder Don Heffner and cash from the Yankees for infielder Bill Knickerbocker. Heffner becomes an infield fixture for the next four seasons.

1982 — The Birds send infielder Wayne Krenchicki to the Reds to complete the deal for hurler Paul Moskau.

February 16

1947 — Terry Crowley (OF-1B-DH 1969-73, 1976-present)

February 17

1890 — Rivington Bisland (SS 1913)

1924 — Bill Sommers (3B-2B 1950)

1934 — Willie Kirkland (OF 1964)

February 18

1889 — George Mogridge (P 1925)

1925 — Joe Lutz (1B 1951)

1954 — The Orioles deal sore-armed outfielder Roy Sievers to Washington for outfielder Gil Coan just two months before opening their first season in Baltimore. Sievers goes on to become a top slugger for the Senators while Coan spends an undistinguished season-and-a-half with the Birds.

February 19

1957 — Sammy Stewart (P 1978-present)

February 20

1896 — Herold (Muddy) Ruel (C 1915, 1933; MGR 1947)

1920 — Frankie Gustine (3B 1950)

1922 — Jim Wilson (P 1948, 1955-56)

February 21

1879 — Ed Smith (P 1906)

1907 — Roy Hansen (P 1935)

1945 — Tom Shopay (OF-C-DH 1971-72, 1975-77)

1978 — The O's release first baseman Tony Muser.

February 22

1919 — Johnny Lucadello (2B-3B-SS-OF 1938-41, 1946)

1929 — Ryne Duren (P 1954)

1930 — Karl Drews (P 1948-49)

1939 — Steve Barber (P 1960-67)

February 23

1890 — John Black (1B 1911)

1958 — John Shelby (OF 1981)

February 24

1911 — Gerard Lipscomb (2B-P-3B 1937)

1956 — Eddie Murray (1B-DH-OF-3B 1977-present)

February 25

1908 — Al Hollingsworth (P 1942-46)

1941 — Dave Vineyard (P 1964)

1975 — The Birds obtain catcher Dave Duncan and outfielder Alvin McGrew from Cleveland for first baseman Boog Powell and pitcher Don Hood. An Oriole crowd favorite, Powell enjoys one more good season, banging out 27 homers for the Indians and their manager Frank Robinson, Powell's former teammate.

February 26

1896 — Harry Collins (P 1929-31)

1923 — Frank Raney (P 1949-50)

February 27

1886 — Walter Moser (P 1911)

1937 — Carl Warwick (OF 1965)

February 28

1896 — Homer Ezzell (3B-2B 1923)

1928 — Dick Kokos (OF 1948-50, 1953-54)

1929 — Ed Albrecht (P 1949-50)

1943 — Bob Oliver (1B-DH 1974)

1958 — Dallas Williams (OF 1981)

MARCH

March 1

1921 — Howie Fox (P 1954)

1928 — Bert Hamric (PH 1958)

1940 — Larry Brown (3B-2B 1973)

March 2

1907 — Jack Knott (P 1933-38)

1921 — Dick Starr (P 1949-51)

1924 — Cal Abrams (OF-1B 1954-55)

March 3

1867 — Jack O'Connor (C 1904, 1906-7, 1910, MGR 1910)

1946 — The Brownies sign outfielder Joe Medwick, who had been released by the Boston Braves. He is released a month later before ever playing a regular season game with St. Louis.

1950 — Jesse Jefferson (P 1973-75)

March 4

1888 — Edward Peffer (P 1911)

1926 — Cass Michaels (3B-2B 1952)

1936 — Bob Johnson (2B-SS-1B-3B-OF 1963-67)

1939 — Jack Fisher (P 1959-62)

1952 — The Browns sell pitcher Jim Suchecki to Pittsburgh.

March 5

1891 — Walt Alexander (C 1912-13, 1915)

1896 — Bernie Hungling (C 1930)

1897 — Lu Blue (1B 1928-30)

　　　Fred (Cactus) Johnson (P 1938-39)

1915 — Stan Ferens (P 1942, 1946)

March 6

1915 — Bob Swift (C 1940-42)

1917 — Pete Gray (OF 1945)

March 7

1890 — Dave Danforth (P 1922-25)

1914 — Joe Gallagher (OF 1939-40)

1924 — Alva (Bobo) Holloman (P 1953)

March 8

1934 — Marv Breeding (2B-SS-3B 1960-62)

March 9

1890 — Rolla Mapel (P 1919)

1908 — Myril Hoag (OF-P 1939-41)

March 10

1880 — Danny Hoffman (OF 1908-11)

1921 — George Elder (OF 1949)

1929 — John (Bud) Thomas (SS 1951)

March 11

Nothing of significance happened on this date.

March 12

1884 — Pat Hynes (OF–P 1904)

1885 — Dode Criss (P–1B–OF 1908–11)

1892 — George Maisel (OF 1913)

1931 — Chuck Oertel (OF 1958)

1936 — Ray (Buddy) Barker (OF 1960)

March 13

1899 — Otis Brannan (2B 1928–29)

1909 — Harry Kimberlin (P 1936–39)

1918 — Eddie Pellagrini (SS 1948–49)

1920 — Frank Biscan (P 1942, 1946, 1948)

1922 — Cliff Mapes (OF 1951)

March 14

1885 — Walt Devoy (OF–1B 1909)

1900 — Marty McManus (2B–3B–1B–SS–OF 1920–26)

1921 — Bill (Lefty) Kennedy (P 1948–51)

March 15

1876 — Bill Hallman (OF 1901)

1902 — Fred Bennett (OF 1928)

March 16

1910 — Bob Poser (P 1935)

1927 — Clint (Scrap Iron) Courtney (C 1954, 1960–61)

1930 — Hobie Landrith (C 1962–63)

1953 — Owner Bill Veeck's bid to move the team from St. Louis to Baltimore is rejected by the other American League owners. They cite the short time before the opening of the season as the reason for denial.

1954 — The Birds acquire first baseman Eddie Waitkus from the Phillies. He splits the first base job with Dick Kryhoski in the first Oriole season before going back to Philadelphia in 1955.

March 17

1869 — George Hogriever (OF 1901)

1895 — Lyman Lamb (3B-OF-2B 1920-21)

1899 — Charlie Root (P 1923)

March 18

1888 — Wiley Taylor (P 1913-14)

1890 — Tommy Mee (SS-3B-2B 1910)

1919 — Hal White (P 1953)

1926 — Dick Littlefield (P 1952-54)

1953 — Randy Miller (P 1977)

March 19

1874 — LeRoy Evans (P 1903)

1884 — Bobby Messenger (OF 1914)

March 20

1907 — Vern Kennedy (P 1939-41)

1915 — Stan Spence (OF-1B 1949)

1925 — Al Widmar (P 1948, 1950-51)

1928 — Rufus Crawford (OF 1952)

March 21

1927 — Owen Friend (2B-3B-SS 1949-50)

1936 — The Browns obtain first baseman Sunny Jim Bottomley from Cincinnati for infielder John Burnett. After a strong season as a starter in 1936, Bottomley is named the team's manager midway through 1937.

1939 — Tommy Davis (DH-OF-1B 1972-75)

March 22

1906 — Julius (Moose) Solters (OF 1935-36, 1939)

1909 — Ed Cole (P 1938-39)

1926 — Billy Goodman (3B-OF-1B-2B-SS 1957)

1978 — The Orioles release pitcher Tommy Moore.

17

March 23

1886 — Clyde Wares (SS-2B 1913-14)

1939 — Sam Bowens (OF 1963-67)

1943 — Bruce Howard (P 1968)

       Lee May (1B-DH 1975-80)

March 24

1893 — George Sisler (1B-OF-P-3B-2B 1915-22, 1924-27; MGR 1924-26)

1925 — Dick Kryhoski (1B 1952-54)

1965 — The O's sell outfielder John Jeter to Pittsburgh.

March 25

1932 — Woodie Held (2B-OF-3B-SS 1966-67)

1953 — The Browns sign outfielder-third baseman Bob Elliott as a free agent. He plays just 48 games with St. Louis before moving on to the White Sox in a trade.

1972 — The Birds obtain reliever Bob Reynolds from the Brewers as the player to be named for Curt Motton. Reynolds proves an effective bullpen artist for Baltimore in 1973 and 1974.

March 26

1874 — Gene De Montreville (2B 1904)

1879 — Charlie Moran (3B-2B-OF 1904-5)

1914 — Hal Epps (OF 1943-44)

1979 — The O's remove catcher Elrod Hendricks from the active list and name him a full-time coach.

March 27

1891 — Bill Rumler (C-OF 1914, 1916-17)

1895 — Bill Burwell (P 1920-21)

1910 — Steve Sundra (P 1942-44, 1946)

March 28

1875 — Harry Gleason (3B-SS-2B-OF 1904-5)

1890 — Johnny Johnston (OF 1913)

1920 — Boris Martin (OF-1B-C 1944-46, 1953)

March 29

1908 — Bill Strickland (P 1937)

1978 — In a wholly uncharacteristically poor judging of talent, the Orioles release reliever Ed Farmer. Farmer ultimately surfaces again as a top reliever for the White Sox.

March 30

1885 — Herman (Dutch) Bronkie (3B-2B-1B 1919, 1922)

March 31

1920 — Dave Koslo (P 1954)

1969 — The Orioles trade pitcher Gene Brabender and infielder Gordon Lund to the expansion Seattle Pilots for utility man Chico Salmon. Chico proves a valuable sub in three pennant-winning seasons (1969-71)

APRIL

April 1

1876 — Bill Friel (2B-3B-1B-SS-C-P 1902-3)

1889 — Tom Phillips (P 1915)

1912 — Jake Wade (P 1939)

1914 — George Bradley (OF 1946)

1915 — Jeff Heath (OF 1946-47)

1958 — Baltimore trades outfielder Larry Doby and pitcher Don Ferrarese to Cleveland for outfielders Gene Woodling and Dick Williams and pitcher Bud Daley. The Birds get the better of the deal as Williams proves a valuable reserve and Woodling enjoys three productive seasons, including a .300 year in 1959.

1959 — The O's trade pitcher Billy Loes to Washington for hurler Vito Valentinetti. The deal is voided a week later because of Loes' sore arm.

1981 — The Birds deal shortstop Kiko Garcia to the Astros in exchange for minor league outfielder Chris Bourjos.

1982 — Baltimore trades first baseman Eddie Murray, third baseman Cal Ripken, and outfielder Ken Singleton to San Diego for pitchers Rick Wise and John Curtis, catcher Steve Swisher, and outfielder Dave Edwards. General manager Hank Peters cites the need to return to the traditions established for the franchise in St. Louis. (April Fool, folks!)

April 2

1878 — Jack Harper (P 1902)

Ed Siever (P 1903-4)

1895 — Earl Pruess (OF 1920)

1924 — Bobby Avila (OF-2B-3B 1959)

1930 — Art Ceccarelli (P 1957)

Gordon Jones (P 1960-61)

1972 — The Birds release pitcher Dave Boswell.

1976 — In a blockbuster deal with Oakland's Charlie Finley, Baltimore obtains outfielder Reggie Jackson and pitchers Ken Holtzman and Bill Van Bommel in exchange for outfielder Don Baylor and pitchers Mike Torrez and Paul Mitchell. The deal does not produce big dividends for either club. Both Jackson and Baylor leave their respective clubs after one year via free agency.

April 3

1879 — John Frill (P 1912)

1886 — Bert Graham (1B-2B 1910)

1980 — The Orioles release second baseman Billy Smith. Signed as a free agent before the 1977 season, Smith proved a valuable addition as he started at second that first year and provided infield depth the next two.

April 4

1910 — Joe Vosmik (OF 1937)

1942 — Eddie Watt (P 1966-73)

1943 — Mike Epstein (1B 1966-67)

Tom Fisher (P 1967)

1978 — The O's sell pitcher Andy Replogle to the Milwaukee Brewers.

1979 — Baltimore obtains outfielder Benny Ayala from the Cardinals' organization for outfielder Mike Dimmel. Ayala has developed into a steady reserve in the outfield and at the plate.

April 5

1876 — Bill Dinneen (P 1907-9)

1907 — Merritt Cain (P 1935-36)

1921 — Bobby Hogue (P 1951-52)

1931 — Fred Besana (P 1956)

1937 — Roger Marquis (OF 1955)

1938 — Ron Hansen (SS-2B 1958-62)

1946 — The Browns release outfielder Joe Medwick.

1971 — In a minor deal, the Birds send pitcher Marcelino Lopez to Milwaukee for pitcher Roric Harrison and outfielder Marion Jackson.

1973 — The O's trade reserve infielder Tom Matchick to the Yankees for shortstop Frank Baker.

April 6

1973 — The Orioles open their 20th season with a 10-0 win over the Brewers as Dave McNally hurls a three-hitter. Batting stars are Don Baylor, with three doubles, a homer, and three RBIs, and Brooks Robinson, who has two homers and four RBIs.

April 7

1879 — Art Weaver (C 1905)

1905 — Joe Hassler (SS 1930)

1907 — Oral Hildebrand (P 1937-38)

1942 — Tom Phoebus (P 1966-70)

1952 — The Brownies obtain pitcher Dave (The Squeakin' Deacon) Madison from the Yankees on waivers. Madison pitches in 31 games for St. Louis before being shipped on to Detroit.

April 8

1888 — Ralph Myers (1B 1911)

1916 — St. Louis sells outfielder Tilly Walker to the Red Sox. He becomes a starter in center field for the pennant-bound Beantowners and hits .266 for the season.

1921 — Dee Sanders (P 1945)

1935 — Dick Luebke (P 1962)

April 9

1870 — Ollie Pickering (OF 1907)

1890 — Joe Willis (P 1911)

April 9 (continued)

1905 — Earl Caldwell (P 1935-37)

1953 — In an effort to stay afloat financially, the Browns sell Sportsman's Park to the Cardinals for $800,000. The park is renamed Busch Stadium and the former owners become tenants.

1970 — Don Buford becomes the first Oriole to hit home runs from each side of the plate in one game.

1976 — The O's sign free agent first baseman Tommy Harper. At age 35 and with his once-considerable skills diminished, Harper ends his career with a .234 year in Baltimore.

April 10

1898 — Tom Jenkins (OF 1929-32)

1905 — Ed Strelecki (P 1928-29)

1928 — Frankie Pack (PH 1949)

1934 — Wes Stock (P 1959-64)

1980 — The Orioles win their season opener for the 17th time in 27 seasons with a 5-3 win over the White Sox in Chicago as Jim Palmer outduels Steve Trout.

April 11

1938 — Art Quirk (P 1962)

1954 — Willie Royster (C 1981)

April 12

1887 — Sam Agnew (C 1913-15)

1889 — Bill Bailey (P 1907-12)

1910 — Bill Miller (P 1937)

1922 — Bill Wight (P 1955-57)

1929 — Mel Held (P 1956)

1933 — Charlie Lau (C 1961-67)

1966 — In his first American League at-bat, Frank Robinson is hit by a pitch from the Red Sox' Earl Wilson. The next batter, Brooks Robinson, then homers. The O's go on to win this season opener in Boston in 13 innings on a walk by Jim Lonborg.

1973 — Southpaw Dave McNally and the Birds beat Mickey Lolich and the Tigers 1-0 in 10 innings on a Lolich throwing error.

April 13

1906 — Alfred (Roxie) Lawson (P 1939-40)

1933 — Outfielder Sammy West goes 6 for 6 in 11 innings for the Browns, banging out five singles and a double.

1954 — The Orioles, in their first game ever, lose to the Tigers in Detroit 3-0 before 46,994 Tiger fans as Steve Gromek outpitches Don Larsen.

1961 — The Birds trade pitcher Jerry Walker and outfielder Chuck Essegian to the Athletics for outfielder Dick Williams and pitcher Dick Hall. A good deal for Baltimore, as Hall becomes a bullpen ace. The trade marks Williams' third and final tour of duty with the Orioles.

1966 — The Robinson boys, Frank and Brooks, deliver back-to-back home runs in the first inning of an Oriole 8-1 win over Boston.

1967 — Jim Palmer and Tommy Phoebus spin twin shutouts over the Senators, 6-0, 9-0.

1969 — After two years of arm trouble, Jim Palmer shuts out Washington 2-0 on a four-hitter.

1973 — The Orioles sell reliever John Montague to Montreal and receive pitcher Mickey Scott almost a year later (4/4/74) to complete the deal.

April 14

1898 — Jess Doyle (P 1931)

1917 — White Sox hurler Eddie Cicotte throws a no-hitter to beat Earl Hamilton and the Browns 11-0 in St. Louis.

1925 — The Browns drop their home opener to Cleveland 21-14 as the Indians bomb Brownie pitching for 12 runs in the 8th inning. To add insult to injury, first sacker George Sisler makes four errors.

1931 — Kal Segrist (3B-2B-1B 1955)

1944 — Frank Bertaina (P 1964-67, 1969)

1954 — The Orioles win their first game, beating the Tigers 3-2 in Detroit as right-hander Duane Pillette goes the distance.

April 15

1915 — The White Sox, paced by the pitching of Red Faber, blast the Browns 16-0.

1954 — In their first home game ever, the Birds beat the White Sox 3-1 as Bob Turley hurls a seven-hitter and strikes out nine. A crowd of 46,354, including Vice President Richard Nixon (who threw out the first ball), is thrilled by homers by Vern Stephens and Clint Courtney off lefty Virgil Trucks. Courtney's home run is the first by an Oriole and the first in Memorial Stadium.

23

April 15 (continued)

1980 — The Orioles enjoy their biggest Opening Day crowd ever, 50, 244, as Jim Palmer and company beat the Royals 12-2.

April 16

1880 — Phil Stremmel (P 1909-10)

1946 — Sergio Robles (C 1972-73)

April 17

1892 — Scott Perry (P 1915)

1924 — Outfielder Baby Doll Jacobson hits for the cycle for the Browns.

1944 — On Opening Day for the Browns in Detroit, right-hander Jack Kramer starts off a pennant-bound Browns squad with a 2-1 win over Dizzy Trout.

1968 — The Orioles ruin the Athletics' debut in Oakland as Dave McNally hurls a two-hitter to beat Lew Krausse 4-1.

1970 — Former catcher Dick Brown dies with a brain tumor at age 35.

1973 — Earl Williams blasts his first American League home run, a three-run shot off Sparky Lyle, to give the O's a 4-3 victory over the Yankees.

1975 — The Birds trade catcher/first baseman Earl Williams to Atlanta for pitcher Jimmy Freeman and $75,000. The deal ends a disappointing period for Baltimore, which had waited in vain for Williams to regain the power of his early years.

April 18

1877 — Tully Sparks (P 1901)

1899 — Bill Bayne (P 1919-24)

1955 — The Orioles release third baseman Vern Stephens, who then signs with the White Sox on May 2.

April 19

1885 — Roy Mitchell (P 1910-14)

1892 — Joseph Bennett (P 1918, 1921) (He played as Bugs Morris in 1921.)

Chick Shorten (OF 1922)

1915 — Glenn McQuillen (OF 1938, 1941-42, 1946-47)

1922 — First sacker George Sisler scores five runs in one game.

April 20

1876 — Charlie Hemphill (OF-2B 1902-4, 1906-7)

1902 — Frank (Squash) Wilson (OF 1928)

1912 — The Browns' George Baumgardner and the White Sox' James Scott battle in a classic 0-0 pitching duel that ends scoreless after 15 innings in St. Louis.

1924 — Jim Bilbrey (P 1949)

1938 — Brownie catcher Billy Sullivan's bunt in the sixth inning spoils Indian Bob Feller's no-hit bid. Feller ends up with a one-hitter and 9-0 win.

April 21

1919 — Stan Rojak (SS-2B 1952)

1947 — Al Bumbry (OF-DH-3B 1972-present)

1954 — The first night game in Memorial Stadium proves memorable as the Birds' Bob Turley loses his bid for a no-hitter with one out in the ninth as Indian Al Rosen hits a single. A Larry Doby home run proves the margin of victory for Cleveland in this 2-1 thriller before 43,000. Turley also notches 14 strikeouts in this superior pitching effort.

1956 — The Birds purchase infielder Billy Gardner from the New York Giants for $20,000. Gardner becomes a fixture at second base for the next four seasons.

1957 — A power failure, the first in league history to end a game, leaves the Senators and Orioles suspended after five innings.

1980 — The Orioles sign free agent pitcher Paul Hartzell, who pitches just a few games before being sent to the minors.

April 22

1922 — Against the White Sox, slugging outfielder Ken Williams of the Browns hits three homers with George Sisler on base each time. Williams in doing so becomes the first American Leaguer in modern history to accomplish this feat.

1938 — John Orsino (C-1B 1963-65)

1947 — Brownie outfielder Al Zarilla's single in the seventh is the sole hit off Indian Bob Feller in a 5-0 Cleveland win.

1981 — Oriole hurler Dennis Martinez is injured when hit by a bottle thrown by a hoodlum fan in Chicago's Comiskey Park.

April 23

1896 — Elam Vangilder (P 1919-27)

April 23 (continued)

1900 — Jim Bottomley (1B 1936–37, MGR 1937)

1915 — Walter Brown (P 1947)

1925 — Carl Peterson (SS 1957)

1939 — Chico Fernandez (SS-2B 1968)

1946 — The Browns purchase first baseman Babe Dahlgren from the Pirates. He appears in just 28 games before calling it a career.

1952 — Second baseman Bobby Young's triple in the first inning is the Browns sole tally off Cleveland's Bob Feller, marking the fourth time that a Brownie has spoiled a no-hit bid by Feller. The Browns win this duel 1–0 as lefty Bob Cain also hurls a one-hitter, yielding a single to Luke Easter in the fifth. The Browns score when Young triples and then Indian third sacker Al Rosen boots Marty Marion's grounder, allowing Young to score. A crowd of 7,110 Brown fans are on hand to see the team win and take temporary possession of first place.

April 24

1913 — Browns' outfielder Gus Williams bangs three consecutive triples against the White Sox in Chicago.

1944 — The Browns sweep a doubleheader from the White Sox, 5–2 and 4–3, to extend their season-opening winning streak to six games. In the first game, Jack Kramer helps his pitching with a two-run homer.

1960 — The Birds' Albie Pearson and Billy Klaus each hit grand slam homers in a losing cause to the Yankees in New York, 15–9.

1962 — The O's sign catcher Darrell Johnson as a player–coach.

April 25

1883 — Elmer Brown (P 1911–12)

1898 — Fred Haney (MGR 1939–41)

1911 — Bobby Estalella (OF 1941)

1918 — Alvis (Tex) Shirley (P 1944–46)

1924 — Art Schallock (P 1955)

1953 — Brown first sacker Dick Kryhoski belts a pinch grand slam off the White Sox' Harry Dorish.

April 26

1919 — Virgil Trucks (P 1953)

1922 — Sam Dente (SS–3B 1948)

1935 — Nate Smith (C 1962)

April 27

1896 — Rogers Hornsby (2B–1B–3B–OF 1933–37, MGR 1935–37, 1952)

1909 — John Whitehead (P 1939–40, 1942)

1914 — George Archie (1B 1946)

1925 — Brownie Harry Rice gets two pinch-hits in the ninth inning.

1944 — The Browns tie the Yankees' league record of seven straight wins to open a season as they beat Cleveland 5–2 at home. Steve Sundra outpitches Allie Reynolds for the win. A triple by Don Gutteridge and a double by Vern Stephens highlight a four-run rally in the sixth inning. Only 960 fans are in attendance.

1968 — Oriole pitcher Tommy Phoebus thrills the hometown fans with a 6–0 no-hitter over the Red Sox. Phoebus strikes out nine and enjoys the benefit of a Brooks Robinson diving catch of a Rico Petrocelli line drive in the eighth.

April 28

1916 — Mike Chartak (OF–1B 1942–44)

1925 — Clarence (Cuddles) Marshall (P 1950)

1927 — Charlie Maxwell (OF 1955)

1934 — Jackie Brandt (OF–3B–1B 1960–65)

1944 — Behind the pitching of Nelson Potter, the Browns set a new American League record with eight straight wins to open the season in beating Cleveland 5–1.

1953 — The Yankees and Brownies get into a wild mêlée as Scrap Iron Courtney slides spikes up into Phil Rizzuto. In the resulting brawl, umpire John Stevens suffers a dislocated collarbone. Among the six players fined are Courtney, who coughs up $250, and shortstop Billy Hunter, who pays $150.

April 29

1888 — Ernie Johnson (SS–3B–2B 1916–18)

1893 — Allen Sothoron (P 1914–15, 1917–21, MGR 1933)

1896 — Johnnie Heving (PH 1920)

1931 — Cleveland's Wes Ferrell no-hits the Browns 9–0 in St. Louis.

April 29 (continued)

1934 — Luis Aparicio (SS 1963-67)

1935 — The Tigers bomb the Browns 18-0.

1944 — The Browns' season-opening win streak extends to nine games as Jack Kramer beats the Indians 3-1 to give the team a 3½-game first-place lead over the Senators.

1962 — Outfielder Russ Snyder becomes the first Oriole to get two pinch-hits in one inning.

1970 — Center fielder Paul Blair, known best for his slick glove, slams three homers to pace an 18-2 Oriole win over the White Sox.

April 30

1912 — Chet Laabs (OF 1939-46)

1960 — The Yankees blast the Birds 16-0 behind the shutout pitching of Jim Coates.

1961 — Jim Gentile, Gus Triandos and Ron Hansen pound consecutive home runs for the Orioles in one inning.

1967 — Southpaw Steve Barber and righty Stu Miller combine for an Oriole no-hitter against Detroit, but lose on a wild pitch and error to Earl Wilson, 2-1. Barber yields 10 walks in one of history's strangest games.

1980 — In the rain and mud, the Birds beat the Yankees 7-4 as Tim Stoddard gets Reggie Jackson to fly out with the bases loaded in the ninth to preserve a win for Steve Stone.

MAY

May 1

1896 — Henry Meine (P 1922)

1910 — Sam Harshaney (C 1937-40)

1916 — Bob Harris (P 1939-42)

1917 — Johnny Berardino (2B-SS-3B-1B 1939-42, 1946-47, 1951)

1919 — Al Zarilla (OF 1943-44, 1946-49, 1952)

1966 — The Birds extend their winning streak to 10 games, beating Detroit 4-1. Brooks Robinson drives in two runs, raising his RBI total to 21 in just 13 games. The O's won-lost record stands at 12-1.

May 2

1891 — John Leary (1B-C 1914-15)

1942 — The Browns lose to Boston in Fenway Park 11-10 on a Ted Williams ninth-inning homer. Brown pitcher Eldon Auker goes the distance, giving up 17 hits and 11 runs.

May 3

1951 — Against St. Louis, Yankee Gil McDougald drives in six runs in one inning with a triple and a grand slam. The Bronx Bombers score 11 runs in the ninth inning to beat the Brownies in St. Louis 17-3.

1963 — In his only plate appearance as an Oriole, pitcher Buster Narum hits a home run in his first major league at-bat off Detroit pitcher Don Mossi in Tiger Stadium. He is optioned to Rochester six days later.

May 4

1875 — Lou Gertenrich (OF 1901)

1892 — Jack Tobin (OF-1B 1916, 1918-25)

1915 — John Miller (P 1943, 1945-46)

1927 — Hal Hudson (P 1952)

May 5

1917 — Brown southpaw Ernie Koob no-hits the White Sox and Eddie Cicotte 1-0, just 20 days after Cicotte's no-hitter versus St. Louis. Koob originally gives up a single in the infield in the first inning, which is later changed to an error on the shortstop after the game following a meeting of the writers.

1922 — Lefty Bill Bayne has a no-hitter for the Browns against the Tigers going into the eighth inning. The Tigers send up five straight pinch-hitters, including one who hits safely to open the ninth and spoil the no-hit bid. Tiger manager Ty Cobb pinch-hit Bob Fothergill for himself in this game. Fothergill struck out and earned the distinction of being the only man to pinch-hit for Cobb.

1925 — Tiger Ty Cobb goes six for six against the Browns, including three homers, for a total of 16 bases. The next day, he hits two more homers against Brown pitching.

1932 — Charlie Locke (P 1955)

1949 — St. Louis obtains outfielder Stan Spence and $100,000 from the Red Sox for flyhawk Al Zarilla: A bad deal for the Browns, as Zarilla goes on to hit .281 this year and .325 the following year for Boston.

1962 — Former Oriole farmhand Bo Belinsky hurls a no-hitter for the Angels against the Orioles in Dodger Stadium. He beats his former minor league roommate Steve Barber 2-0 and becomes an overnight Hollywood celebrity.

May 6

1907 — Ivy Andrews (P 1934-36)

1917 — Not to be outdone by teammate Ernie Koob, Brown right-hander Bob Groom hurls a no-hitter for St. Louis, the second in two days versus the White Sox. He beats Joe Berry 3-0 in the second game of a doubleheader. More interestingly, Groom had pitched two hitless innings in relief in the first game of the twin bill.

1934 — Leo Burke (OF-3B-2B 1958-59)

1953 — Brown rookie right-hander Bobo Holloman throws a no-hitter against Philadelphia in his first major league start. He beats Morris Martin and the Athletics 6-0 and drives in three runs with two singles in three at-bats. Only 2,473 Brown fans are on hand for this hometown gem.

May 7

1888 — Gus Williams (OF 1911-15)

1896 — Tom Zachary (P 1926-27)

1910 — Harry (Stinky) Davis (1B-OF 1937)

1919 — Al Papai (P 1949)

1928 — Dick Williams (OF-3B-2B-1B 1956-58, 1961-62)

May 8

1891 — Chester Hoff (P 1915)

1893 — Ed Hemingway (3B 1914)

1895 — Ed Murray (SS 1917)

1937 — Mike Cuellar (P 1969-76)

1963 — The Orioles sell catcher Hobie Landrith to the Senators.

1966 — Slugging outfielder Frank Robinson hits the first homer ever out of Memorial Stadium, a 451-foot shot off Cleveland's Luis Tiant over the left field bleachers before a home crowd of 49,000.

1979 — Eddie Murray, Lee May, and Gary Roenicke hit consecutive homers in the sixth inning of an 8-2 triumph over Oakland.

May 9

1904 — Brad Springer (P 1925)

1950 — St. Louis buys pitcher Harry Dorish from the Red Sox for $10,000. Dorish has a mediocre season in St. Louis before moving on to the White Sox.

1955 — Tom Chism (1B 1979)

1961 — Oriole first sacker Jim Gentile becomes the first player to hit grand slams in consecutive at-bats in a 13-5 mauling of the Twins. He belts his first slam off Pete Ramos in the first inning and the next off Paul Giel in the second inning. A sacrifice fly in the game gives him a club record total of 9 RBIs in one game.

1962 — Third baseman Brooks Robinson hits his second grand slam in as many games becoming only the fifth American Leaguer to do so. His blast comes off Kansas City's Ed Rakow.

1973 — Al Bumbry and Rich Coggins hit their first major league home runs back-to-back off Catfish Hunter in a 4-3 loss to Oakland.

1979 — Left fielder Gary Roenicke spoils the A's Mike Norris' bid for a no-hitter with a seventh-inning double. Norris winds up with a 4-2 one-hit victory over the Orioles.

May 10

1914 — Russ Bauers (P 1950)

1972 — Oriole southpaw Dave McNally blanks the Rangers 1-0 for his fourth shutout of the season. He beats Pete Broberg, who gives up only two hits.

May 11

1890 — Ed Hawk (P 1911)

1906 — Tom Jones of the Browns records 22 putouts at first base, the first to accomplish the feat at his position.

1933 — St. Louis trades catcher Rick Ferrell and pitcher Lloyd Brown to the Red Sox for catcher Merv Shea and cash. Boston gets the best of the deal as Ferrell settles in as a .300-hitting catcher for the next four seasons while Shea lasts only one year in a Brown uniform.

1939 — Milt Pappas (P 1957-65)

1954 — The Orioles purchase infielder Jim Brideweser from the Yankees. He spends the year on the bench before going on to the Chisox.

1955 — The Birds buy pitcher Art Schallock from the Yankees. Art appears in 30 games and then fades into the woodwork.

May 12

1899 — Earl McNeely (OF-1B 1928-31)

1902 — Frank Henry (P 1921-22)

1910 — Howard (Lefty) Mills (P 1934, 1937-40)

1911 — Archie McKain (P 1941, 1943)

1922 — Johnny Hetki (P 1952)

1951 — Joe Nolan (C present)

1956 — Southpaw Don Ferrarese loses his chance for a no-hitter when Yankees Andy Carey and Hank Bauer single to open the ninth inning. He hangs on for a two-hit 1-0 Oriole win for his first major league victory.

1978 — Center fielder Al Bumbry breaks his leg sliding into second base against the Rangers.

May 13

1901 — Pat Burke (3B 1924)

1924 — Cliff (Mule) Fannin (P 1945-52)

1939 — In a major deal, the Browns trade shortstop Red Kress, outfielder Roy Bell, and pitchers Bobo Newsom and Jim Walkup to the Tigers for third baseman Mark Christman, outfielder Chet Laabs, and pitchers Vern Kennedy, Roxie Lawson, George Gill, and Bob Harris. Newsom becomes a key in Detroit's drive to the top of the American League in 1940.

1952 — St. Louis obtains pitcher Stubby Overmire from the Yankees on waivers.

1967 — Oriole reliever Stu Miller gives up Mickey Mantle's 500th career home run, a seventh-inning game-winning shot at Yankee Stadium in a 3-2 Oriole loss.

1980 — The Birds sell reserve catcher Dave Skaggs to California. He subsequently breaks his ankle, a career-ending injury.

May 14

1913 — The Browns end Senator Walter Johnson's streak of 56 scoreless innings in the fourth inning of a 10-5 loss at home.

1915 — Myron (Red) Hayworth (C 1944-45)

1925 — Les Moss (C 1946-55)

1955 — Dennis Martinez (P 1976-present)

1956 — The Orioles purchase pitcher John Schmitz from the Red Sox.

1957 — The Birds sell pitcher Sandy Consuegra to the New York Giants.

1961 — The Indians edge Baltimore 1-0 in 15 innings.

1969 — Center fielder Paul Blair bangs two homers, then makes a great catch of a Rod Carew drive to preserve a 9-8 Oriole win over the Twins in the ninth inning.

May 15

1895 — Joe Evans (OF 1924-25)

1905 — Chet Falk (P 1925-27)

1941 — The Browns sell outfielder Rip Radcliff to the Tigers for $25,000. Rip hits .317 for Detroit in 96 games that season.

1950 — St. Louis buys pitcher Clarence Marshall from the Yankees.

1969 — Dave McNally's try for a no-hitter is ruined by a Cesar Tovar single with one out in the ninth. Dave winds up with a one-hit, 5-0 win over the Twins.

May 16

1919 — Frank (Stubby) Overmire (P 1950-52)

1920 — Dave Philley (OF-3B-1B 1955-56, 1960-61)

May 17

1907 — Ed Baecht (P 1937)

1927 — Jim McDonald (P 1951, 1955)

1932 — Billy Hoeft (P 1959-62)

1933 — Ozzie Virgil (PH 1962)

1947 — A seagull flying over Boston's Fenway Park drops a smelt on Brown pitcher Ellis Kinder.

1951 — The Browns trade catcher Les Moss to the Red Sox for catcher Matt Batts and pitcher Jim Suchecki, plus a player to be named and $100,000. The deal is completed July 18 when pitcher Jim McDonald is sent to St. Louis from Boston's Louisville farm club.

1967 — Baltimore beats Boston 12-8 on the strength of seven home runs, including four in the seventh inning by Andy Etchebarren, Sam Bowens, Boog Powell, and Dave Johnson. The other three homers are supplied by Paul Blair, Frank Robinson and Brooks Robinson.

1968 — Oriole Curt Motton hits his second pinch homer in as many at-bats.

May 18

1922 — Gil Coan (OF 1954-55)

1923 — Don Lund (OF 1948)

1937 — Brooks Robinson (3B-2B-SS 1955-77)

1938 — Brown hurler Bobo Newsom strikes out six consecutive Yankees.

May 18 (continued)

1946 — Reggie Jackson (OF-DH 1976)

1957 — A Dick Williams home run off the White Sox' Paul LaPalme ties the game 4-4 just seconds before a 10:20 P.M. curfew would have given Chicago a 4-3 win over Baltimore.

May 19

1886 — Albert Nelson (P 1910-12)

1895 — Ray Kennedy (PH 1916)

1910 — Tommy Thompson (OF 1939)

1915 — Jake Early (C 1947)

1952 — Dan Ford (OF-DH present)

1959 — Bird pitcher Billy (Digger) O'Dell wins the game with a 120-foot home run to beat Billy Pierce and the White Sox 2-1. Digger lofts a fly ball over first base which strikes the wooden right field foul line in Memorial Stadium and bounces over the head of right fielder Al Smith. Billy Gardner scores ahead of O'Dell.

May 20

1904 — Pete Appleton (P 1942, 1945)

1919 — Red Sox pitcher Babe Ruth hits his first major league grand slam off Brown pitcher Dave Davenport.

1921 — Earl Rapp (OF 1951-52)

1953 — Brownie outfielder Don Lenhardt hits a ball out of Fenway Park, just to the left of the flag pole between the last upright of the screen and the center field wall. He hits this shot off Red Sox hurler Skinny Brown. The Red Sox win 3-2 in 14 innings on catcher Del Wilber's pinch homer.

May 21

1935 — St. Louis sells pitcher Bobo Newsom to Washington for $40,000.

1951 — Bob Molinaro (OF 1979)

1956 — The Orioles obtain third baseman George Kell, outfielder Bob Nieman, and pitchers Mike Fornieles and Connie Johnson from the White Sox for outfielder Dave Philley and pitcher Jim Wilson. The deal is a plus for Baltimore: Kell and Nieman step into the starting lineup and Johnson joins the starting rotation.

1957 — Second baseman Billy Gardner registers 12 putouts for the Orioles in a 16-inning contest.

1959 — The Birds sell second baseman Bobby Avila to the Red Sox.

1962 — In a smart move, the O's sign pitcher Robin Roberts who had been released by the Yankees on April 30. Roberts wins 42 games in 3½ seasons with Baltimore before moving on to Houston.

1973 — The Orioles sell reliever Mickey Scott to the Expos.

May 22

1893 — Pat Parker (OF 1915)

1938 — Brownie second baseman Don Heffner registers 12 assists in a 13-inning game.

1959 — Knuckleballer Hoyt Wilhelm hurls a one-hit, 5-0 win over the Yankees, with Jerry Lumpe's eighth-inning single the only hit. Six days later, Wilhelm shuts out the Yanks again 5-0.

May 23

1892 — Luke Stuart (2B 1921)

1906 — Willis Hudlin (P 1940, 1944)

1918 — Frank Mancuso (C 1944-46)

1923 — Jerry McCarthy (1B 1948)

1943 — Lee May (1B-DH 1975-80)

1955 — The Orioles sell pitcher Bob Kuzava to the Phillies.

1963 — The Birds' Robin Roberts shuts out the Senators 6-0 on two hits, both by weak-hitting Eddie Brinkman.

May 24

1891 — Pete Sims (P 1915)

1926 — Willie Miranda (SS-3B-2B 1952-53, 1955-59)

1929 — Brownie flyhawk Heinie Manush belts two doubles and two triples in a single game.

1940 — The first Brown night game in St. Louis draws 24,827 to see Eldon Auker lose to Bob Feller and the Indians. Feller helps himself with a home run.

1962 — Oriole manager Billy Hitchcock accuses Tiger ace Jim Bunning of notching balls with his belt buckle.

1963 — The Birds release pitcher Pete Burnside, who then signs with the Senators.

1964 — Twin slugger Harmon Killebrew hits the longest measured homer up to that point in Memorial Stadium, a 471-foot shot over the hedge in left-center off Milt Pappas.

May 24 (continued)

1970 — Third sacker Brooks Robinson is beaned by a pitch from Red Soxer Mike Nagy in the fourth inning, but stays in the game to hit a game-winning homer in the 10th inning off Sparky Lyle in Memorial Stadium.

May 25

1889 — John Daley (SS 1912)

1897 — Jim Riley (2B 1921)

1932 — Jim Marshall (1B–OF 1958)

1945 — Bill Dillman (P 1967)

1954 — The O's acquire outfielder Cal Abrams and $10,000 from the Pirates for pitcher Dick Littlefield. Abrams takes over right field for the next two seasons.

1955 — Andres Mora (OF–DH–3B 1976-78)

1965 — Oriole board chairman Joseph Iglehart sells his 64,000 shares to the National Brewing Company for $1.6 million. Brewery chairman Jerold Hoffberger becomes the new team chairman.

May 26

1891 — Gene Paulette (1B-2B-3B 1916-17)

1894 — Bill Fincher (P 1916)

1959 — The Birds deal outfielder Lenny Green to Washington for the diminutive flychaser Albie Pearson. The Senators get the upper hand in this trade as Green becomes a fixture in the outfield and accompanies the team to Minnesota.

1963 — Oriole reliever Wes Stock becomes the first Bird to win both ends of a doubleheader in a twin bill with Cleveland.

1976 — The O's sign outfielder Terry Crowley following his release by Atlanta and send him to Rochester. He rejoins the team later and has remained a key utility player.

May 27

1913 — Hal Spindel (C 1939)

1935 — The Browns obtain outfielder Moose Solters from the Red Sox, along with cash, for second baseman Oscar Melillo. The Browns are glad to add this slugger to their outfield and move Tom Carey into the keystone spot.

1955 — Center fielder Chuck Diering makes a memorable catch of a 440-foot Mickey Mantle drive in the hedge at Memorial Stadium just 10 feet from the scoreboard.

1960 — The Orioles unveil the "big mitt" catcher's glove designed by Paul Richards to handle Hoyt Wilhelm's knuckleball. The mitt is 50 percent bigger than the standard glove. In its first tryout, the glove aids Clint Courtney in allowing no passed balls in a 3-2 win at Yankee Stadium as Wilhelm goes the distance.

1961 — The Birds release first baseman Walt Dropo to make room for relief pitcher Dick Hyde.

May 28

1918 — Bob Malloy (P 1949)

1923 — Bob Kuzava (P 1954-55)

1926 — Frank Saucier (OF 1951)

1971 — The Orioles trade pitcher Jim Hardin to the Yankees for hurler Bill Burbach and also sign pitcher Dave Boswell, who had been released by Detroit.

1978 — Jim Palmer becomes the Orioles' first 200-game winner as he shuts out Mike Paxton and the Indians 3-0 at home.

May 29

1909 — George McQuinn (1B 1938-45)

1927 — Brown catcher Leo Dixon records an unassisted double play.

1934 — Outfielder Ray Pepper scores five runs in a game for the Browns.

1946 — Dyar Miller (P 1975-77)

1952 — Fred Holdsworth (P 1976-77)

1967 — The Orioles obtain pitcher Pete Richert from Washington for first baseman Mike Epstein and pitcher Frank Bertaina.

1970 — Oriole hurler Mike Cuellar strikes out four Angels in one inning (Alex Johnson, Ken McMullen, Tommy Reynolds, and Jim Spencer, although Johnson gets on base following a dropped third strike).

1971 — Baltimore blows a 7-0 lead over the Twins in Minnesota only to rally for an 11-8 win as Dave Boswell gets his first win as an Oriole in his first outing.

1975 — On his birthday, the Birds obtain pitcher Fred Holdsworth from Detroit for reliever Bob Reynolds.

May 30

1926 — Roy Upright (PH 1953)

1941 — John Miller (P 1962-63, 1965-67)

1955 — Baltimore sells utility player Bob Kennedy to the White Sox.

May 31

1950 — Tippy Martinez (P 1976-present)

1967 — The O's sell reserve catcher Charlie Lau to Atlanta.

1971 — A brawl with the White Sox marks a turning point in the season. Don Buford, after being hit by a Bart Johnson pitch, charges the mound to set off the fireworks. When he took his left field position in the bottom of the eighth, the White Sox fans began to shower him with debris. The umpires removed Buford from the game for his own safety in the ninth inning after a fan left the stands and jumped him in the on-deck circle. The Orioles scored five runs to go on to an 11-3 win and the beginning of a nine-game winning streak.

JUNE

June 1

1891 — Hank Severeid (C-1B-3B 1915-25)

1901 — Fred Stiely (P 1929-31)

1926 — Ray Moore (P 1955-57)

1937 — The White Sox' Bill Dietrich no-hits the Browns 8-0 in Chicago.

1954 — The Orioles trade first baseman/outfielder Vic Wertz to the Indians for pitcher Bob Chakales. They also release pitcher Dave Koslo.

1960 — A homer by Mickey Mantle ruins the no-hit bid of Oriole hurler Skinny Brown.

1975 — Nolan Ryan records the fourth no-hitter of his career as he beats Ross Grimsley and the Orioles 1-0. In this gem before his home fans, Ryan fanned nine Orioles.

June 2

1869 — Tom Leahy (C-OF-2B 1901)

1876 — Charlie Jones (OF 1908)

1899 — Hollis (Sloppy) Thurston (P 1923)

1941 — Bob Saverine (OF-SS-2B 1959, 1962-64)

1946 — Roger Freed (1B-OF 1970)

1950 — Browns pitcher Harry Dorish steals home in the fifth inning against Washington.

1959 — In pursuit of his eighth straight win, Bird hurler Hoyt Wilhelm is attacked by gnats in the first inning at Comiskey Park. After a futile effort by the groundskeeper to chase the pesky pests, a fireworks display originally scheduled for after the game chases the gnats away and Wilhelm goes on to win 3-2.

1980 — Batting for the first time against his former team, Lenn Sakata homers as a pinch-hitter leading off the 11th inning to beat the Brewers 9-8. In this same game, second baseman Rich Dauer gets five hits.

1982 — Hurler Steve Stone announces his retirement due to recurring tendinitis in his pitching arm.

June 3

1887 — Jim Duggan (1B 1911)

1919 — George Sisler raps a homer and a double for the Browns in the fifth inning of a single game.

1934 — Jim Gentile (1B 1960-63)

1941 — Outfielder Roy Cullenbine gets a double and a triple in the same inning for the Browns.

1945 — Pitcher Tex Shirley hurls 13 scoreless innings for the Browns against the Athletics in a 0-0 tie.

1964 — First sacker Boog Powell belts two homers for the Birds, including a 430-foot shot off the Kansas City scoreboard, to pace a 5-1 win. The triumph is the 21st Oriole victory in 27 games.

June 4

1889 — Lee Magee (3B-2B-1B-OF 1917)

1922 — Ray Coleman (OF 1947-48, 1950-52)

1928 — Billy Hunter (SS 1954)

1954 — Oriole catcher Clint Courtney records an unassisted double play, the first in Baltimore history for a catcher.

1967 — Catcher Andy Etchebarren slugs a homer off Senator hurler Bob Priddy in the bottom of the 19th inning to end the longest game in Oriole history.

June 5

1874 — Frank Huelsman (OF 1904)

1878 — Billy Maloney (C-OF 1901-2)

1881 — Albert Jacobson (P 1906-7)

1896 — Ray Richmond (P 1920-21)

1942 — St. Louis beats Philadelphia in 16 innings 1-0.

June 5 (continued)

1951 — The Browns obtain first baseman Dale Long from Pittsburgh on waivers. Ironically, Dale would return to the Pirates and set a record in 1956 for eight home runs in eight straight games.

1971 — With a 12-4 win over Milwaukee, the Orioles move into first place to stay for the rest of the season.

1979 — Baltimore trades outfielder Larry Harlow to California for infielder Floyd Rayford and cash.

June 6

1914 — Eddie Silber (OF 1937, 1939)

1943 — Merv Rettenmund (OF 1968-73)

1955 — The Birds trade catcher Les Moss to the White Sox for pitcher Harry Dorish.

1967 — Outfielder Curt Blefary belts three homers in one game for the Orioles.

June 7

1900 — Ed Wells (P 1933-34)

1944 — Roger Nelson (P 1968)

1950 — Boston bombs the Browns 20-4 with 23 hits, a prelude to the next day's 29-4 massacre in Fenway Park.

1953 — Yankee catcher Yogi Berra connects for a pinch grand slam off ace Brown reliever Satchel Paige.

1959 — The O's Hoyt Wilhelm wins his ninth in a row as he pitches his third shutout in a row to lower his ERA to 0.996.

June 8

1911 — The Red Sox permit four Brownies to reach first base on errors in the fourth inning.

1925 — Eddie Gaedel (PH 1951)

1935 — George Brunet (P 1963)

1942 — The Browns trade outfielder Roy Cullenbine and pitcher Bill Trotter to the Yankees for outfielder Mike Chartak and pitcher Steve Sundra. From a deal of little consequence for both clubs in the first year, Sundra becomes the Browns' staff ace in 1943.

1944 — Mark Belanger (SS-2B-3B 1965-81)

1950 — The Browns suffer the worst defeat in major league history as the Red Sox pummel them 29-4 in Fenway Park. The Red Sox attack features 17 extra-base hits, including seven homers, and 28 hits. Boston's 29 runs mark the most ever scored by a major league club.

1954 — Lenn Sakata (SS-2B-DH 1980-present)

1963 — The O's sign veteran hurler Ike Delock one week after his release by the Red Sox. After appearing in just seven games with little success, Ike hangs them up.

June 9

1931 — Ray Shore (P 1946, 1948-49)

1952 — Rogers Hornsby is fired as manager of the Browns for the second time.

1959 — The Orioles move into first place in a tie with Chicago after beating Cleveland 7-5 before 46,601 hometown fans. This win marks the first time the Orioles have held first place past the second day of a season. They hold a 29-24 record.

1960 — The Orioles obtain outfielder Gene Stephens from the Red Sox for outfielder Willie Tasby.

June 10

1900 — Garland Braxton (P 1931, 1933)

1908 — Mike Kreevich (OF 1943-45)

1910 — Frank Demaree (OF 1944)

1928 — Ken Lehman (P 1957-58)

1929 — Hank Foiles (C 1961)

1947 — Ken Singleton (OF-DH 1975-present)

1959 — Indian flyhawk Rocky Colavito ties a major league record by hitting four consecutive home runs at Memorial Stadium against the Birds. Billy Martin and Minny Minoso also homer to lead the Tribe over Baltimore 11-8.

1972 — The O's trade infielder Jerry DaVanon to the Angels for outfielder Roger Repoz.

June 11

1878 — Jim Buchanan (P 1905)

1903 — Ernie Nevers (P 1926-28)

1919 — Earl Jones (P 1945)

June 11 (continued)

1944 — Outfielder Gene Moore pinch-hits a grand slam off the Indians' Joe Heving.

1962 — At Yankee Stadium, Bud Daley beans left fielder Boog Powell in the top of the fourth inning. Powell is removed on a stretcher. In the bottom of the fourth, Bird hurler Robin Roberts throws a ball close to Roger Maris, precipitating a free-for-all. Both managers Hitchcock and Houk are ejected and the Birds go on to win 5–3 as Hoyt Wilhelm gets a save, to give Roberts his first American League win.

June 12

1903 — Jack Crouch (C 1930–31, 1933)

1951 — Dave Skaggs (C 1977–80)

1953 — The Browns sell shortstop Willie Miranda to the Yankees.

1962 — The Orioles release catcher Darrell Johnson as a player but keep him as a coach.

1966 — The Birds trade second baseman Jerry Adair and minor league first baseman John Riddle to the White Sox for reliever Eddie Fisher. Fisher pays immediate dividends as a key bullpen ace for Baltimore.

1972 — Oriole Pat Dobson hurls a four-hitter to beat the A's sensation, Vida Blue, before 50,182 Oakland fans 1–0. The Birds purchase catcher Francisco Estrada from the Angels and send him to Rochester.

1981 — Madness reigns on a day that will live in infamy—baseball begins its first mid-season strike.

June 13

1895 — Emilio Palmero (P 1921)

1929 — Sherwin Swartz (P 1947)

1932 — Tommy Gastall (C 1955–56)

1937 — The Yankee Clipper, Joe DiMaggio, hits three consecutive homers in the nightcap of a doubleheader with the Browns. The game ends in an 8–8 tie due to darkness. The Browns lose the first game 16–9 as the Yanks score seven runs in the top of the ninth.

1939 — The Browns obtain outfielder Joe Gallagher from the Yankees for infielder Roy Hughes. Gallagher goes on to hit .282 for the year as the starting left fielder.

1953 — St. Louis trades outfielder/third baseman Bob Elliott and pitcher Virgil Trucks to the White Sox for catcher Darrell Johnson, pitcher Lou Kretlow, and $75,000. Trucks quickly established himself as the ace of the Chicago staff and Elliott took over third base.

1957 — The Birds trade outfielder Dick Williams to Cleveland for flyhawk Jim Busby. The deal works to Baltimore's advantage as Busby becomes the center fielder and Williams is reobtained for 1958.

1977 — The O's trade reliever Dyar Miller to California for pitcher Dick Drago.

1978 — Slugger Eddie Murray hits switch-hit homers in a 3–2 win over Seattle.

June 14

1889 — Bill Harper (P 1911)

1930 — In a major deal, the Browns send outfielder Heinie Manush, pitcher General Crowder, and $20,000 to Washington for outfielder Goose Goslin. Although all three players perform at All-Star levels, the deal ultimately helps Washington to a pennant in 1933 as Crowder leads the league with 24 wins.

1934 — Brown outfielder Sammy West gets the sole hit, a third-inning single, off Yankee hurler Johnny Broaca in a 7–0 loss at home.

1957 — The O's acquire infielder Billy Gardner from Boston for pitcher Mike Fornieles. Gardner becomes the embodiment of the saying, "Good field, no hit."

1962 — Catcher Charlie Lau registers three passed balls in one inning for the Orioles and four in the game while attempting to control Hoyt Wilhelm's knuckleball.

1972 — The Birds extend their winning streak to seven games as second baseman Bobby Grich hits a 10th-inning homer to give southpaw Dave McNally a 2–1 win over Oakland's Catfish Hunter.

June 15

1890 — Harry (Dutch) Schirick (PH 1914)

1891 — Frank Crossin (C 1912–14)

1912 — Ellsworth (Babe) Dahlgren (1B 1942, 1946)

1926 — The Browns trade outfielder Baby Doll Jacobson to the Athletics for outfielder Bing Miller—a good deal for St. Louis, as Miller becomes a solid .300 hitter in the outfield.

1950 — In a big trade with the Yankees, the Browns send third baseman Leo Thomas and pitchers Tom Ferrick, Joe Ostrowski, and Sid Schact to New York for infielder Snuffy Stirnweiss, outfielder Jim Delsing, and pitchers Don Johnson and Duane Pillette, plus $50,000.

1951 — St. Louis trades pitcher Stubby Overmire to the Yankees for pitcher Tommy Byrne and $25,000. Byrne moves right into the Browns' rotation.

June 15 (continued)

1955 — Baltimore trades outfielder Gene Woodling and third baseman Billy Cox to Cleveland for outfielders Dave Pope and Wally Westlake. When Cox refuses to report, the O's substitute cash.

1959 — The O's obtain pitcher Billy Hoeft from the Red Sox for hurler Jack Harshman.

1964 — The Birds trade pitcher Wes Stock to Kansas City for catcher Charlie Lau. Stock steps in as the A's bullpen ace.

1967 — Baltimore obtains reliever Marcelino Lopez from California for utility man Woodie Held.

1968 — Outfielder Fred Valentine is obtained from Washington for pitcher Bruce Howard — in a deal that means very little to Baltimore.

1970 — In two separate and minor deals, the Orioles trade outfielder Dave May to Milwaukee to obtain pitchers Dick Baney and Buzz Stephen and send infielder Bobby Floyd to the Royals to reacquire reliever Moe Drabowsky.

1973 — The Birds sell reliever Orlando Pena to the Cardinals.

1975 — Baltimore sells catcher Andy Etchebarren to the Angels and trades pitcher Jesse Jefferson to the White Sox for first baseman Tony Muser.

1976 — In one of the team's best trades ever, the Orioles send pitchers Ken Holtzman, Doyle Alexander, Grant Jackson, and Jimmy Freeman to the Yankees for catcher Rick Dempsey and pitchers Rudy May, Scott McGregor, Dave Pagan, and Tippy Martinez. Dempsey, McGregor, and Martinez all have kept the Orioles in contention and continue to be part of the team nucleus.

June 16

1924 — Ernie Johnson (P 1959)

1938 — Red Sox slugger Jimmy Foxx walks six times in a 12-8 win over the Browns in St. Louis.

1973 — Bird ace Jim Palmer retires 25 straight Rangers before catcher Ken Suarez singles with one out in the ninth. Palmer winds up with a two-hit, 9-1 win.

June 17

1881 — Claude Rossman (OF 1909)

1915 — Brown outfielder Burt Shotton walks twice in the same inning.

1925 — Dave Pope (OF 1955-56)

1944 — Brown right-hander Sig Jakucki shuts out the Tigers on a seven-hitter. Third baseman Mark Christman leads the attack with a three-run homer.

1946 — Brown hurler Jack Kramer stops Boston's string of 13 consecutive games with at least one home run.

June 18

1927 — Irv Medlinger (P 1949, 1951)

1953 — In the seventh inning, the Red Sox bomb Brown pitching for 17 runs. Bosox outfielder Gene Stephens gets three hits in the inning and catcher Sammy White scores three times.

1974 — Second baseman Bobby Grich belts three consecutive homers for the Birds against the Twins at home. Baltimore wins 10-1 behind the pitching of Ross Grimsley.

June 19

1906 — George (Buck) Stanton (OF 1931)

1912 — Don Gutteridge (2B-OF-3B 1942-45)

1918 — St. Louis sells flyhawk Ham Hyatt to the Yankees. Hyatt hits .299 as a reserve.

1929 — Don Ferrarese (P 1955-57)

1960 — Orioles Hoyt Wilhelm and Milt Pappas spin a twin shutout of the Tigers, 2-0, 1-0.

June 20

1879 — Jim Delahanty (3B-OF-2B 1907)

1918 — The Browns sell pitcher John Robinson to the Yankees.

1926 — Brown outfielder Ken Williams slugs a pinch three-run homer off the Senators' ace Walter Johnson.

1928 — Bob Mahoney (P 1951-52)

1943 — Andy Etchebarren (C 1962, 1965-75)

1947 — St. Louis sends pitcher Denny Galehouse, a starter in the '44 pennant drive, to the Red Sox for cash. Galehouse pitches well, winning 11 games for Boston.

1954 — Tony Chavez (P 1977)

1964 — The Birds score six runs in the first inning against Boston before a single batter is retired.

1970 — Third sacker Brooks Robinson records his 2,000th career hit, a three-run homer off the Senators' Joe Coleman in the fifth inning, to snap a 2-2 tie and give the Birds a 5-4 win.

June 21

1876 — Billy Gilbert (2B 1901)

1879 — Hunter Hill (3B-OF 1903-4)

1897 — Spencer Adams (2B-3B 1927)

1906 — Russ (Sheriff) Van Atta (P 1935-39)

1918 — Ed Lopat (P 1955)

1948 — Brown southpaw Bill Kennedy walks 12 Athletics in a single game.

1951 — Dave Skaggs (C 1977-80)

1956 — Bird pitchers Connie Johnson and George Zuverink combine to one-hit the White Sox, but lose to Jack Harshman's own one-hitter, 1-0.

1966 — Right fielder Frank Robinson makes a sensational, game-saving catch of Roy White's drive with two out and two on, falling into the right field seats at Yankee Stadium. The O's win this first game of a doubleheader 7-5. After winning the pennant later in the season, Manager Hank Bauer calls this play the biggest play of the season.

June 22

1887 — John (Red) Fisher (OF 1910)

1888 — Dick Kaufmann (1B-OF 1914-15)

1900 — Bill Mizeur (PH 1923-24)

1906 — George (Count) Puccinelli (OF 1934)

1913 — The White Sox' Jim Scott strikes out six straight Browns.

1914 — Maurice Newlin (P 1940-41)

1931 — Second baseman Oscar Melillo scores five runs for the Browns.

1934 — Russ Snyder (OF 1961-67)

1951 — Mike Anderson (OF 1978)

1962 — Boog Powell becomes the first batter to hit a homer over the center field hedge in Memorial Stadium, blasting a 469-foot drive off Boston's Don Schwall.

1966 — Curt Blefary's three-run homer and Steve Barber's four-hitter beat out the Yankees 3-0 in Yankee Stadium.

1970 — Merv Rettenmund walks twice in the seventh inning of a 9-8 win over Boston.

1979 — Third baseman Doug DeCinces raps a game-winning home run off Tiger Dave Tobik with two out and Eddie Murray on base for a 6-5 win before 35,456 Oriole fans.

June 23

1906 — Brownie Harry Howell shuts out Cleveland 4-0, despite giving up 11 hits.

1913 — Bill Cox (P 1938-40)

1915 — In a game with Detroit, the Browns fall victim to an unusual play and a display of Ty Cobb's amazing speed. With Cobb at second, Sam Crawford hits a ball back to Brown pitcher Grover Lowdermilk, who does a somersault going for the ball. Cobb goes to third and then streaks home as Lowdermilk sits on the mound with the ball in his hand.

1918 — First sacker George Sisler steals four bases for the Browns.

1930 — The Yankees shellac the Browns 15-0 behind the pitching of Henry Johnson in the first game of a twin bill.

1932 — Brown flyhawk Goose Goslin hits three consecutive homers.

1954 — The O's hang on to beat the Red Sox 8-7 in 17 innings in a game that lasts four hours and 58 minutes. During the game, both teams use 42 players (Red Sox 22, Orioles 20), leave 38 players on base (Boston 21, Baltimore 17) and send up to the plate 11 pinch-hitters (Red Sox 6, Orioles 5).

1959 — In a waiver deal with Cincinnati, Baltimore obtains first baseman Walt Dropo for utility player Whitey Lockman. Walt proves a valuable addition to the Bird bench.

1964 — Reserve catcher Charlie Lau gets two pinch-hits in the eighth inning of a 9-8 win over New York. The Birds rally from a 7-2 deficit to score seven runs with two out in the eighth. In the Yankee ninth, Roger Maris homers, but Stu Miller fans Tommy Tresh to end the game.

1973 — In his first major league game, Oriole Jesse Jefferson pitches 10 innings to beat Boston 2-1 in Fenway Park. He misses his first shutout when he yields a homer to Rico Petrocelli with two out in the ninth.

1978 — The Birds sign free agent outfielder Mike Anderson.

June 24

1907 — Rollie Hemsley (C-OF-1B 1933-37)

1917 — Al Gerheauser (P 1948)

1957 — Skinny Brown blanks the Tigers 6-0, starting a four-day string of Oriole shutouts, tying a league record. In the next three days, Billy Loes beats the Athletics 5-0, Connie Johnson whitewashes Kansas City 1-0, and Ray Moore beats the Indians 6-0.

47

June 25

1890 — Fred Walden (C 1912)

1914 — Brown catcher Frank Crossin records an unassisted double play.

1945 — Dick Drago (P 1977)

1956 — The Orioles buy outfielder Dick Williams from the Brooklyn Dodgers and sell pitcher Harry Dorish to the Red Sox.

1970 — Trailing the Red Sox 7–0 in Boston in the fifth inning, the Orioles rally for a tie in the ninth on a Rettenmund homer and Etchebarren double. In the 14th, the Birds explode for six runs and win as Frank Robinson makes a game-saving catch in the bottom of the inning, on a Reggie Smith drive, to end a potential Red Sox rally.

June 26

1908 — Debs Garms (OF 1932–35)

1921 — Willard Brown (OF 1947)

1933 — Gene Green (OF 1960)

1941 — Brown outfielder Glenn McQuillen ruins Yankee Marius Russo's bid for a no-hitter with a home run.

1966 — The Orioles tie the club record of 20 hits in a nine-inning game in a 12-7 win over the Angels in Anaheim. Outfielder Russ Snyder gets five hits and Boog Powell has four RBIs.

1970 — In an awesome offensive display, Frank Robinson hits two grand slams for eight RBIs in a 12-2 win over the Senators. He hits his first homer in the fifth off Joe Coleman and the other in the sixth off Joe Grzenda. Southpaw Dave McNally is the beneficiary of Robinson's slugging performance.

1978 — The Blue Jays humiliate the Orioles 24-10 in Toronto. In recognition of the day's futility, Manager Earl Weaver pitches sub flyhawk Larry Harlow and catcher Elrod Hendricks. Harlow yields five runs in two-thirds of an inning and Hendricks gives up just one hit and no runs in two and one-third innings.

June 27

1918 — Albert White (PH 1940)

1923 — Lou Kretlow (P 1950, 1953–55)

1964 — Outfielder Boog Powell hits three homers against the Senators in Washington.

1967 — Frank Robinson suffers a concussion by banging his head into the knee of White Sox second sacker Al Weis on a play at second. Robbie is out for a month while Weis sits out the season.

1970 — Oriole catcher Clay Dalrymple breaks his ankle in a home plate collision with Senator Mike Epstein, who was out on the play.

June 28

1890 — Ken Williams (OF–2B 1918-27)

1915 — George Sisler makes his pitching debut for the Browns with three scoreless innings at the end of a 4-2 loss in Chicago.

1949 — Don Baylor (OF–1B–DH 1970-75)

1973 — Center fielder Paul Blair makes a spectacular catch of a Roy White drive to preserve an eventual 6-3 Bird win over the Yanks.

June 29

1880 — Bill (Parson) McGill (P 1907)

1915 — Paul (Dizzy) Trout (P 1957)

June 30

1880 — Davy Jones (OF 1901-2)

1905 — Art (Scoop) Scharein (3B–SS–2B 1932-34)

1921 — Brownie George Sisler scores five runs in a game.

1975 — In an 8-2 Oriole win over the Red Sox in Boston, a line drive off the bat of Tony Muser breaks the cheekbone of Red Sox hurler Dick Pole. In this game, the Oriole catcher, Dave Duncan, belts four doubles to pace the attack.

JULY

July 1

1905 — White Sox hurler Frank Owen beats St. Louis twice, 3-2, 3-0.

1910 — The White Sox open their new stadium, soon to be called Comiskey Park, with a 2-0 loss to the Browns before 28,000 fans (24,900 paid). Barney Pelty gets the shutout for St. Louis.

1920 — Paul Lehner (OF–1B 1946-49, 1951)

1924 — Ken Wood (OF 1948-51)

Jack Bruner (P 1950)

1963 — The O's sell catcher Charlie Lau to the Athletics for $20,000.

July 2

1888 — Grover (Slick) Hartley (C–SS–3B 1916-17, 1934)

1930 — Pete Burnside (P 1963)

1975 — Don Baylor slugs three consecutive homers against the Tigers in a 13-5 road win, giving him four consecutive home runs in two days. The day before, he had hit a homer in his last at-bat versus Boston.

July 3

1882 — Tom Tennant (PH 1912)

1889 — Mike Balenti (SS-OF 1913)

1892 — Anthony (Bunny) Brief (1B-OF 1912-13)

1915 — George Sisler hurls his first complete game win over the Indians 3-1.

1930 — Al Pilarcik (OF 1957-60)

1955 — Jeff Rineer (P 1979)

1972 — In a nationally televised game, the O's set a club record of 21 hits in a nine-inning 15-3 win over Detroit. The Birds belt 17 hits and score 15 runs in the last four innings.

July 4

1880 — Edward (Pinky) Swander (OF 1903-4)

1887 — William Kenworthy (2B 1917)

1893 — Frank Thompson (3B-2B 1920)

1912 — On his 32nd birthday, Tiger ace George Mullin no-hits Willie Adams and the Browns 7-0 in Detroit. Mullin aids his cause with two singles, a double, and two RBIs. In the fifth inning, the great Ty Cobb steals second, third, and home.

1928 — Werner (Babe) Birrer (P 1956)

1944 — Second baseman Don Gutteridge records 12 assists in a 14-inning game for the Browns.

1949 — Tim Nordbrook (SS-2B 1974-76)

1954 — The Orioles sell pitcher Marlin Stuart to the Yankees on waivers.

1960 — The Birds sign outfielder Bobby Thomson, who is at the end of a good career. The Staten Island Scot bats six times in three games before being let go without getting an Oriole hit.

1967 — The O's trade pitcher Steve Barber to the Yankees for first baseman Ray Barker, outfielder Chet Trail, flyhawk Joe Brody, and cash.

July 5

1884 — Ward (Windy) Miller (OF-2B 1916-17)

1904 — Irving (Bump) Hadley (P 1932-34)

1931 — Arnold Portocarrero (P 1958-60)

1943 — Curt Blefary (OF-1B-C 1965-68)

1955 — After just three weeks with the team, outfielder Wally Westlake is released by Baltimore.

July 6

1876 — John (Snags) Heidrick (OF-SS-3B-C-P 1902-4, 1908)

1881 — Roy Hartzell (3B-OF-SS-2B 1906-10)

1891 — Steve O'Neill (C 1927-28)

1917 — Ken Sears (C 1946)

1924 — Frank Kellert (1B 1953-54)

1938 — Barry Shetrone (OF 1959-62)

1966 — Boog Powell drives in 11 runs in a doubleheader, tying the American League record, against Kansas City. Powell bangs out two homers, including a grand slam, along with two doubles and a sacrifice fly for 4 RBIs in the first game and seven RBIs in the second.

July 7

1893 — Franklin (Buzz) Wetzel (OF 1920-21)

1906 — Leroy (Satchel) Paige (P 1951-53)

1911 — Red Sox pitcher Smoky Joe Wood strikes out 11 Brownies.

1927 — In a waiver deal, the Browns send pitcher Tom Zachary to Washington and get hurler General Crowder in return. A great deal for St. Louis as Crowder wins 21 the next season to lead the staff and nets 17 wins in 1929.

1931 — Brown pitcher Chad Kimsey hits a pinch homer.

1935 — Outfielder Moose Solters hits three consecutive homers for the Browns.

1961 — Oriole Jim Gentile belts a pinch grand slam off Kansas City's Ed Rakow.

1970 — Brooks Robinson's grand slam off Lindy McDaniel in the 10th inning gives the Birds a 6-2 win over New York.

July 7 (continued)

1973 — A Baltimore Helmet Night crowd of 42,180 sees an around-the-horn Oriole triple play in a 5–4 loss to Oakland. A Deron Johnson grounder to Brooks Robinson starts the play, which then goes to Bobby Grich and first sacker Enos Cabell to complete the triple killing.

July 8

1889 — Joe Crisp (C 1910–11)

1893 — Bill Brown (OF 1912)

1909 — The Senators' ace, Walter Johnson, strikes out seven consecutive Browns.

1929 — Johnny Powers (OF 1960)

1958 — The O's host their first All-Star game ever before 48,829 fans. Oriole catcher Gus Triandos starts for the American League and pitcher Billy O'Dell stars in relief by retiring nine straight National Leaguers on 27 pitches to protect a 4–3 American League win. For his sterling effort, O'Dell is named the game's Most Valuable Player.

1969 — The Orioles score 10 runs on nine hits in the fourth inning, including seven runs in a row off Yankees Fritz Peterson and Mike Kekich, to beat New York 10–3 in the first game of a twin bill. O's pitcher Tom Phoebus gets the win.

1970 — Trailing New York 8–6 in the bottom of the ninth, the Birds strike with a Frank Robinson homer and two-out Don Buford single to win 9-8.

1971 — Frank Robinson notches his 2,500th career hit, a three-run homer off Senator Horacio Pina, as Mike Cuellar gets his 11th straight win 7–3. The victory is the Cuban's 13th out of 14 decisions.

July 9

1874 — Jack Powell (P 1902–3, 1905–12)

1887 — Bill McCorry (P 1909)

1901 — Lou Polli (P 1932)

1915 — Tony Criscola (OF 1942–43)

1949 — Steve Luebber (P 1981)

1955 — After his release by the Orioles, pitcher Saul Rogovin signs with the Phillies.

1959 — Two 20-year-olds, Milt Pappas and Jerry Walker, shut out the Senators for the Orioles 8–0, 5–0, in Washington. This same day, rookie third baseman Brooks Robinson is recalled from the minors for good.

July 10

1864 — Jimmy McAleer (OF 1902, 1907; MGR 1902-9)

1903 — Johnny Niggeling (P 1940-43)

1917 — Yankee Ray Caldwell hurls nine and two-thirds innings of no-hit relief to beat the Browns as the Yanks score twice in the 17th inning to win 7-5 in St. Louis.

1918 — Chuck Stevens (1B 1941, 1946, 1948)

1926 — The Senators score 12 runs in an inning against St. Louis.

1947 — Yankee reliever Joe Page hits a ninth-inning homer to beat the Browns 4-3 in St. Louis.

1951 — Bob Bailor (SS-2B-DH 1975-76)

July 11

1911 — Vito Tamulis (P 1938)

1914 — George (Bingo) Binks (OF-1B 1948)

1968 — First base coach Earl Weaver is named manager by the Orioles, succeeding Hank Bauer and beginning one of the most successful managing careers in history. In his first game at the helm, the Orioles beat the Senators 2-0 behind the two-hit pitching of lefty Dave McNally.

July 12

1907 — Bob Looney (P 1931-32)

1913 — Tom Hafey (OF-1B 1944)

1927 — Jack Harshman (P-OF 1958-59)

July 13

1879 — John (Jiggs) Donahue (C-1B 1901-2)

1902 — Bill Lasley (P 1924)

1921 — Harry (Fritz) Dorish (P 1950, 1955-56)

1946 — Outfielder Al Zarilla hits two triples in an inning for the Browns.

1948 — The Browns host the All-Star Game before a crowd of 34,009. The fans go home happy as the American League wins, 5-2.

1955 — The Birds purchase pitcher Bill Wight from Cleveland. Wight is strictly a journeyman for Baltimore.

1962 — Catcher Charlie Lau hits four doubles in a game with the Indians.

July 14

1911 — Julio Bonetti (P 1937–38)

1916 — Pitcher Ernie Koob goes the distance for the Browns in a 17-inning 0–0 deadlock with Boston. Poor base-running by Koob in the 15th inning costs him a win as he fails to touch third base before scoring on a Ward Miller single. For the Red Sox, Carl Mays pitches 15 innings before yielding to Dutch Leonard for the last two.

1920 — Bryan Stephens (P 1948)

1947 — Steve Stone (P 1979–81)

1948 — Earl Williams (C–1B–DH 1973–74)

1953 — Billy Smith (2B–SS–1B–3B 1977–79)

1977 — The Orioles trade pitcher Fred Holdsworth to Montreal for a player to be named. The Expos send pitcher Dennis Blair to the O's on September 6 to complete the deal.

1980 — Eddie Murray's streak of 444 consecutive games ends when he is struck in the eye by a bad-hop grounder off the bat of George Brett. Murray misses four games before returning to the lineup.

July 15

1904 — Brown right-hander Fred Glade strikes out 15 Senators.

1917 — The Browns trade outfielder Armando Marsans to the Yankees for outfielder Lee Magee. A deal of little consequence for both clubs.

1943 — St. Louis obtains pitcher Bobo Newsom from Brooklyn for pitchers Archie McKain and Fritz Ostermueller.

1960 — Brooks Robinson hits for the cycle.

July 16

1936 — Eddie Fisher (P 1966–67)

1941 — Outfielder Chet Laabs slugs two homers, a triple, and a double for the Browns.

1951 — The Browns buy outfielder Jack Maguire from Pittsburgh.

1953 — Catcher Clint Courtney, first sacker Dick Kryhoski, and outfielder Jim Dyck hit consecutive homers for the Browns.

1958 — Oriole pitcher Jack Harshman hits two homers in one game.

July 17

1902 — The Browns win a forfeit from Baltimore when the latter club fails to show up for one of its home games. The club had been purchased the day before by New York Giant owner Andrew Freedman, who transferred four players to the Giants and released two others.

1919 — The Browns beat the Yanks 7-6 in 17 innings on a squeeze play. In this contest, the Browns rap out 17 hits while the New Yorkers get 21 hits.

1947 — Hank Thompson becomes the first black player for the St. Louis Browns. The 21-year-old second baseman later becomes the third baseman for the pennant-winning Giants of the early Fifties.

1964 — Robin Roberts blanks the Tigers 5-0 for the Birds, despite giving up 11 hits.

1969 — Oriole catcher Clay Dalrymple creates a controversy when he takes his position with a catcher's mitt on his hand and a fielder's glove in his back pocket. He plans to use the fielder's glove for close plays at the plate but is told by the umpires that he cannot.

July 18

1914 — Ben Huffman (C 1937)

1944 — Rudy May (P 1976-77)

1954 — Red Sox pitcher Russ Kemmerer hurls a one-hitter against the Orioles in his first major league start.

July 19

1891 — Earl Hamilton (P 1911-17)

1916 — Brown pitcher Dave Davenport throws two complete game wins, 3-1, 3-2, over the Yankees.

1927 — Billy Gardner (2B-SS-3B 1956-59)

1941 — St. Louis first baseman George McQuinn hits for the cycle.

1954 — Dan Graham (C-3B-DH-OF 1980-81)

1963 - - The O's release pitcher Ike Delock.

1966 — Slugger Boog Powell strikes out twice in the same inning.

1968 — The Orioles suffer one of their tougher defeats as Tiger Tom Matchick hits a Moe Drabowsky pitch out of sight with two outs in the ninth, one on base, and a full count. The 5-4 Detroit win was a critical victory in the Bengals' pennant drive.

1973 — The Orioles beat the Angels 3-1 in 11 innings as Mike Cuellar goes the distance and strikes out 12. Angel hurler Nolan Ryan has a no-hitter going until Mark Belanger singles in the eighth. The Birds win as Terry Crowley doubles in two runs off Dave Sells, who came in to relieve Ryan. Ryan sends 13 Orioles down in defeat at the plate on strikes.

July 20

1901 — Heinie Manush (OF 1928-30)

1937 — The Browns fire manager Rogers Hornsby and replace him with Sunny Jim Bottomley.

1944 — Umpire Cal Hubbard throws Brown pitcher Nelson Potter out of a game against the Yankees for violating the rules by wetting his fingers. Potter receives a 10-day suspension.

July 21

1888 — Walt Leverenz (P 1913-15)

1910 — Eight St. Louis errors contribute heavily to a 19-2 Yankee win.

1935 — Moe Drabowsky (P 1966-68, 1970)

1946 — In the second game of a doubleheader, Ted Williams hits for the cycle against the Browns. In both games, the Red Sox superstar records seven consecutive hits.

1979 — Against the Angels, Bird handyman John Lowenstein plays all three outfield positions, walks three times, and drives in three runs with a triple.

July 22

1891 — George Baumgardner (P 1912-16)

1905 — Philadelphia's Weldon Henley no-hits the Browns, beating Barney Pelty 6-0 in the first game of a home twin bill.

1918 — The Browns battle the Yankees to a 15-inning 4-4 draw.

1921 — Al La Macchia (P 1943, 1945-46)

1922 — Jim Rivera (OF 1952)

1935 — Red Sox hurler Wes Ferrell belts a homer in the ninth to beat the Browns 2-1.

1945 — Rookie sensation Dave (Boo) Ferriss gets his 17th win for the Red Sox by beating St. Louis 3-2 before a crowd of 34,810 in Fenway Park. Thousands of fans who try to get in to see the game are turned away.

1973 — Brooks Robinson drives in five runs with three hits, including a homer, to pace an 8-2 Oriole win over the Angels.

July 23

1915 — The Browns sell outfielder Elmer Miller to the Yanks.

1926 — Johnny Groth (OF 1953)

1979 — Tippy Martinez retires 23 straight hitters and pitches seven and two-thirds innings of perfect relief as the O's beat Oakland 7-4 on a Pat Kelly grand slam.

July 24

1913 — Senator ace Walter Johnson fans 15 Brownies in 11 and one-third innings in relief, a strikeout record for relievers.

1922 — A trade between the Red Sox and Yankees involving third baseman Joe Dugan enrages the contending Browns, who argue that it gives the Yankees an unfair advantage in the pennant chase. This trade leads Judge Landis to establish the June 15 trading deadline.

Duane Pillette (P 1950-55)

1934 — Yankee outfielder Earle Combs suffers a fractured skull crashing into the center field wall in St. Louis in pursuit of a fly ball. The Browns win the contest 4-2.

1943 — A line drive off the bat of Red Sox hitter Oscar Judd strikes Brown pitcher Bobo Newsom in the head. Newsom escapes with no serious injury.

1949 — The Red Sox pound Brown pitching for 25 hits.

1979 — Outfielder John Lowenstein drives in six runs for the Orioles and goes three for five with a grand slam off Seattle's Odell Jones in an 11-3 win. Scott McGregor is the beneficiary of Lowenstein's slugging in this second game of a twin bill.

July 25

1913 — Brown pitcher Carl Weilman sets a major league record as he strikes out six times in a 15-inning game with Washington.

1918 — The Browns lose a tough one to the Senators 1-0 in 15 innings.

1926 — Carroll (Whitey) Lockman (1B-2B-OF 1959)

1947 — Mickey Scott (P 1972-73)

1955 — The O's release first baseman Eddie Waitkus.

1967 — Racial strife in the streets of Detroit forces a postponement of the Orioles-Tigers game. The remaining two games in the set are shifted to Baltimore for July 26 and 27.

July 25 (continued)

1969 — In a 17-inning game with the White Sox, the Orioles team up with the Chisox for 154 fielding chances, including 100 putouts and 54 assists.

July 26

1892 — Sam Jones (P 1927)

1914 — Ellis Kinder (P 1946-47)

1923 — Hoyt Wilhelm (P 1958-62)

1924 — Leo Thomas (3B-SS-2B 1950, 1952)

1926 — Tito Herrera (P 1951)

 Bill (Hooks) Miller (P 1955)

1933 — Norm Siebern (1B 1964-65)

1935 — Lou Jackson (OF 1964)

1939 — Yankee catcher Bill Dickey belts three consecutive homers in a 14-1 win over the Browns as the Yanks score in every inning.

 Pete Ward (OF 1962)

1980 — Bird pitcher Steve Stone beats the Brewers and Mike Caldwell 4-1 to record his 14th straight win.

July 27

1883 — Harry (Klondike) Kane (P 1902)

1898 — Benny Bengough (C 1931-32)

 Zack Taylor (MGR 1946, 1948-51)

1908 — Southpaw Rube Waddell strikes out 16 Athletics to break Fred Glade's team record for the Browns and set a new American League record.

1933 — Rogers Hornsby is named manager of the Browns, succeeding Bill Killefer and interim skipper Allan Sothoron.

1945 — The Browns purchase first baseman Lou Finney from the Red Sox. Finney hits .277 coming off the bench.

1946 — Rudy York slugs two grand slams and a double for the Red Sox against the Browns to give him 15 RBIs in two games.

1947 — Red Sox first sacker Jake Jones is awarded a 60-foot triple by umpire Cal Hubbard after Brown pitcher Fred Sanford throws his glove at Jones's rolling hit to keep it from going into fair territory.

1952 — Rich Dauer (2B–3B–DH 1976–present)

1957 — Floyd Rayford (3B–2B–DH 1980, present)

1959 — Baltimore native outfielder Barry Shetrone goes two for four with a triple against the Tigers in Detroit as he becomes the first Baltimore city native to play for the Orioles.

1965 — The Orioles release pitcher Robin Roberts after he contributes three strong seasons as a member of the starting rotation.

1969 — The O's score their biggest shutout win ever, a 17–0 whitewash of the White Sox. Jim Hardin throws a two-hitter for the Birds, who bang out 20 hits for 39 total bases.

1973 — Indian George Hendrick's single in the eighth spoils Jim Palmer's bid for a no-hitter. Palmer beats Cleveland 9–0 in the first game of a doubleheader.

1977 — The Orioles buy reserve catcher Ken Rudolph from the Giants.

July 28

1917 — In a doubleheader with the Red Sox that covers 20 innings, the Browns' pitchers do not record a single strikeout.

1952 — The Browns sell catcher Darrell Johnson and outfielder Jim Rivera to the White Sox. In return, the Browns obtain from Chicago outfielder Ray Coleman and minor league catcher J. W. Porter. This is not a sterling deal for St. Louis as Rivera goes on to have a decent major league career with Chicago and Kansas City.

1971 — Frank Robinson blasts a three-run homer off Oakland's bullpen ace Rollie Fingers to get a 3–2 win in the ninth. Oddly enough, Brooks Robinson has one of the worst days of his career, with three errors in the fifth inning and going 0-for-3 while hitting into two double plays.

July 29

1908 — Just two days after a record-setting performance, Brown ace Rube Waddell repeats his 16-strikeout effort once more against Philadelphia.

1911 — Boston's Smoky Joe Wood throws a no-hitter to beat St. Louis 5–0. He strikes out 12 Browns in this first game of a twin bill in Boston.

1954 — Baltimore sells outfielder Sam Mele to the Red Sox.

July 30

1915 — The Browns send catcher Walt Alexander to the Yanks for cash.

Jerry Witte (1B 1946–47)

1922 — Joe Coleman (P 1954–55)

1930 — Gus Triandos (C–1B–3B 1955–62)

1944 — Pat Kelly (OF–DH 1977–80)

1953 — The Browns obtain shortstop Vern Stephens from the White Sox on waivers. The former star of the 1944 Brown pennant drive raps .321 in 46 games at third base for the Brownies.

1954 — Utility player Bob Kennedy hits the first grand slam in Oriole history off Yankee hurler Allie Reynolds in Memorial Stadium.

1969 — Dave McNally beats the Royals 4–2 for his 15th straight win without a defeat and 17th over two seasons. This game allows the Oriole hurler to tie the record set by Cleveland's Johnny Allen.

1971 — A Frank Robinson home run ruins the no-hit bid of Kansas City's Dick Drago.

1979 — Steve Stone's try for a no-hitter is spoiled by a homer by Brewer Charlie Moore. Stone ends up with a one-hitter for eight and two-thirds innings in a 2–1 Oriole win. Al Bumbry's two-run homer is the winning margin.

July 31

1870 — Joe Sugden (C–1B–P 1902–5)

1910 — Glenn Liebhardt (P 1936, 1938)

1916 — Billy Hitchcock (2B–3B–SS–1B 1947; MGR 1962–63)

1922 — Hank Bauer (MGR 1964–68)

1931 — Joe Durham (OF 1954, 1957)

   Walter (Rip) Coleman (P 1959–60)

1941 — The Browns win a three-hour and 11 minute marathon with the Red Sox 16–11. It is the longest nine-inning game in league history up to that point.

1947 — Earl Stephenson (P 1977–78)

1951 — The Browns trade third baseman Kermit Wahl, shortstop Tom Upton, and pitchers Bob Hogue and Lou Sleater to the Yankees for outfielder Cliff Mapes.

1971 — Bird hurler Pat Dobson wins his 12th straight, beating Kansas City 4–0.

AUGUST

August 1

1917 — Chet Johnson (P 1946)

1925 — George Bamberger (P 1959)

1937 — Yankee great Lou Gehrig hits for the cycle against the Browns in a 14-5 New York win.

1941 — Yankee hurler Lefty Gomez walks 11 Brownies in a game.

1947 — Tony Muser (1B-DH-OF 1975-77)

August 2

1876 — William (Doc) Nance (OF 1904)

1886 — Dwight Stone (P 1913)

1951 — Brown pitcher Satchel Paige gives up a pinch grand slam to Boston's Charlie Maxwell.

1981 — Memorial Stadium opens the gates free to 4,791 fans to watch the Orioles' first workout since the settlement of the strike.

August 3

1889 — Wally Mayer (C 1919)

1894 — George Hale (C 1914, 1916-18)

1928 — Dick Hyde (P 1961)

1949 — Red Sox hurler Ellis Kinder fans 14 Brownies in a 9-3 Boston win.

1955 — The O's turn the first triple play in their history when Kansas City pitcher Art Ceccarelli grounds into a double play and the runner is thrown out at home. The play goes from first sacker Gus Triandos to shortstop Willie Miranda to catcher Hal Smith.

1969 — Southpaw Dave McNally's 17-game win streak, including 15 in a row this season, ends as the Twins' Rich Reese hits a pinch grand slam in the seventh inning of a 5-2 Minnesota win behind the pitching of Jim Kaat.

1970 — The Birds beat the Royals 10-8 for a record 23rd-straight win.

1973 — Oriole pitcher Jesse Jefferson strikes out nine and retires 17 men in a row in an 8-2 win over the Red Sox.

August 4

1899 — Oscar Melillo (2B-3B 1926-35)

1907 — George Caster (P 1941-45)

1948 — In a home game with the Red Sox, the Browns give up six runs in the top of the first inning only to come back with seven of their own in the bottom of the inning.

August 4 (continued)

1952 — St. Louis purchases pitcher Bob Hogue from the Yankees.

1975 — In a night game at Fenway Park, the Birds hang on to beat the Red Sox 12–8 before 35,866 disappointed Beantowners.

August 5

1905 — Ray Pepper (OF 1934–36)

1933 — Brown outfielder Sammy West belts two triples, a double, and a homer.

1940 — In the second half of a twin bill at home, Brown right-hander Silent John Whitehead hurls a rain-shortened, six-inning 4–0 no-hitter over the Tigers for his only win of the season. His season is curtailed by an ankle injury.

1943 — Nelson Briles (P 1978)

August 6

1903 — Hal (Whitey) Wiltse (P 1928)

1904 — Herb Cobb (P 1929)

1905 — Chad Kimsey (P 1929–32)

Ed Roetz (SS–1B–2B–3B 1929)

1922 — St. Louis outfielder John Tobin blasts a game-winning grand slam off Washington ace Walter Johnson. It is the first of only two grand slams given up by the Big Train in his Hall-of-Fame career.

1926 — Ralph (Blackie) Schwamb (P 1948)

1937 — Camilo Carreon (C 1966)

1943 — Jim Hardin (P 1967–71)

1949 — Mike Reinbach (OF–DH 1974)

1952 — In one of baseball's greatest pitching performances, 46-year-old Brown hurler Satchel Paige beats Virgil Trucks and the Tigers 1–0 in 12 innings.

1959 — With the White Sox' Billy Pierce and the Birds' Billy O'Dell locked in a 1–1 tie in the ninth, the Orioles send Hoyt Wilhelm into the game in relief of O'Dell. Wilhelm proceeds to throw 8⅔ innings of no-hit relief before giving up a hit. The game is called after 18 innings, still 1–1, because of the midnight curfew.

August 7

1876 — Lou Noroyke (1B 1906)

1883 — Tom Richardson (PH 1917)

1899 — Guy Sturdy (1B 1927-28)

1902 — Brown outfielder Snags Heidrick hits two doubles and two triples in a game.

1912 — First sacker George Stovall records seven assists in a game for St. Louis.

1915 — Brown third baseman Jimmy Austin explodes at the plate, going 8 for 10 in a doubleheader, including a triple and a homer.

1922 — Bob Alexander (P 1955)

Slugging Brown outfielder Ken Williams hits two homers in a single inning.

1927 — Art Houtteman (P 1957)

1929 — Don Larsen (P-OF 1953-54, 1965)

1932 — St. Louis catcher Benny Bengough registers an unassisted double play.

1936 — Bob Nelson (OF-1B 1955-57)

1954 — The Birds obtain pitcher Bob Kuzava from the Yankees.

August 8

1918 — Marlin Stuart (P 1952-54)

1920 — First baseman George Sisler hits for the cycle for St. Louis.

1928 — Johnny Temple (2B 1962)

1936 — Ray Pepper gets two pinch-hits in the eighth inning for the Browns.

1970 — A grand slam by left fielder Don Buford lifts the Orioles to a 7-4 win over Milwaukee. Milwaukee reliever Dave Baldwin had walked Boog Powell intentionally to load the sacks for Buford.

August 9

1886 — Bob Clemons (OF 1914)

1887 — Willis (Kid) Butler (2B-3B-SS 1907)

1908 — Third baseman Hobe Ferris hits the first grand slam in Browns' history.

1919 — Fred Sanford (P 1943, 1946-48, 1951)

1921 — In a 19-inning contest with Washington, Browns' star George Sisler goes 6 for 9, with a triple and five singles. St. Louis right-hander Dixie Davis goes the distance for an 8-6 win over the Senators, yielding 13 hits and striking out eight.

1931 — Chuck Essegian (OF 1961)

August 9 (continued)

1948 — The Browns obtain pitcher Karl Drews from the Yankees on waivers. Drews contributes little this season and goes 4 and 12 the next as a starter.

1975 — Oriole second sacker Bobby Grich walks five times in a game with the White Sox.

August 10

1895 — Joe Schepner (3B 1919)

1908 — Bill Trotter (P 1937-42)

1927 — Bob Chakales (P 1954)

1944 — The Browns win their tenth straight as right-hander Denny Galehouse shuts out the Yankees 3-0.

1962 — The Birds sell second baseman Johnny Temple to Houston.

1963 — Left fielder Boog Powell becomes the first Oriole to hit three home runs in a game, as he belts two off Bennie Daniels and one off Steve Ridzik in DC Stadium in a loss to the Senators.

1967 — Indian hurler Stan Williams strikes out 14 Birds in 13 innings.

1969 — For the second time in a season, Minnesota's Cesar Tovar ruins an Oriole's bid for a no-hitter. This time Mike Cuellar is the victim of a ninth-inning Tovar single.

1971 — Bird southpaw Mike Cuellar gives up Harmon Killebrew's 500th career home run in the first inning of a 4-3 win at Minnesota.

1981 — The Orioles open the second half of the strike-torn season with a 3-2 win over the Royals in 12 innings. John Lowenstein drives in the winning run with a single and Tippy Martinez gets the win in relief before 19,850 Bird fans.

August 11

1907 — Norman (Bobo) Newsom (P 1934-35, 1938-39, 1943)

1943 — Steve Sundra's bid for a Brown no-hitter is ruined by a homer by the Yankees' King Kong Keller.

1950 — Brown right fielder Ken Wood records two assists in the eighth inning.

1966 — Frank Robinson continues his fielding magic with a great catch to rob Clete Boyer of a homer that would have tied the score in a game at Yankee Stadium.

1975 — The O's acquire outfielder Andres Mora, the "Mexican Babe Ruth," from Saltillo of the Mexican League. Mora managed to hit 27 home runs in three seasons as a part-timer with the Birds before mercifully returning to his native land.

August 12

1887 — Marc Hall (P 1910)

1912 — Harlond Clift (3B-2B-SS 1934-43)

1948 — The Indians shellac the Browns 26-3 in the second game of a double-header, pounding out 26 hits.

1956 — Bob Bonner (SS 1980-present)

1964 — The Birds sell outfielder Willie Kirkland to the Senators.

1981 — In his major league debut, lefty reliever Jeff Schneider gives up a grand slam to the Royals' Frank White in a 10-0 Oriole loss to Kansas City.

August 13

1874 — Fielder Jones (MGR 1916-18)

1886 — Thomas (Lefty) George (P 1911)

1908 — George Susce (C 1940)

1910 — Lou Finney (OF-1B-3B 1945-46)

1921 — First baseman George Sisler hits for the cycle, including two doubles, in a 10-inning game with Detroit.

1969 — Oriole ace Jim Palmer no-hits Oakland 8-0 in his second start since coming off the disabled list four days earlier. He strikes out eight in this thrill for the home crowd.

1978 — With the help of a rain-out rule, the Orioles beat New York 3-0. The Yankees scored five runs in the top of the seventh, but heavy rain called the game in the bottom of the inning, with the score reverting to the score at the end of the last completed frame. Subsequently, this rule was changed in 1980.

August 14

1888 — Al Clancy (3B 1911)

William (Babe) Borton (1B 1916)

1903 — The Senators hang on through 15 innings to beat the Browns 1-0.

1913 — Paul (Daffy) Dean (P 1943)

1929 — Jim Pisoni (OF 1953)

1930 — Earl Weaver (MGR 1968-present)

1937 — The Tigers score 36 runs against the Browns in a doubleheader, a major league offensive record.

August 14 (continued)

1952 — The Browns obtain pitchers Dick Littlefield and Marlin Stuart, first baseman Vic Wertz, and outfielder Don Lenhardt from Detroit for pitchers Ned Garver, Dave Madison, and Bud Black and outfielder Jim Delsing. The Tigers get the best of this deal, which helps both clubs, as Garver becomes a top starter and Delsing takes over center field.

1973 — Right fielder Don Baylor goes 5 for 5 in a 12-10 Bird win over Texas, giving him nine hits in two days.

August 15

1891 — Tim Bowden (OF 1914)

1936 — John Buzhardt (P 1967)

1966 — Boog Powell's three homers pace a 4-2 win over the Red Sox in 11 innings at Fenway Park. The slugging left fielder hits all three shots over left field and racks up 13 total bases for the day.

The O's sell pitcher Billy Short to the Red Sox.

1979 — First baseman Eddie Murray steals home in the 12th inning with two out to beat the White Sox and Guy Hoffman 2-1. Mike Flanagan gets the win.

August 16

1885 — Herb Northen (OF 1910)

1890 — William (Baby Doll) Jacobson (OF-1B, 1915, 1917, 1919-26)

1922 — Gene Woodling (OF 1955, 1958-60)

1941 — Gene Brabender (P 1966-68)

1969 — Boog Powell hits an inside-the-park home run off former teammate Steve Barber in Seattle.

1980 — The Birds draw their biggest night crowd ever at Memorial Stadium, 51,649, but lose to Gaylord Perry and New York 4-1.

August 17

1888 — Vince Molyneaux (P 1917)

1920 — Vern Bickford (P 1954)

1923 — Harry Markell (P 1951)

1941 — John (Boog) Powell (1B-OF-DH 1961-74)

1956 — In a waiver deal, the O's send catcher Hal Smith to Kansas City for catcher Joe Ginsberg. The Athletics benefit more as Smith becomes a starter.

1963 — Reliever Dick Hall pitches a perfect inning for the Orioles against Kansas City to extend his string of consecutive batters retired to 28 in five appearances during 25 days.

1966 — For the second day in a row, the Orioles score five runs in the ninth to win, beating Boston 8-4. They had won 6-4 the previous day.

1972 — The O's draw their smallest crowd ever at Memorial Stadium, 655 for a game with the White Sox.

1980 — Southpaw Scott McGregor hurls a six-hitter to beat Luis Tiant and the Yankees 1-0 before 50,073 fans at Memorial Stadium.

August 18

1891 — Wally Gerber (SS-2B-3B 1917-28)

1913 — Tommy Heath (C 1935, 1937-38)

1915 — Max Lanier (P 1953)

> The Browns trade pitcher William James to Detroit for outfielder Baby Doll Jacobson. A great deal for St. Louis as Jacobson hits above .300 for seven of eight seasons as a star center fielder.

1920 — Bob Kennedy (3B-OF-1B 1954-55)

1951 — Owner Bill Veeck pulls his most famous stunt, delighting the home crowd at Sportsman's Park by sending up midget Eddie Gaedel to pinch-hit for Frank Saucier. The little batter draws a walk off Tiger Bob Cain in his only big-league appearance.

1969 — Light-hitting shortstop Mark Belanger enjoys a big day for the O's against the Pilots in Seattle, hitting two doubles in one inning and finishing the day with three doubles, a single, and five RBIs.

1972 — The Orioles trade catcher Elrod Hendricks to the Cubs for first baseman Tommy Davis. A valuable deal for Baltimore as Davis becomes the designated hitter for three seasons.

August 19

1918 — St. Louis second sacker Joe Gedeon records 12 assists in a 14-inning game.

1928 — Jim Finigan (3B-2B-SS 1959)

1930 — Brown left fielder Goose Goslin slugs three consecutive homers.

1937 — Jim Lehew (P 1961-62)

1950 — Paul Mitchell (P 1975)

1980 — Steve Stone wins his 20th game of the season, beating the Angels 5-2. Stone had a no-hitter going for $7\frac{1}{3}$ innings until Bert Campaneris rapped a single.

August 20

1907 — Roy (Beau) Bell (OF–1B–3B 1935–39)

1909 — Sig Jakucki (P 1936, 1944–45)

1919 — Earl Harrist (P 1952)

1924 — George Zuverink (P 1955–59)

August 21

1905 — Frank Waddey (OF 1931)

1907 — Wally (Preacher) Herbert (P 1931–33)

1911 — Tom Cafego (OF 1937)

1914 — St. Louis commits eight errors that lead to a 4–3 Yankee win.

1917 — St. Louis sells catcher Muddy Ruel to the Yankees.

1920 — Mizell (Whitey) Platt (OF–1B 1948–49)

1931 — Babe Ruth slugs his 600th career home run in an 11–7 New York win over the Browns.

1945 — Jerry DaVanon (2B–SS–3B–1B 1971)

1961 — The Birds purchase catcher Charlie Lau from the Braves.

1967 — Baltimore buys pitcher John Buzhardt from the White Sox. Buzhardt appears in just seven games for the O's.

August 22

1879 — John McAleese (OF–3B 1909)

1889 — Wally Schang (C–OF 1926–29)

1890 — Urban Shocker (P 1918–24)

1899 — Ernest Dudley (SS–2B–3B 1920–21)

1934 — Angelo (Junior) Dagres (OF 1955)

1951 — The Red Sox strand 22 runners in a 13-inning game with St. Louis.

1966 — At a private team swim party at the home of funeral director Leonard Ruck, catcher Andy Etchebarren saves Frank Robinson from drowning.

1972 — Baltimore releases utility player Chico Salmon.

August 23

1886 — Fletcher Allen (C-1B 1910)

1888 — Paul Meloan (OF 1911)

1889 — Ed Hallinan (SS-2B-3B 1911-12)

1890 — Hal Schwenk (P 1913)

1896 — Cedric Durst (OF-1B 1922-23, 1926)

1905 — Brown left fielder George Stone tallies an unassisted double play versus the Yankees.

1911 — Nelson Potter (P 1943-48)

1918 — Ken Holcombe (P 1952)

1922 — George Kell (3B-1B-2B 1956-57)

1924 — Sherman Lollar (C-3B 1949-51)

1931 — Philadelphia's Lefty Grove sees his 16-game win skein stopped as Dick Coffman and the Browns beat him 1-0. The Browns score when Athletic rookie left fielder Johnny Moore misjudges a fly ball by Oscar Melillo, which falls for a double to drive in Fred Schulte, who had singled.

1936 — In his first major league start after several relief appearances, 17-year-old Bob Feller of Cleveland beats St. Louis 4-1. He delights the home crowd by fanning 15 Brownies.

1941 — John Morris (P 1968)

1945 — Ed Barnowski (P 1965-66)

1957 — Mike Boddicker (P 1980-81)

August 24

1918 — In a rare feat for a pitcher, Red Sox lefty Babe Ruth steals home against the Browns.

1960 — Cal Ripken Jr. (SS-3B 1981-present)

August 25

1889 — Fred Graff (3B 1913)

Les Nunamaker (C-OF-1B 1918)

1924 — Senator ace Walter Johnson throws a rain-shortened, seven-inning no-hitter for a 2-0 win over the Browns.

August 25 (continued)

1926 — Jim Suchecki (P 1951)

1928 — Darrell Johnson (C 1952, 1962)

1930 — Tiger hurler Tommy Bridges walks 12 Browns in a game.

1968 — The Orioles beat Boston 3-2 in 18 innings at home.

August 26

1909 — Gene Moore (OF–1B 1944–45)

1913 — Hank Helf (C 1946)

1916 — A Yankee triple play kills a Browns' rally with the bases loaded in the seventh inning of a 10-6 New York win.

1925 — Billy De Mars (SS–3B 1950–51)

1962 — Robin Roberts helps the Orioles cap a five-game sweep of the Yankees at home with a five-hitter to beat Whitey Ford 2-1.

1966 — Vic Roznovsky and Boog Powell belt back-to-back pinch homers off Lee Stange in the ninth inning against the Red Sox.

1968 — Dave McNally hits a grand slam for the Birds off Oakland's Chuck Dobson.

1971 — In an uncharacteristic performance, Don Buford strikes out five times against his former team, the White Sox.

1973 — In a 10-1 Oriole win over the Royals, Paul Blair hits an inside-the-park grand slam off Paul Splittorff as his drive falls between outfielders Amos Otis and Steve Hovley. Otis and Hovley collide in mid-air while chasing the ball.

August 27

1874 — George Bone (SS 1901)

1893 — Carl East (P 1915)

1910 — Ewald (Lefty) Pyle (P 1939, 1942)

1925 — Bullet Joe Bush hurls a one-hitter for St. Louis.

1961 — Bird pitcher Milt Pappas hits two homers in a game.

1973 — The Orioles win their 14th straight game, beating Texas 6-1 with sparkling defensive play.

August 28

1875 — Joe Yeager (3B-2B-SS 1907-8)

1887 — Byron (Duke) Houck (P 1918)

1903 — A train carrying the Browns and Indians derails near Napoleon, Ohio. Among the St. Louis players injured are pitcher Bill Sudhoff, who suffers a cut and sprained wrist, and center fielder Snags Heidrick, who gets a cut face and bruised leg. The Indians' star, Nap Lajoie, suffers a face cut and a sprained knee.

1943 — Lou Piniella (PH 1964)

1946 — Mike Torrez (P 1975)

1957 — Baltimore pounds Cleveland 19-6, with a 19-hit attack led by catcher Gus Triandos' two home runs.

1960 — The Orioles get an assist from the rule book to take away a game-winning homer from the White Sox. With a 3-1 lead in the top of the eighth, Oriole hurler Milt Pappas serves up a three-run homer to White Sox slugger Ted Kluszewski. Third-base umpire Ed Hurley had called time just before the pitch because Chisox Earl Torgeson and Floyd Robinson were warming up outside the prescribed bullpen area. So Big Klu's homer was nullified.

August 29

1915 — In a great pitching performance, George Sisler outduels Walter Johnson as St. Louis beats Washington 2-1.

1917 — Brown pitcher Bob Groom strikes out twice in one inning.

1918 — Joe Schultz (C 1943-48)

1919 — Billy Cox (3B-2B-SS 1955)

1927 — Al Naples (SS 1949)

1939 — Dave Nicholson (OF 1960, 1962)

Frank Zupo (C 1957-58, 1961)

1947 — Tiger pitcher Fred Hutchinson takes advantage of Brown hurler Ellis Kinder's big windup to steal home in the third inning. Hutchinson also has a single and triple for the day.

1950 — Doug DeCinces (3B-2B-SS-1B-DH 1973-81)

1966 — Tiger pitcher Denny McLain beats the O's 6-3, despite giving up eight hits and nine walks while throwing 229 pitches. The Detroit hurler strikes out 11 en route to winning his 16th game.

August 29 (continued)

1979 — Slugger Eddie Murray hits three consecutive home runs, including switch-hit homers, in a 7-4 road win over the Twins.

August 30

1878 — Charlie Starr (2B-3B 1905)

1886 — Wilbur Smith (C-1B 1909)

1894 — Bing Miller (OF 1926-27)

1912 — Southpaw Earl Hamilton becomes the first Brown to throw a no-hitter, with a 5-1 win over the Tigers in Detroit, beating Jean Dubuc.

1916 — Dutch Leonard and the Red Sox no-hit St. Louis 4-0 in Boston.

1917 — Charles (Red) Embree (P 1949)

1922 — The Browns blow a four-run lead in the ninth to lose to the Indians and fall 2½ games out of first place.

1927 — Gordon Goldsberry (1B-OF 1952)

1938 — Red Sox outfielder Doc Cramer hurls four innings in relief against the Browns.

1958 — Baltimore's Dick Williams plays all three outfield positions, but doesn't record a put-out or an assist in a 7-2 win over Boston.

1961 — In his last game as Oriole manager, Paul Richards leads the team to an 11-5 win over the Angels at Wrigley Field in Los Angeles. The Bird attack is paced by five homers and Jack Fisher pitches the distance despite 12 walks. Richards returns to his native Texas as general manager of the Houston Colt 45s. Luman Harris is named interim manager by Baltimore.

1965 — Baltimore sells pitcher Harvey Haddix to Milwaukee, but he elects to retire rather than report to his new team.

August 31

1875 — Eddie Plank (P 1916-17)

1883 — Syd Smith (C 1908)

1907 — Jack Burns (1B 1930-36)

1935 — Frank Robinson (OF-1B 1966-71)

1942 — Tom Dukes (P 1971)

1943 — The Browns sell pitcher Bobo Newsom to Washington.

1955 — After Bird starter Bill Wight gives up two walks, five hits, and five runs in the first inning against the Indians, Skinny Brown comes in in relief and throws eight no-hit innings, striking out 10 Tribesmen. But the Indians win 5-1 as Herb Score fans 13 Orioles.

1966 — On his 31st birthday, Frank Robinson hits a two-run homer off Luis Tiant in the eighth inning to lead Baltimore to a 5-1 win over Cleveland. The victory snaps a four-game losing streak.

1979 — The Birds purchase outfielder Bob Molinaro from the White Sox.

SEPTEMBER

September 1

1885 — Chuck Rose (P 1909)

1900 — Hubert (Hub) Pruett (P 1922-24)

1905 — The Browns buy pitcher Jack Powell from the Yankees. Powell becomes a key starter for the next seven seasons with St. Louis.

1918 — Two all-time greats, George Sisler and Ty Cobb, both pitch in relief for their respective teams, St. Louis and Detroit. Sisler hurls one scoreless inning as the Browns win 6-2. Cobb pitches two innings and gives up a double to Sisler.

1930 — Dean Stone (P (1963)

1968 — The O's pennant hopes suffer as Tiger hurler Denny McLain kills off a potential Baltimore rally by turning Boog Powell's liner into a triple play. The Tigers win 7-3.

1978 — Right-hander Sammy Stewart sets a major league record by striking out seven consecutive White Sox in his major league debut for Baltimore. He sets down Jorge Orta, Chet Lemon, Thad Bosley, Mike Colbern, Kevin Bell, Claudell Washington, and Greg Pryor.

September 2

1933 — Marv Throneberry (OF-1B 1961-62)

1951 — Dave Criscione (C 1977)

1954 — John Flinn (P 1978-79)

1957 — Connie Johnson fans 14 Yankees to tie Bob Turley's Oriole club record in a 6-1 win.

1959 — Drungo Hazewood (OF 1980)

1960 — The O's begin a three-game sweep of New York at home as Milt Pappas beats Whitey Ford 5-0 with a three-hitter.

September 2 (continued)

1964 — The Twins' Zorro Versalles ruins Milt Pappas' no-hit bid with a single.

1974 — Orioles Ross Grimsley and Mike Cuellar blank Boston, 1-0, 1-0, beating Luis Tiant and Bill Lee respectively.

1978 — In his major league debut, Dave Ford pitches seven-hit shutout ball for 8⅓ innings against the White Sox. Tippy Martinez preserves a 1-0 Baltimore win in relief of Ford.

September 3

1873 — Mike Kahoe (C-OF 1902-4)

1876 — George Stone (OF 1905-10)

1915 — Weldon (Lefty) West (P 1944-45)

1920 — Sandy Consuegra (P 1956-57)

1922 — Morrie Martin (P 1956)

1960 — Jack Fisher shuts out the Yankees 2-0 on seven hits as Brooks Robinson drives in both Oriole runs. During the game, plate umpire Larry Napp is carried off the field after being struck for the third time by a foul ball.

September 4

1887 — John (Red) Corriden (SS-3B 1910)

1889 — Clarence (Tilly) Walker (OF 1913-15)

1919 — Eddie Waitkus (1B 1954-55)

1922 — George Sisler scores seven runs for St. Louis in a doubleheader as the Browns regain first place by a half game.

1944 — The Browns drop out of first place as the Yankees sweep Philadelphia 10-0, 14-0.

1950 — Doyle Alexander (P 1972-76)

1953 — Outfielder Vic Wertz hits the last grand slam in Browns' history.

1957 — The 18-year-old Oriole bonus baby, Jerry Walker, hurls a four-hit, 10-inning 1-0 shutout over the Senators.

1960 — The Birds extend their win streak to seven as Chuck Estrada and Hoyt Wilhelm combine to beat New York 6-2. Estrada loses his chance for a no-hitter in the seventh inning with two out when Yankee first sacker Moose Skowron singles.

1969 — Frank Robinson, Boog Powell, and Brooks Robinson hit consecutive home runs in the ninth inning of a 5-4 win over the Tigers in Detroit.

September 5

1883 — Albert (Lefty) Leifield (P 1918-20)

1900 — Merv Shea (C 1933)

1915 — Despite a complete-game pitching effort by George Sisler, St. Louis loses to Detroit 6-5.

1919 — Tom Jordan (PH 1948)

1920 — Gene Bearden (P 1952)

1935 — Tom Patton (C 1957)

1953 — Brown ace Bob Turley strikes out 14 Tigers in a 12-inning game.

September 6

1896 — Leo Dixon (C 1925-27)

1908 — Tiger hurler Wild Bill Donovan strikes out six consecutive Browns.

1913 — Branch Rickey is named manager of the Browns.

1924 — Urban Shocker pitches the Browns to two complete game wins over the White Sox, 6-2, 6-2.

George Schmees (OF-1B 1952)

Jim Fridley (OF 1954)

1959 — Baltimore buys pitcher Rip Coleman from the Athletics.

1974 — Southpaws Dave McNally and Mike Cuellar both blank Cleveland, 2-0, 1-0.

September 7

1907 — Bill McAfee (P 1934)

1917 — Roy Partee (C 1948)

1943 — Tommy Matchick (3B 1972)

1962 — The O's sell pitcher Skinny Brown to the Yankees.

1977 — Baltimore sends third baseman Taylor Duncan to the Cardinals.

September 8

1891 — Verne Clemons (C 1916)

1893 — Bill Gleason (2B 1921)

September 8 (continued)

1896 — Johnny Schulte (C-1B 1923, 1932)

1905 — Yankee pitcher Doc Newton walks 11 Browns.

     Ed Grimes (3B-2B-SS 1931-32)

1916 — Tom Turner (C 1944)

1926 — Lou Sleater (P 1950-52, 1958)

1929 — The Browns' George Blaeholder and the Red Sox' Milt Gaston hook up in a 10-inning 0-0 tie in Fenway Park.

1938 — George Werley (P 1956)

1953 — The Browns obtain infielder Johnny Lipon from the Red Sox.

September 9

1908 — Johnny (Footsie) Marcum (P 1939)

1922 — In the most lopsided Brown win in the team's history, Baby Doll Jacobson belts three triples to lead the Browns to a 16-0 romp over the Tigers behind the pitching of Elam Vangilder.

1926 — Ed Mickelson (1B 1953)

1945 — In the second game of a twin bill in Philadelphia, Athletic hurler Dick Fowler no-hits the Browns to beat Ox Miller 1-0.

1954 — An Enos Slaughter single over the head of second baseman Bobby Young ruins Joe Coleman's bid for a no-hitter. Coleman goes on to gain a one-hit 1-0 Oriole win over the Yankees.

September 10

1880 — Harry Niles (2B-OF-3B 1907-7)

     Barney Pelty (P 1903-12)

1896 — Sammy Hale (3B 1930)

1965 — Brooks Robinson, Curt Blefary, and Jerry Adair hit consecutive home runs for the O's.

1980 — Pat Kelly belts a pinch grand slam off the Tigers' Dave Rozema in an 8-4 Oriole win.

September 11

1892 — Ernie Koob (P 1915-17, 1919)

1911 — Les (Toots) Tietje (P 1936-38)

1916 — Ellis (Cat) Clary (3B-2B 1943-45)

1926 — Eddie Miksis (OF 1957-58)

1958 — In a game with Kansas City, Oriole manager Paul Richards lists three pitchers in his starting lineup: pitcher Billy O'Dell and Jack Harshman in center field and Milt Pappas at second base. He then introduced Jim Busby into center field and Billy Gardner at second base when the Birds got two runners on with two out.

1959 — Two 20-year-old phenoms, Jack Fisher and Jerry Walker, shut out the White Sox in a doubleheader. Fisher wins the opener 3-0 and Walker hurls 16 innings of shutout ball before Brooks Robinson singles in the only run to win 1-0.

1974 — The Orioles purchase first baseman Bob Oliver from the Angels and assign pitcher Mickey Scott to the Angels' farm system on October 3 to complete the deal.

September 12

1884 — Bob Groom (P 1916-17)

1903 — Len Dondero (3B-2B 1929)

1907 — Aloysius (Ollie) Bejma (2B-SS-3B-OF 1934-36)

1909 — The Browns bang out 25 hits versus the Tigers, the most in team history.

1925 — George Sisler walks twice in one inning.

1926 — Despite giving up 12 hits to the Red Sox, Brownie moundsman Milt Gaston hurls a 1-0 shutout.

1934 — Albie Pearson (OF 1959-60)

1951 — The Browns buy second sacker Mike Goliat from the Phillies. He plays little and contributes even less.

1962 — Washington hurler Tom Cheney strikes out a major league record 21 Orioles in a 16-inning 2-1 complete-game win. Russ Snyder, Jim Gentile, Dave Nicholson, Marv Breeding, and Dick Hall each whiff three times. Ten different Orioles strike out during the game.

1964 — Southpaw Frank Bertaina pitches a one-hitter to beat Kansas City for the Orioles 1-0. Athletic hurler Bob Meyer also throws a one-hitter. The victory is Bertaina's first major league win.

1966 — The Birds purchase first baseman Dave Roberts from the Pirates.

September 13

1896 — Pat Collins (C-1B 1919-24)

September 13 (continued)

1906 — Brown pitcher Barney Pelty duels Chisox hurler Frank Owen in Chicago in a 10-inning 0-0 deadlock.

Jim Levey (SS 1930-33)

1922 — The Browns announce that first baseman George Sisler has severely sprained ligaments in his right arm, the result of catching a ball hit by Ty Cobb of the Tigers.

1947 — Mike Adamson (P 1967-69)

1948 — Cleveland pitcher Don Black suffers a cerebral hemmorhage while batting against the Browns. He eventually recovers.

1949 — Rick Dempsey (C 1976-present)

1971 — In the first of a twin bill with the Tigers at home, lefty Dave McNally wins his 13th straight game as Frank Robinson slugs his 499th career home run. In the second game, Robby hits number 500 off Fred Scherman in a losing effort.

September 14

1884 — Willie (Happy) Hogan (OF-1B 1911-12)

1951 — St. Louis outfielder Bob Nieman homers in his first two major league at-bats, the only player ever to do so. Both shots come off Red Sox hurler Mickey McDermott.

1954 — White Sox manager Paul Richards resigns and signs a three-year contract as the manager and general manager of the Orioles, replacing field boss Jimmy Dykes and front-office chief Arthur Ehlers. Dykes is permitted to finish out the season.

1976 — In his major league debut, as the first Nicaraguan to play major league baseball, Dennis Martinez gets a win in relief over the Tigers with 5⅔ scoreless innings. He strikes out the first three batters he faces.

1980 — First baseman Eddie Murray ties the club record of 13 total bases with three home runs and a single against the Blue Jays. But the Birds still lose to the Blue Jays 4-3 in 13 innings in Toronto.

September 15

1893 — Elwood (Speed) Martin (P 1917)

1903 — Russ Young (C 1931)

1907 — Fritz Ostermueller (P 1941-43)

1912 — Boston's Smoky Joe Wood wins his 16th consecutive game, tying the record of Walter Johnson, with a 2-1 win over the Browns in St. Louis. Wood scores the winning run when Earl Hamilton uncorks a wild pitch with the bases full. The game is called in the eighth because of darkness. The victory is Wood's 33rd of the season.

1944 — Radio announcer Bill Stern warns of a scandal involving the Browns. A Chicago publication attributes the recent Brown slump to the fact that the major league leaders want a bigger park for the World Series. Stern repudiates his story four days later.

1946 — Brown right-hander Fred Sanford throws a 1-0 shutout over the Yankees in his first major league game.

1950 — Dave Pagan (P 1976)

1966 — Rookie Tom Phoebus pitches a 2-0 shutout over California in his major league debut before the hometown fans. The Baltimore native gives up four hits and fans eight.

1977 — Baltimore forfeits a game to Toronto in the fifth inning as manager Earl Weaver removes his team from the field in protest of umpire Marty Springstead's refusal to make the Toronto bullpen remove a tarpaulin.

September 16

1899 — Clarence (Heinie) Mueller (1B-OF 1935)

1904 — Ed Barnhart (P 1924)

1908 — Buster Mills (OF 1938)

1912 — Emil Bildilli (P 1937-41)

1922 — With a half-game lead over the Browns, the Yankees come to St. Louis for a three-game set. New York's Bob Shawkey outduels Brownie Urban Shocker before a sellout crowd of 18,000 in Sportsman's Park. Yankee center fielder Whitey Witt is carried from the field in the ninth inning after being hit by a pop bottle. Many in the crowd begin cheering for the Yankees after the bottle incident. Brown star George Sisler later remarks that "the bottle throwing had taken the heart out of the Browns."

1940 — Second sacker Johnny Lucadello of the Browns becomes the first American Leaguer to hit a home run from each side of the plate in a single game.

1944 — Jack Kramer's one-hitter versus the White Sox vaults the Browns into first place.

1949 — Red Sox Lou Stringer scores from third on a pop foul to Brown catcher Les Moss when baserunner Birdie Tebbetts on first starts for second, drawing the throw from Moss and allowing Stringer to come home.

September 16 (continued)

1960 — The Orioles arrive in New York for a crucial four-game series just .001 percentage points behind New York. Whitey Ford beats Steve Barber 4–2 and the O's go on to lose the next three games too, including a September 18 doubleheader (7–3, 2–0) before 53,876 Yankee fans.

1968 — Don Buford's grand slam caps a five-run inning off Boston's Jim Lonborg in an 8–1 Oriole win.

1974 — Baltimore buys outfielder Jim Northrup from Montreal and sells pitcher Larry McCall to the Angels.

September 17

1870 — Dick Padden (2B 1902–5)

1874 — Willie Sudhoff (P–OF 1902–5)

1886 — Robert Ray (P 1910)

1887 — Nick Cullop (P 1921)

1890 — Ernie Walker (OF 1913–15)

1899 — John (Sheriff) Blake (P 1937)

1916 — George Sisler hurls a six-hit, 1–0 victory over Walter Johnson and the Senators.

1918 — Bob Dillinger (3B–SS 1946–49)

1922 — In the second game of a crucial three-game set, southpaw Hub Pruett beats Waite Hoyt and the Yankees 5–1. Outfielder Ken Williams homers and George Sisler hits in his 41st consecutive game despite a bad right arm. The only Yankee run comes on a Babe Ruth home run.

1930 — The Browns absorb their worst shutout loss ever, a 17–0 whitewash by the Yankees behind Red Ruffing.

1934 — In his first major league start, Red Sox rookie George Hockette shuts out the Browns.

1954 — Wayne Krenchicki (SS–3B–2B–DH 1979–81)

1960 — Oriole catcher Clint Courtney records the second unassisted double play of his career, becoming the only player in history to do so.

September 18

1922 — In the rubber game of a three-game series, the Browns blow a 2–1 lead over the Yanks in the ninth and go on to lose 3–2. Dixie Davis yields a single to Wally Schang and then throws a wild pitch. Manager Lee Fohl brings Hub Pruett in to relieve. A bunt by Mike McNally should have been an easy out, but catcher Hank Severeid throws high to third sacker Kid Foster, allowing Schang to advance. Pruett then walks Everett Scott, to load the bases. Fohl then brings in Urban Shocker, who gives up a single to Whitey Witt, scoring two runs to win the game for the Yankees. Fans upset by the loss get into an altercation with several New York writers.

1925 — Harvey Haddix (P 1964-65)

1934 — Brown pitcher Bobo Newsom pitches nine hitless innings against the Red Sox but loses 2-1 in 10 innings to Wes Ferrell. Walks prove Newsom's downfall as he walks two batters and then gives up his only hit to Roy Johnson, who drives in the winning runs.

1951 — Pitcher Tommy Byrne hits a grand slam for the Browns off the Senators' Sid Hudson in the ninth inning.

1963 — Steve Barber becomes the first 20-game winner in Oriole history by beating the Angels 3-1 in Los Angeles with relief from Dick Hall.

1968 — Orioles' pitching strikes out 17 Red Sox.

1977 — The Birds draw their largest regular season crowd ever, 51,798, on a "Thanks Brooks" salute to the great third baseman against Boston. The Birds lose 10-4.

September 19

1900 — Jim Wright (P 1927-28)

1913 — John (Red) Barkley (2B 1937)

1916 — Browns' catcher Grover Hartley records an unassisted double play.

1930 — Bob Turley (P 1951, 1953-54)

1977 — Baltimore purchases pitcher Nelson Briles from Texas.

September 20

1946 — Roric Harrison (P 1972)

1956 — Oriole catcher Tom Gastall is killed when the small plane he is piloting crashes into Chesapeake Bay.

1958 — Hoyt Wilhelm throws the first no-hitter in Oriole history, beating New York 1-0. Gus Triandos' 30th home run is the winning margin and ties an American League record for home runs by catchers set by Yogi Berra.

1966 — In his second major league start, Tom Phoebus throws his second shutout, beating Kansas City 4-0. He becomes only the sixth pitcher since 1900 to hurl shutouts in his first two starts. Frank Robinson hits a two-run homer, his 47th of the year. He breaks Jim Gentile's club record of 46 homers.

1973 — Jim Palmer notches his 22nd win by blanking the Tigers 9-0 with the help of a triple play.

September 21

1886 — Art Bader (OF 1904)

1896 — Herschel Bennett (OF 1923-27)

1910 — Eldon Auker (P 1940-42)

1971 — Southpaw Dave McNally wins his 20th game, marking his fourth straight season with 20 or more wins. He blanks the Yankees 5-0.

September 22

1905 — Larry Bettencourt (OF-3B-C 1928, 1931-32)

1923 — Tom Wright (OF 1952)

1930 — Bob Harrison (P 1955-56)

1936 — The Browns fall victim to their biggest doubleheader shutout loss ever as Tigers Eldon Auker and Tommy Bridges beat them 12-0, 4-0.

1961 — First sacker Jim Gentile sets an American League record and ties the major league mark of Ernie Banks with his fifth grand slam of the season, this one off Don Larsen in Chicago.

1966 — The O's clinch the pennant, their first ever, with a 6-1 win over the Athletics in Kansas City. Jim Palmer throws a five-hitter and both Frank and Brooks Robinson contribute two RBIs each. The game ends as Russ Snyder makes a diving catch after a long run to snare a Dick Green drive with two on.

1973 — The Birds clinch their division title against the Brewers in Milwaukee as designated hitter Al Bumbry belts three triples. Doyle Alexander gets the win in the 7-1 triumph.

September 23

1900 — Walter (Lefty) Stewart (P 1927-32)

1943 — Marcelino Lopez (P 1967, 1969-70)

1958 — For the second time in the season, Oriole pitcher Jack Harshman hits two homers in a game.

September 24

1894 — Otto Nye (SS 1917)

1896 — George Pennington (P 1917)

1921 — Brown pitcher Dixie Davis hurls both ends of a doubleheader with the Red Sox, losing 2-1 and winning 11-0.

1940 — Curt Motton (OF-DH 1967-74)

1956 — In his major league debut, rookie Charlie Beamon pitches a 1-0 win for the Orioles over Whitey Ford and the Yankees.

1963 — The White Sox shellac the Orioles 15-0, an easy win for Ray Herbert.

1971 — The Orioles clinch their division as Mike Cuellar wins his 20th game, beating the Indians in Cleveland 9-2. In the second game of the double-header, Pat Dobson notches his 20th win too, with a 7-0 shutout.

1974 — Baltimore native Al Kaline, a Tiger great, doubles into right field off Dave McNally in the fourth inning for his 3,000th career hit at Memorial Stadium.

September 25

1904 — Paul Hopkins (P 1929)

1926 — The Yankees sweep the Browns 10-2, 10-4, to clinch the pennant.

1944 — The Browns pull into a tie with Detroit for first place as Nelson Potter shuts out the Red Sox 3-0 while the Athletics beat Detroit 2-1.

September 26

1906 — Jack Powell and Harry Howell pitch the Browns to a shutout of Philadelphia, 5-0, 0-0.

1926 — The Browns and Yankees play the shortest doubleheader in history, two hours and seven minutes. The Browns win the opener 6-1 in one hour and 12 minutes and the second game 6-2 in 55 minutes.

1941 — Rick Ferrell's bunt in the fifth inning is the only Brown tally off Cleveland's Bob Feller in a 3-2 Brown loss.

1944 — Sig Jakucki's 1-0 whitewash of Boston keeps the Browns in a tie for first place.

1945 — Dave Duncan (C 1975-76)

1961 — Oriole hurler Jack Fisher gives up Roger Maris' 60th home run in a 3-2 loss at Yankee Stadium.

1962 — In his first major league game, southpaw Dave McNally hurls a 3-0 shutout over Kansas City.

1971 — Jim Palmer becomes the fourth Oriole 20-game winner of the season and the third in three days as he beats the Indians 5-0 in Cleveland.

1978 — Oriole Mike Flanagan loses a no-hitter with two out in the ninth to Indian Gary Alexander's homer.

September 27

1890 — Willie Adams (P 1912-13)

September 27 (continued)

1904 — Willie Sudhoff and Philadelphia's Chief Bender lock horns in a 10-inning 0-0 standoff in St. Louis.

1914 — Cleveland's Nap Lajoie gets his 3,000th career hit against the Browns.

1928 — Perry Currin (SS 1947)

1930 — Dick Hall (P 1961-66, 1969-71)

1938 — Tiger Hank Greenberg hits his 57th and 58th homers of the year against the Browns. His 58th homer is an inside-the-park shot which ends in a close play at home plate.

1950 — Carlos Lopez (OF 1978)

1963 — Stu Miller sets an American League record for appearances (71) and games finished (59) while notching his 26th save for the Birds against Detroit.

1974 — Baltimore goes 17 innings to beat Milwaukee 1-0.

September 28

1889 — Pete Compton (OF 1911-13)

1917 — Glen Moulder (P 1947)

1925 — Bill Jennings (SS 1951)

1942 — Grant Jackson (P 1971-76)

1947 — Radio announcer Dizzy Dean is activated and starts for the Browns against Chicago. He pitches four shutout innings, giving up three hits.

1960 — In his final major league game, Bosox slugger Ted Williams hits a home run off Jack Fisher in his last at-bat for a career total of 521. Outfielder Al Pilarcik had deprived the Splendid Splinter of a homer in his previous at-bat with a leaping catch in right center field.

1973 — The O's set a Memorial Stadium record by scoring 18 runs against the Indians. Shortstop Frank Baker hits his first major league homer, a grand slam off Dick Bosman.

September 29

1911 — The Browns lose to New York 16-12 as the Yankees draw 13 walks and steal 15 bases. The Yanks steal six bases in the second inning alone.

1938 — Mike McCormick (P 1963-64)

1944 — The Browns sweep a crucial doubleheader from New York, 4-1, 1-0. Nellie Potter throws a six-hitter in the second game while Jack Kramer wins the opener behind George McQuinn's two-run homer in the eighth.

1953 — American League owners approve the shift of the St. Louis Browns franchise to Baltimore. A group headed by attorney Clarence Miles pays Bill Veeck $2,475,000 for 79 percent of the team's stock.

1963 — Billy Hitchcock is told he will not return as Oriole manager after two mediocre seasons.

September 30

1882 — Charles (Gabby) Street (MGR 1938)

1904 — Johnny Allen (P 1941)

1906 — Red Sox rookie Floyd Kroh shuts out St. Louis 2-0 in his first big league start.

1924 — Bennie Taylor (1B 1951)

1926 — Robin Roberts (P 1962-65)

1934 — Two Browns coaches play against the Tigers in the second game of a twin bill. Grover Hartley, age 46, catches and 53-year-old Charlie O'Leary pinch-singles and scores, the oldest player to do so.

1944 — Denny Galehouse shuts out New York 2-0, backed up by fine defensive outfield play by Mark Christman and Mike Kreevich.

OCTOBER

October 1

1894 — Ray Kolp (P 1921-24)

1897 — Tony Rego (C 1924-25)

1926 — Bob Boyd (1B-OF 1956-60)

1944 — The Browns clinch the only pennant in their history with a 5-2 win over the Yankees at home. A crowd of 37,815 is on hand to see Sig Jakucki hurl a six-hitter to stymie the Yanks. The offense is led by homers from Chet Laabs and Vern Stephens. The win marked the Browns' fourth straight down the stretch over the Bronx Bombers, a great surge of clutch baseball. More than 15,000 fans are turned away at the gate for this game, the only pennant-clincher in Browns' history.

October 2

1958 — Baltimore trades outfielder Dick Williams to Kansas City for shortstop Chico Carrasquel and sells pitcher Ken Lehman to the Phillies.

1960 — The Orioles clinch second place, their best finish in their brief history, by beating the Senators on the last day of the season 2-1. A Jackie Brandt homer in the eighth provides the winning margin.

October 2 (continued)

1964 — In the next to the last game of the year, the O's take advantage of a thick fog to score six runs in the second inning against Detroit as Tiger flyhawks lose two routine flies for extra-base hits. Final score of this fog-bound contest: 10-4.

October 3

1887 — Armando Marsans (OF-3B-2B 1916-17)

1970 — In the opening game of the American League championship series, the Birds score seven runs in the fourth inning and go on to beat the Twins, 10-6. A grand slam by pitcher Mike Cuellar paces the Oriole attack.

1971 — A four-run surge in the seventh inning against A's ace Vida Blue gives Baltimore a 5-3 win in the first game of the league playoffs.

1972 — With the coming of the DH rule in 1973, Roric Harrison's homer versus the Indians is the last by an American League pitcher in regulation play. The four-bagger is hit off Ray Lamb in the sixth inning of a 4-3 Oriole win.

1979 — A dramatic 10th-inning three-run homer by John Lowenstein with two men out lifts the O's over the Angels in the opening game of the American League championship series.

The Birds sell outfielder Bob Molinaro to the White Sox.

October 4

1884 — Harry Ables (P 1905)

1889 — Maurice (Shorty) Dee (SS 1915)

1922 — Don Lenhardt (OF-1B 1950-54)

1944 — The Browns open game one of the World Series with a 2-1 win over the National League champion St. Louis Cardinals. Denny Galehouse hurls a seven-hitter to top the Redbirds' Mort Cooper. The Brownies win despite only two hits, a single by right fielder Gene Moore and a homer by first baseman George McQuinn in the fourth inning.

1948 — Dave Johnson (P 1974-75)

1969 — Paul Blair's suicide squeeze with two out in the 12th scores Mark Belanger to beat Minnesota 4-3 in the first game ever of a championship series between the Eastern and Western Division winners of the American League.

1970 — Southpaw Dave McNally spins a six-hitter to beat Minnesota 11-3 in game two of the league championship series.

1971 — The Orioles take a 2-0 lead over the A's in the league playoffs with a 5-1 win on the strength of four home runs, including two by Boog Powell. The other power shots are supplied by Brooks Robinson and Elrod Hendricks.

1979 — The O's hang on to beat the Angels in game two of the league series 9-8 after giving Mike Flanagan a 9-1 lead.

October 5

1890 — Rollin Cook (P 1915)

1893 — Paul Speraw (3B 1920)

1895 — Norm McMillan (2B-3B-SS-1B 1924)

1904 — Sammy West (OF 1933-38)

1944 — In game two of the World Series, the Cardinals beat St. Louis 3-2 in 11 innings on Ken O'Dea's pinch-single off Bob Muncrief.

1966 — In their first World Series game ever, the Birds beat the Los Angeles Dodgers with the help of sterling relief by Moe Drabowsky, 5-2. Moe hurls $6\frac{2}{3}$ innings of one-hit, shutout relief and strikes out 11 Dodgers. The Orioles have a big first inning with homers by Frank and Brooks Robinson.

1969 — Dave McNally goes 11 innings and strikes out 10 to beat Minnesota 1-0 in game two of the league title series. The Birds win the game on a pinch single by Curt Motton that scores Boog Powell.

1970 — Baltimore wraps up the American League pennant with a 6-1 win over Minnesota in game three of the American League championship series.

1971 — Despite yielding two homers to Reggie Jackson and another round-tripper to Sal Bando, Jim Palmer hangs on to beat Oakland 5-3 for the American League title.

1974 — The Birds win the first and their only game of the American League championship series over Oakland 6-3. Home runs by Paul Blair, Brooks Robinson, and Bobby Grich lead the O's attack.

1980 — Scott McGregor wins his 20th game, beating the Indians and Len Barker 7-1. The O's win denies Barker's bid for 20 wins. For the second straight year, Baltimore attains the 100-win mark.

October 6

1893 — Johnny Tillman (P 1915)

1922 — Joe Frazier (OF 1956)

1944 — As the home team in game three of the World Series, the Browns beat the Redbirds 6-2 as Jack Kramer throws a seven-hitter and strikes out 10. The Brownies score four runs on five hits off Card rookie Ted Wilks after two outs in the third.

1954 — Mike Parrott (P 1977)

October 6 (continued)

1966 — Behind Jim Palmer's four-hit shutout, the Birds beat Sandy Koufax and the Dodgers in game two of the World Series 6-0. Three errors by Dodger center fielder Willie Davis in the fifth inning lead to three runs for Baltimore.

1969 — The O's beat the Twins 11-2 to win the American League pennant. Center fielder Paul Blair stars with a homer and two doubles for five RBIs.

1973 — The Birds open the league playoffs with a 6-0 win over Oakland, paced by Jim Palmer's five-hitter. Baltimore pounds Vida Blue for four runs in the first inning, giving Palmer a cushion to work with.

1979 — The Orioles clinch the American League pennant in game four of the title series, as Scott McGregor hurls a six-hitter to beat California 8-0. Great fielding by third baseman Doug DeCinces kills any hopes of an Angel rally.

October 7

1898 — Joe Giard (P 1925-26)

1922 — Grady Hatton (2B-3B 1956)

1939 — John O'Donoghue (P 1968)

1944 — The Cardinals even the World Series at two games each with a 5-1 win over the Browns. The American League champs strand 10 men on base against Harry Brecheen.

October 8

1887 — James (Doc) Crandall (P-PH 1916)

1929 — Bob Mabe (P 1960)

1944 — Game five of the Fall Classic is a pitching duel once more between Denny Galehouse and Mort Cooper. This time Cooper and the Cardinals get the win as Galehouse yields solo home runs to Ray Sanders and Danny Litwhiler. Cooper strikes out 12 Brownies while giving up seven hits.

1949 — Enos Cabell (1B-OF-3B-2B 1972-74)

1966 — Wally Bunker hurls a six-hit shutout to win game three of the World Series 1-0. The only Bird tally is a homer by Paul Blair off the Dodgers' Claude Osteen.

October 9

1873 — Bill Reidy (P 1901-3)

1890 — Ernie Manning (P 1914)

1944 — The Browns dream of a world title dies as the Cardinals clinch the championship with a 3-1 win behind the three-hit pitching of Max Lanier and Ted Wilks, who retires the last 11 Brownies in a row.

1959 — The Birds release pitcher Ernie Johnson.

1966 — The Orioles win their first World Series with a four-game sweep of the Dodgers, as Dave McNally throws a four-hit 1-0 shutout. The Birds win the game on the strength of a Frank Robinson round-tripper.

1971 — In game one of the World Series versus the Pirates, Dave McNally hurls a three-hitter to top the Buccos 5-3. Homers by Frank Robinson and Merv Rettenmund pace the O's attack.

October 10

1887 — Bill Killefer (C 1909-10; MGR 1930-33)

1904 — Fay Thomas (P 1935)

1914 — Tom Fine (P 1950)

1916 — Floyd Baker (SS-2B-3B 1943-44)

1922 — Saul Rogovin (P 1955)

1937 — Gordie Sundin (P 1956)

1970 — In the first World Series game ever played on artificial turf, the Orioles beat the Reds in Cincinnati 4-3 on a Brooks Robinson homer.

1973 — Bobby Grich's eighth-inning home run gives Baltimore a 5-4 comeback win to tie Oakland at two games each in the American League championship series.

1979 — The Orioles win game one of the World Series 5-4 in the rain and cold, thanks to three costly Pirate errors.

October 11

1878 — Frank Roth (C 1905)

1908 — Tom Carey (2B-SS-3B 1935-37)

1926 — Joe Ginsberg (C 1956-60)

1944 — Mike Fiore (1B-OF 1968)

1963 — The Orioles sell outfielder Fred Valentine to Washington. Squeaky puts in two seasons as a reliable starter for the Senators before returning to Baltimore finally in 1968 for his swan song.

1969 — The opening game of the World Series gives the Birds their only win against the Amazin' New York Mets as Mike Cuellar tosses a six-hitter to win 4-1.

October 11 (continued)

1970 — The O's win game two of the World Series 6-5 over the Reds behind solid relief pitching by Tom Phoebus, Moe Drabowsky, Marcelino Lopez, and Dick Hall.

1971 — Brooks Robinson's three hits pace the Orioles to an 11-3 win over Pittsburgh in game two of the World Series.

1973 — Oakland ace Catfish Hunter shuts out Baltimore 3-0 to win the American League pennant.

October 12

1874 — Jimmy Burke (3B 1901; MGR 1918-20)

1882 — Ivan Howard (1B-3B-OF-SS-2B 1914-15)

1890 — Joe Jenkins (C 1914)

   Frank (Dixie) Davis (P 1920-26)

1902 — Stew Bolen (P 1926-27)

1905 — Rick Ferrell (C 1929-33, 1941-43)

1917 — Ray (Deacon) Murray (C 1954)

1962 — Baltimore sells outfielder Dick Williams to the Houston Colt 45s.

1979 — Four hits by shortstop Kiko Garcia, including a bases-loaded triple, pace the Birds to an 8-4 win over Pittsburgh in game three of the World Series.

October 13

1876 — Rube Waddell (P 1908-10)

1887 — Ham Patterson (1B-OF 1909)

1910 — In an appearance before league president Ban Johnson, Brown third baseman Red Corriden denies deliberately letting Cleveland's Nap Lajoie get hits in order to win the batting title over Detroit's Ty Cobb. Johnson accepts Corriden's explanation for his shoddy fielding in late-season games.

1914 — Frankie (Blimp) Hayes (C-1B 1942-43)

1938 — Ron Moeller (P 1956, 1958)

1970 — Southpaw Dave McNally goes the distance in game three of the World Series and hits a grand slam to beat the Reds 9-3. Sensational fielding by Brooks Robinson at third gives him his first national recognition as the premier player at the hot corner.

1979 — The O's explode for six runs in the eighth inning to beat Pittsburgh 9-6 in game four of the World Series.

October 14

1891 — Bert Gallia (P 1918-20)

1914 — Harry (The Cat) Brecheen (P 1953)

1940 — Tommy Harper (OF-1B-DH 1976)

1953 — Kiko Garcia (SS-2B 1976-80)

October 15

1875 — Emil Frisk (OF 1905, 1907)

1881 — Charlie O'Leary (PH 1934)

1897 — Sam Gray (P 1928-33)

1910 — Manager Jack O'Connor and scout Harry Howell are fired by the Browns following the controversy over the Nap Lajoie batting title.

1945 — Jim Palmer (P 1965-67, 1969-present)

1965 — Frank Cashen is named executive vice president of the Orioles.

1970 — The Orioles win the World Series in five games over the Reds with a 9-3 win behind Mike Cuellar's six-hitter.

October 16

1885 — Dan Howley (MGR 1927-29)

1900 — Leon (Goose) Goslin (OF-3B 1930-32)

1904 — Walter (Boom-Boom) Beck (P 1924, 1927-28)

1921 — Matt Batts (C 1951)

1924 — Bob Cain (P 1952-53)

1949 — Don Hood (P 1973-74)

1959 — The Orioles release hurler Lou Sleater.

1971 — In game six, the Birds even the World Series with a 3-2 win over the Pirates in 10 innings. Brooks Robinson's sacrifice scores Frank Robinson with the winner.

October 17

1900 — Ernie Wingard (P 1924-27)

October 17 (continued)

1947 — Jim Hutto (C 1975)

1971 — The Pirates win the 1971 World Series as Steve Blass stops Baltimore 2-1 with a four-hitter.

1979 — Willie Stargell's two-run homer leads the Bucs to a 4–1 win over Baltimore and a comeback World Series championship in seven games.

October 18

1884 — Burt Shotton (OF 1909, 1911-17)

1885 — Jack Gilligan (P 1909-10)

1914 — Roy Cullenbine (OF-1B 1940-42)

1917 — Loy Hanning (P 1939, 1942)

1949 — Ed Farmer (P 1977)

1954 — Mike Dimmel (OF 1977-78)

October 19

1894 — Tim McCabe (P 1915-18)

1905 — Mike Meola (P 1936)

1938 — Vic Roznovsky (C 1966-67)

October 20

1909 — Bruce Campbell (OF 1932-34)

1943 — Bobby Floyd (SS-2B-3B 1968-70)

1978 — The Orioles release reserve outfielder Mike Anderson.

October 21

1913 — Mark Christman (3B-SS-1B-2B 1939, 1943-46)

1930 — Valmy Thomas (C 1960)

October 22

1900 — Jim Elliott (P 1923)

October 23

1910 — Billy Sullivan (C-OF-1B 1938-39)

1920 — Vern (Junior) Stephens (SS-3B-OF 1941-47, 1953-55)

October 24

1888 — Emmett (Parson) Perryman (P 1915)

October 25

1923 — Bobby Thomson (PH 1960)

October 26

1887 — Harry Chapman (C 1916)

1918 — George (Snuffy) Stirnweiss (2B-3B-SS 1950)

1938 — The Browns obtain catcher Joe Glenn and outfielder Myril Hoag from the Yankees for pitcher Oral Hildebrand and outfielder Buster Mills. A good deal for both clubs as Hildebrand wins 10 games for the pennant-winning New Yorkers in 1939 and both Glenn and Hoag start for the Browns.

1950 — Wayne Garland (P 1973-76)

October 27

1894 — Charlie Bold (1B 1914)

1922 — Del Rice (PH 1960)

1972 — The Orioles trade catcher Francisco Estrada to the Cubs to reacquire a Memorial Stadium favorite, catcher Ellie Hendricks.

October 28

1879 — Ben Bowcock (2B 1903)

1890 — John (Doc) Lavan (SS 1913-17)

1910 — George Hennessey (P 1937)

1954 — Sammy Stewart (P 1979-present)

October 29

1909 — Ralph Winegarner (P 1949)

1939 — Pete Richert (P 1967-71)

1946 — Frank Baker (SS-2B-3B-1B 1973-74)

1953 — The Baltimore Orioles officially come into being as the local buyers complete the purchase of the St. Louis Browns.

October 30

1891 — Charlie Deal (3B-2B 1916)

1896 — Clyde Manion (C 1928-30)

October 31

1886 — Alex Malloy (P 1910)

1942 — Dave McNally (P 1962-74)

NOVEMBER

November 1

1904 — Johnny Burnett (3B-SS-2B 1935)

1932 — Jim Pyburn (OF-3B-C 1955-57)

November 2

1903 — Elon (Chief) Hogsett (P 1936-37)

1904 — John Kloza (OF 1931-32)

1920 — John Sullivan (SS-3B-2B 1949)

1953 — Paul Hartzell (P 1980)

November 3

1878 — Ike Rockenfeld (2B 1905-6)

1886 — Clyde Southwick (C 1911)

1919 — Mike Goliat (2B 1951-52)

1936 — Earl Robinson (OF 1961-62, 1964)

1945 — Ken Holtzman (P 1976)

1955 — Mark Corey (OF-DH 1979-81)

November 4

1873 — Bobby Wallace (SS-3B-2B-OF-P 1902-16; MGR 1911-12)

1885 — Jack Enzenroth (C 1914)

1889 — George O'Brien (C 1915)

1915 — Sig Gryska (SS 1938-39)

1933 — John (Tito) Francona (OF-1B 1956-57)

November 5

1895 — Wayne Wright (P 1917-19, 1922-23)

1897 — Jack Ogden (P 1928-29)

1904 — Ollie Sax (3B 1928)

1905 — Carl Fischer (P 1932)

1958 — Lee McPhail replaces Paul Richards as general manager of the Orioles. Richards retains his duties as field boss.

November 6

1907 — Earl Clark (OF 1934)

November 7

1909 — Alan Strange (SS-3B-2B-1B 1934-35, 1940-42)

1933 — Bob Hale (1B 1955-59)

November 8

1901 — Frank McGowan (OF 1928-29)

1920 — Wally Westlake (OF 1955)

November 9

1911 — Ed Linke (P 1938)

1917 — Bob Neighbors (SS 1939)

1919 — Jerry Priddy (2B 1948-49)

1931 — Dorrel (Whitey) Herzog (OF 1961-62)

1944 — Al Severinsen (P 1969)

1981 — Baltimore owner Edward Bennett Williams proposes construction of a new stadium downtown, within walking distance of the Harborplace development on the Inner Harbor. He said the facility should be named "Babe Ruth Stadium" in honor of Baltimore's famous native son.

November 10

1878 — Cy Morgan (P 1903-5, 1907)

1892 — Jim Park (P 1915-17)

1896 — Jimmy Dykes (MGR 1954)

November 10 (continued)

1922 — Johnny Lipon (3B-2B 1953)

1950 — *The Sporting News* reports that William Zeckendorf of New York is interested in buying the Browns and moving them to Houston.

November 11

1929 — Ike Delock (P 1963)

November 12

1926 — Don Johnson (P 1950-51, 1955)

November 13

1922 — Andy Anderson (SS-2B-3B-1B 1948-49)

1925 — Jim Delsing (OF 1950-52)

1951 — Larry Harlow (OF-P-DH 1975, 1977-79)

November 14

1876 — Harry Howell (P-3B-OF 1904-10)

November 15

1916 — Milt Byrnes (OF-1B 1943-45)

Joe Ostrowski (P 1948-50)

November 16

1940 — Leslie (Buster) Narum (P 1963)

November 17

1906 — Rollie Stiles (P 1930-31, 1933)

1933 — Orlando Pena (P 1971, 1973)

1947 — The Browns obtain pitchers Joe Ostrowski, Jim Wilson, and Al Widmar, catchers Roy Partee and Don Palmer, shortstop Eddie Pellagrini, outfielder Pete Layden, and $310,000 for pitcher Jack Kramer and shortstop Vern Stephens in a deal with the Red Sox. A deal bad enough to show that quantity does not equal quality. Kramer becomes the top pitcher in '48 for Boston and Stephens a key performer at short. At least the Browns got a little cash.

1965 — General manager Lee McPhail leaves the Orioles to become executive administrator to the new commissioner, William (Spike) Eckert.

1979 — Ace reliever Don Stanhouse abandons the Orioles via free agency to sign with the Los Angeles Dodgers.

November 18

1886 — Howie Gregory (P 1911)

1912 — Charlie Fuchs (P 1943)

1922 — Kermit Wahl (3B 1951)

1926 — Roy Sievers (OF-1B-3B 1949-53)

1947 — The Browns trade pitcher Ellis Kinder and infielder Billy Hitchcock to the Red Sox for pitcher Clem Dreisewerd, infielder Sam Dente, third baseman Bill Sommers, and $65,000. Another gross error for the Browns as Kinder becomes a top pitcher for the Bosox.

1954 — The Orioles and Yankees embark on the biggest trade in history, a 17-player deal that takes until December 3 to complete. The Birds get: pitchers Harry Byrd, Bill Miller, and Jim McDonald; catchers Hal Smith and Gus Triandos; infielders Don Leppert, Kal Segrist, and Willie Miranda; and outfielder Gene Woodling. In return, New York obtains: pitchers Bob Turley, Don Larsen, and Mike Blyzka; catcher Darrell Johnson; infielder Billy Hunter; first baseman Dick Kryhoski; and outfielders Ted del Guercio and Jim Fridley. The blockbuster trade helps both teams as Turley and Larsen prove good starters while Triandos, Smith, and Miranda stick in the O's starting lineup.

1963 — The Orioles name coach Hank Bauer their new manager after Eddie Stanky, Cardinal director of player development, turns the job down. The move proves fortuitous as Bauer leads the Birds to a pennant and world's championship in 1966.

1976 — Baltimore obtains outfielder Pat Kelly from the White Sox for catcher Dave Duncan. Kelly provides the Orioles with solid play for the next four seasons.

November 19

1908 — Joe Glenn (C 1939)

1937 — The Browns give first baseman Sunny Jim Bottomley his unconditional release.

1942 — Larry Haney (C 1966-68)

1976 — Free agent Wayne Garland, a 20-game winner, leaves Baltimore to sign with the Cleveland Indians.

November 20

1880 — George McBride (SS 1901)

1887 — John Scheneberg (P 1920)

November 20 (continued)

1930 — Don Leppert (2B 1955)

1938 — Herm Starrette (P 1963-65)

November 21

1908 — Paul Richards (MGR 1955-61)

1962 — The Orioles acquire catcher Jim Coker from the Phillies.

November 22

1901 — Harry Rice (OF-3B-1B-2B-SS-C 1923-27)

1936 — Joe Gaines (OF 1963-64)

November 23

1878 — George Stovall (1B 1912-13; MGR 1912-13)

1897 — Claude Jonnard (P 1926)

1932 — John Anderson (P 1960)

1951 — St. Louis trades pitcher Jim McDonald to the Yankees for catcher Clint Courtney. A solid deal for the Browns as Scrap Iron moves in effectively behind the plate for the Browns.

November 24

1888 — Ed Miller (1B-OF-SS-2B-3B 1912, 1914)

1912 — Tony Giuliani (C 1936-37)

1939 — Jim Northrup (OF-DH-SS 1974-75)

1942 — Fred Beene (P 1968-70)

1954 — The Orioles purchase outfielder Charlie Maxwell from the Red Sox.

1976 — The Orioles lose second baseman Bobby Grich to the Angels via free agency.

November 25

1903 — Jim Weaver (P 1934, 1938)

November 26

1866 — Hugh Duffy (OF 1901; MGR 1901)

1916 — Bob Elliott (3B 1953)

1927 — Pete Taylor (P 1952)

1951 — St. Louis trades pitcher Al Widmar, catcher Sherman Lollar, and shortstop Tommy Upton to the White Sox for pitcher Dick Littlefield, catcher Gus Niarhos, first baseman Gordon Goldsberry, shortstop Joe DeMaestri, and outfielder Jim Rivera. Chicago gets the real benefit in this deal as Lollar blooms into an All-Star catcher.

1962 — Baltimore trades catcher Gus Triandos and outfielder Whitey Herzog to Detroit for catcher Dick Brown. This same day, the Birds draft speedy flyhawk Paul Blair from the Mets' organization.

1976 — After one season, Reggie Jackson forsakes Baltimore for the Yankees as a free agent.

November 27

1892 — Joe Bush (P-OF 1925)

1920 — Johnny Schmitz (P 1956)

1937 — Billy Short (P 1962, 1966)

1961 — The O's draft infielder Ozzie Virgil from the Kansas City organization.

1963 — Baltimore trades first baseman Jim Gentile and $25,000 to the Athletics for first baseman Norm Siebern. A disappointing deal as Gentile hits 28 home runs with his new club.

1978 — The Orioles purchase utility player John Lowenstein from the Texas Rangers for $20,000. A steal, Lowenstein remains a top-notch platoon outfielder for the Birds and a steady clutch performer.

November 28

1870 — Lee Fohl (MGR 1921-23)

1891 — Frank (Blackie) O'Rourke (3B-SS-2B-1B 1927-31)

1950 — Jim Fuller (OF-1B-DH 1973-74)

1951 — The Browns trade catcher Gus Niarhos and outfielder Ken Wood to the Red Sox for catcher Les Moss and outfielder Tom Wright.

1967 — The O's draft catcher Ellie Hendricks from Seattle of the California Angels' organization.

1978 — The Birds sign free agent Steve Stone, a pitcher who blossoms into a Cy Young Award winner.

November 29

1889 — Carl (Zeke) Weilman (P 1912-17, 1919-20)

1892 — Charlie Snell (C 1912)

November 29 (continued)

1896 — Joe De Berry (P 1920-21)

1965 — The Birds draft pitcher Moe Drabowsky from St. Louis and hurler Gene Brabender from the Dodgers. Drabowsky proves a key addition to the bullpen.

1967 — The Orioles trade shortstop Luis Aparicio, outfielder Russ Snyder, and first baseman John Matias to the White Sox for outfielder/infielder Don Buford and pitchers Bruce Howard and Roger Nelson. While Aparicio continues to perform well at shortstop, Buford becomes a key part of the Birds' revival in 1969-71.

November 30

1891 — John Billings (C-1B 1919-23)

1897 — Win Ballou (P 1926-27)

1954 — Joe Kerrigan (P 1978-80)

1959 — Baltimore trades pitchers Billy O'Dell and Billy Loes to San Francisco for pitcher Gordon Jones, catcher Roger McCardell, and outfielder Jackie Brandt. The Birds get a solid center fielder in the flaky Brandt, who proves a crowd pleaser.

1970 — The O's send pitcher Moe Drabowsky to St. Louis for utility infielder Jerry DaVanon.

1972 — The Birds obtain catcher Earl Williams and infielder Taylor Duncan from Atlanta for catcher Johnny Oates, second baseman Dave Johnson, and pitchers Pat Dobson and Roric Harrison. Johnson responds to the deal by promptly hitting more home runs (43) than any other second baseman in history. As for Earl Williams, he soon reveals an astonishing lack of prowess defensively, much to the Earl of Weaver's chagrin.

DECEMBER

December 1

1901 — Ed Coleman (OF 1935-36)

1902 — Morris (Red) Badgro (OF 1929-30)

1917 — Marty Marion (SS-3B 1952-53; MGR 1952-53)

1921 — Bob Savage (P 1949)

1949 — The Browns sell pitcher Al Papai to the Red Sox on waivers.

1970 — The Orioles trade pitchers Tom Phoebus, Fred Beene, and Al Severinsen and shortstop Enzo Hernandez to San Diego for pitchers Pat Dobson and Tom Dukes. The deal pays off handsomely for the Birds as Dobson becomes a 20-game winner and Dukes contributes four saves in the bullpen in the '71 pennant drive.

1974 — The O's sell first baseman Bob Oliver to the Yankees.

December 2

1927 — The Browns obtain first baseman Lu Blue and outfielder Heinie Manush from the Tigers for pitcher Elam Vangilder, infielder Chick Galloway, and outfielder Harry Rice. An excellent deal for St. Louis as Manush displays his Hall of Fame form by hitting .378 and leading the league with 241 hits. Blue's .281 average and team-leading 14 homers help contribute to the team's third-place finish.

1936 — St. Louis buys outfielder Ethan Allen from the Cubs. The next summer Allen hits .316 coming off the bench in the clutch.

1937 — The Browns obtain pitcher Bobo Newsom, shortstop Red Kress, and outfielder Buster Mills from the Red Sox for outfielder Joe Vosmik. This deal helps St. Louis avoid the basement of the league as Newsom wins 20 games and both Kress and Mills perform well as starters.

1958 — The Orioles acquire second baseman Bobby Avila from the Indians for pitcher Russ Heman and cash. Avila plays only 20 games with the Birds before being shipped on to Boston.

1959 — Baltimore trades outfielder Bob Nieman to the Cardinals for catchers Gene Green and Chuck Staniland.

1965 — In a deal with California, the O's send first baseman Norm Siebern west for outfielder Dick Simpson.

1971 — Baltimore marks an end of one Robinson era by trading superstar outfielder Frank Robinson and reliever Pete Richert to Los Angeles for pitchers Doyle Alexander and Bob O'Brien, catcher Sergio Robles, and outfielder Royle Stillman.

December 3

1886 — Bill Crouch (P 1910)

1919 — Clarence (Hooks) Iott (P 1941, 1947)

1936 — Clay Dalrymple (C 1969-71)

1940 — Chico Salmon (SS-2B-1B-3B-OF 1969-72)

The Browns pay the Red Sox $30,000 for pitchers Denny Galehouse and Fritz Ostermueller. A good deal for St. Louis as Galehouse produces as a starter for the next four seasons.

1957 — The Orioles trade pitcher Ray Moore, second baseman Billy Goodman, and outfielder Tito Francona to the White Sox for pitcher Jack Harshman, first baseman Jim Marshall, and outfielder Larry Doby.

December 3 (continued)

1974 — Baltimore obtains first baseman Lee May and outfielder Jay Schlueter from Houston for second sacker Rob Andrews and utility player Enos Cabell. This trade is a definite plus for the O's because of the power Lee May brings to their lineup for the next six seasons.

December 4

1868 — Jesse Burkett (OF-P-SS-3B 1902-4)

1952 — The Browns obtain pitchers Virgil Trucks and Hal White and outfielder Johnny Groth from the Tigers in exchange for second baseman Owen Friend, outfielder Bob Nieman, and outfielder/catcher J. W. Porter.

1963 — The Orioles obtain outfielder Willie Kirkland from Cleveland for outfielder Al Smith and $25,000. Both players last less than a full season with their new clubs.

1968 — Baltimore trades first baseman John Mason and outfielder Curt Blefary to the Astros for pitcher Mike Cuellar, first baseman Elijah Johnson, and shortstop Enzo Hernandez. By obtaining the Cuban lefty Cuellar, the O's add a team-leading 23-game winner to their rotation.

1973 — The Birds send outfielder Merv Rettenmund, catcher Bill Wood, and infielder Junior Kennedy to the Reds for pitcher Ross Grimsley and catcher Wallace Williams.

1974 — In one of the team's finest deals ever, Baltimore obtains outfielder Ken Singleton and pitcher Mike Torrez from the Expos for pitchers Dave McNally and Bill Kirkpatrick and flyhawk Rich Coggins. Since '75, Singleton has been the key to the Oriole lineup and one of the finest players in baseball.

December 5

1906 — Lin Storti (3B-2B 1930-33)

1916 — Len Schulte (3B-2B-SS 1944-46)

1940 — John Papa (P 1961-62)

1954 — Gary Roenicke (OF 1978–present)

1969 — The O's sell pitcher Bill Dillman to the Cardinals.

December 6

1881 — Joe Lake (P 1910-12)

1883 — Dave Rowan (1B 1911)

1894 — Joe Gedeon (2B 1918-20)

1953 — Jeff Schneider (P 1981)

1965 — The O's trade center fielder Jackie Brandt and pitcher Darold Knowles to the Phillies for reliever Jack Baldschun.

1973 — In a deal they will later regret, the Orioles sell outfielder/first baseman Terry Crowley to Texas for $100,000.

1979 — Baltimore trades pitcher John Flinn to Milwaukee for second baseman Lenn Sakata. Score one for the O's. The small Hawaiian has proven a valuable player for the Orioles and took over the shortstop position from Mark Belanger in the second half of 1981.

December 7

1877 — Albert (Hobe) Ferriss (3B-2B 1908-9)

1911 — Denny Galehouse (P 1941-44, 1946-47)

1930 — Hal Smith (C 1955-56)

1950 — Rich Coggins (OF-DH 1972-74)

1965 — Harry Dalton is named director of player personnel, succeeding Lee McPhail, who left to join the Commissioner's office.

1973 — The Birds sell reliever Eddie Watt to the Phillies.

1977 — The O's obtain pitcher Tommy Moore and outfielder Carlos Lopez from the Mariners for pitcher Mike Parrott.

1979 — The Orioles trade first baseman Tom Chism to Minnesota for catcher Dan Graham. This deal has been a sleeper for the Birds. Graham assumed an important role as a platoon catcher for the team in 1980 and 1981.

December 8

1879 — Jimmy Austin (3B-SS-2B-C 1911-23, 1925-26, 1929; MGR 1913, 1918, 1923)

1918 — Sam Zoldak (P 1944-48)

1925 — Hank Thompson (2B 1947)

1939 — The Browns obtain first baseman/outfielder Rip Radcliff from the White Sox in exchange for outfielder Moose Solters. The Brownies get the better of this trade as Radcliff strokes a nifty .342 while leading the league with 200 hits.

1977 — The Orioles pick the Expos' pocket one more time by sending pitchers Rudy May, Randy Miller, and Bryn Smith to Montreal for outfielder Gary Roenicke and pitchers Don Stanhouse and Joe Kerrigan.

December 9

1888 — Charles (Lefty) Brown (P 1911-13)

103

December 9 (continued)

1928 — Joe De Maestri (SS-3B-2B 1952)

Billy Klaus (SS-3B-2B 1959-60)

1941 — Darold Knowles (P 1965)

1965 — The Orioles make a deal to remember as they obtain outfielder Frank Robinson from Cincinnati for pitchers Milt Pappas and Jack Baldschun and outfielder Dick Simpson. Most baseball experts rate this trade one of the 10 best of all time.

1971 — The Orioles trade outfielder Curt Motton to the Brewers for cash and a player to be named (pitcher Bob Reynolds joins Baltimore to complete the deal on March 25, 1972).

1980 — Designated hitter Lee May signs with the Royals as a free agent.

December 10

1879 — Charlie Shields (P 1902)

1880 — Pat Newnam (1B 1910-11)

1883 — Art Griggs (OF-1B-2B-SS-3B 1909-10)

Jim Stephens (C 1907-12)

1899 — Verdo Elmore (OF 1924)

December 11

1878 — Clarence Wright (P 1903-4)

1890 — Walt Meinert (OF 1913)

1910 — George (Slick) Coffman (P 1940)

1924 — Hal (Skinny) Brown (P 1955-62)

1959 — Lee McPhail is named president of the Orioles, succeeding James Keelty, Jr.

December 12

1885 — Frank Truesdale (2B 1910-11)

1917 — Clyde Kluttz (C 1951)

December 13

1891 — Charlie Flanagan (OF-3B 1913)

1916 — Hank Majeski (3B-2B 1955)

1929 — Billy Loes (P 1956–59)

1933 — The Browns trade outfielder Carl Reynolds to the Red Sox for pitcher Ivy Andrews and outfielder Smeed Jolley. This deal works to Boston's advantage as Reynolds hits .303 as a starting center fielder.

1948 — St. Louis sends pitcher Fred Sanford and catcher Roy Partee to the Yankees for pitcher Rich Starr, catcher Sherman Lollar, and $100,000. Lollar becomes a starter behind the plate and Starr contributes on the mound in '50 with seven triumphs and two saves.

1949 — The Browns trade third baseman Bob Dillinger and outfielder Paul Lehner to the Philadelphia Athletics for third baseman Frankie Gustine, shortstop Billy DeMars, outfielders Ray Coleman and Rocco Ippolitto, and $100,000: a slight edge to the A's, who gain two starters in Dillinger and Lehner.

December 14

1873 — John Anderson (1B-OF 1901–3)

1876 — Bert Blue (C 1908)

1897 — Syl Simon (3B-SS 1923–24)

1905 — Bob (Lefty) Weiland (P 1935)

1909 — Jim Walkup (P 1934–39)

1914 — Russell (Rusty) Peters (2B-SS 1947)

1921 — Bobby Adams (3B-2B 1956)

1925 — Sam (Toothpick) Jones (P 1964)

1927 — The Browns sell aging superstar George Sisler to the Senators for $25,000. Sisler lasts just 20 games with Washington before changing leagues and finishing out his career with the Boston Braves. In his last two seasons in the National League, George hit .326 and .309.

1932 — St. Louis trades pitcher Walter Stewart and outfielders Goose Goslin and Fred Schulte to the Senators for pitcher Lloyd Brown, outfielders Carl Reynolds and Sammy West, and $20,000. Although Goslin plays a key role in Washington's title in 1933, both Reynolds and West perform well in the outfield as Brownies.

1963 — The Orioles obtain pitcher Harvey Haddix from Pittsburgh for infielder Dick Yencha and cash.

December 15

1882 — Jay (Nig) Clarke (C-1B 1911)

1920 — Eddie Robinson (1B 1957)

December 15 (continued)

1927 — The Browns sell slugging outfielder Ken Williams to the Red Sox for $10,000. Although 38 years old, Williams hits .303 as the starting left fielder for Boston in '28.

1958 — The Orioles trade outfielder Jim Busby to the Red Sox for infielder Billy Klaus.

1959 — Baltimore purchases outfielder Johnny Powers from the Reds.

1962 — The O's send pitchers Jack Fisher and Billy Hoeft and catcher Jim Coker to San Francisco for pitchers Stu Miller and Mike McCormick and catcher John Orsino. Miller promptly leads the American League with 27 saves and sets a new record for appearances with 71.

In a separate transaction, the Birds send pitcher Dick Luebke and infielder Willard Oplinger and cash to Cincinnati for outfielder Joe Gaines.

1966 — Reliever Dick Hall is shipped by the Orioles to the Phillies for reliever John Morris.

1980 — The Orioles release pitcher Paul Hartzell.

December 16

1892 — William (Scrappy) Moore (3B 1917)

1951 — Mike Flanagan (P 1975–present)

1970 — The O's obtain reliever Grant Jackson and outfielders Jim Hutto and Sam Parilla from the Phillies for outfielder Roger Freed. Jackson becomes the Birds' ace southpaw reliever for the next five seasons.

December 17

1892 — Clarence (Tex) Covington (1B 1913)

1924 — The Browns trade pitcher Urban Shocker to the Yankees for pitchers Bullet Joe Bush, Milt Gaston, and Joe Giard.

1936 — Jerry Adair (2B-SS-3B 1958-66)

1976 — The Orioles release outfielder Tommy Harper.

1980 — The Birds sign free agent catcher and designated hitter Jose Morales. The ex-Twin hits just .244 in his first season as an Oriole.

December 18

1889 — Skelton (Buddy) Napier (P 1912)

1906 — Dick Coffman (P 1928-35)

1929 — Gino Cimoli (OF 1964)

1981 — For the second year in a row, the Orioles raise ticket prices. General admission for children under 12 remains $2.50, but the top price for lower-level box seats goes to $8.50 each.

December 19

1882 — Paul Krichell (C 1911-12)

1898 — Lou Koupal (P 1937)

December 20

1876 — Jimmy Williams (2B 1908-9)

1881 — Branch Rickey (C-OF 1905-6, 1914; MGR 1913-15)

December 21

1888 — George Curry (P 1911)

1897 — Hal Haid (P 1919)

1948 — Elliott Maddox (OF-3B 1977)

1976 — The Orioles release pitcher Mike Cuellar, who compiled 143 wins in eight seasons in Baltimore.

December 22

1885 — Owen Shannon (C-1B 1903)

1915 — Another baseball war ends as the Federal League disbands, after two seasons of competition with the existing American and National Leagues. As part of the settlement agreement, Phil Ball, owner of the St. Louis Federals, purchases the St. Louis Browns.

1922 — Johnny Bero (SS-2B 1951)

1940 — Elrod Hendricks (C-1B-DH-P 1968-76, 1978-79)

December 23

1889 — Fritz Maisel (3B-OF 1918)

1899 — Tommy Thomas (P 1936-37)

1943 — Dave May (OF 1967-70)

1959 — The Orioles release shortstop Chico Carrasquel.

1980 — Baltimore signs free agent outfielder Jimmy Dwyer.

December 24

1890 — Tod Sloan (OF 1913, 1917, 1919)

December 24 (continued)

1916 — Jack Graham (1B 1949)

1924 — Chico Garcia (2B 1954)

1954 — The O's buy outfielder Charlie Maxwell from the Red Sox.

December 25

1874 — Barry McCormick (3B-2B-SS-OF 1902-3)

1895 — Frank Ellerbe (3B 1921-24)

1899 — Gene Robertson (3B-SS-2B 1919, 1922-26)

1904 — Lloyd Brown (P 1933)

1925 — Ned Garver (P 1948-52)

1928 — Mike Blyzka (P 1953-54)

1934 — Charlie Beamon (P 1956-58)

December 26

1913 — Al Milnar (P 1943, 1946)

1927 — Stu Miller (P 1963-67)

1936 — Wayne Causey (3B-2B-SS 1955-57)

1961 — George (Storm) Davis (P 1982)

December 27

1922 — Connie Johnson (P 1956-58)

December 28

Nothing of significance happened on this date.

December 29

1889 — Bill McAllester (C 1913)

1890 — George Alton (OF 1912)

1911 — Bill Knickerbocker (SS-2B 1937)

1926 — Tom Upton (SS-2B-3B 1950-51)

1946 — Ken Rudolph (C 1977)

1956 — Dave Ford (P 1978-81)

December 30

1919 — Pete Layden (OF 1948)

1929 — Joe Taylor (OF 1958-59)

1944 — Jose Morales (DH 1981-82)

December 31

1919 — Tommy Byrne (P 1951-52)

1924 — Ted Gray (P 1955)

1933 — Ken Rowe (P 1964-65)

Unknown Birthdates

18?? — Ed Bruyette (OF-2B-SS-3B 1901)
18?? — Fred King (C 1901)
18?? — Pete Dowling (P 1901)
18?? — Claude Gonzzle (2B 1903)
18?? — John Terry (P 1903)
18?? — Bill Graham (P 1908-10)
18?? — Joe McDonald (3B 1910)
18?? — Fred Linke (P 1910)
18?? — Ernie Gust (1B 1911)
18?? — Phil Ketter (C 1912)
18?? — Charlie Miller (SS 1912)
18?? — Lou Proctor (PH 1912)
18?? — Henry Smoyer (SS-3B 1912)
18?? — George Tomer (PH 1913)
18?? — Sam Powell (P 1913)
18?? — Pete Schmidt (P 1913)
18?? — Bob Burkham (PH 1915)
18?? — Reeves McKay (P 1915)
18?? — Alex Remneas (P 1915)
1876 — Pete O'Brien (2B-3B-SS 1906)
1877 — Charlie Gibson (C 1905)
        Ike Van Zandt (OF-1B-P 1905)
1882 — Al Schweitzer (OF 1908-11)
1886 — Frank Spencer (P 1912)
1890 — Ray Jansen (3B 1910)
        Walter Jantzen (OF 1912)
1892 — Thomas Walsh (OF-SS-3B-2B-P 1913-15)
1894 — Roy Sanders (P 1920)

NICKNAMES

What would baseball be without those strange monickers hung on phenoms, flashes, and superstars? Nicknames are a great part of baseball's lore, as well as allure.

The rich history of the Browns and Orioles has produced some nickname classics. So sit back, take a few minutes, and run your eyes over this listing of some of the game's great and not-so-great.

Fletcher Allen	Sled
John Anderson	Honest John
Ivy Andrews	Poison
Luis Aparicio	Little Looie
Hank Arft	Bow Wow
Eldon Auker	Big Six
Jimmy Austin	Pepper
Morris Badgro	Red
Win Ballou	Old Pard
Ray Barker	Buddy
John Barkley	Red
Bill Bayne	Beverly
Walter Beck	Boom-Boom
Aloysius Bejma	Ollie
Roy Bell	Beau
Fred Bennett	Red
Joseph Bennett	Bugs
John Billings	Josh
George Binks	Bingo
Werner Birrer	Babe
Frank Biscan	Porky
Paul Blair	Motormouth
John Blake	Sheriff
William Borton	Babe
Jim Bottomley	Sunny Jim
Bob Boyd	The Rope
Harry Brecheen	The Cat
Anthony Brief	Bunny
Herman Bronkie	Dutch
Charles Brown	Curly, Lefty
Elmer Brown	Shook
Hal Brown	Skinny
Lloyd Brown	Gimpy
Jack Bruner	Pappy
George Brunet	Lefty
Al Bumbry	Bee
Jimmy Burke	Sunset Jimmy
Jesse Burkett	The Crab
Jack Burns	Slug
Joe Bush	Bullet Joe
Willis Butler	Kid
Milt Byrnes	Skippy
Bob Cain	Sugar
Merritt Cain	Sugar

110

Earl Caldwell	Teach
Art Ceccarelli	Chic
Bob Chakales	Chick
Mike Chartak	Shotgun
Gino Cimoli	Thatsa-My-Boy Gino
Jay Clarke	Nig
Ellis Clary	Cat
Verne Clemons	Fats
Harland Clift	Darkie
George Coffman	Slick
Walter Coleman	Rip
Harry Collins	Rip
John Corriden	Red
Clint Courtney	Scrap Iron
Clarence Covington	Tex
James Crandall	Doc
Rufus Crawford	Jake
Bill Crouch	Skip
Jack Crouch	Roxy
Alvin Crowder	General
George Curry	Soldier Boy
Ellsworth Dahlgren	Babe
Dave Danforth	Dauntless Dave
Frank Davis	Dixie
George Davis	Storm
Harry Davis	Stinky
Jay Hanna Dean	Dizzy
Paul Dean	Daffy
Maurice Dee	Shorty
Joe De Maestri	Oats
Billy DeMars	Kid
Sam Dente	Blackie
Bill Dinneen	Big Bill
Francis Donahue	Red
John Donahue	Jiggs
Harry Dorish	Fritz
Walt Dropo	Moose
Joe Durham	Pop
Frank Ellerbe	Governor
Jim Elliott	Jumbo
Charles Embree	Red
Joe Evans	Doc
Walter Evers	Hoot
Chet Falk	Spot
Cliff Fannin	Mule
Ed Farmer	Eatin' Ed
Stan Ferens	Lefty
Don Ferrarese	Midget
Albert Ferris	Hobe
Mike Fiore	Lefty
George Fisher	Showboat
John Fisher	Red

Dan Ford	Disco Dan
Eddie Foster	Kid
John Francona	Tito
Joe Frazier	Cobra Joe
Jim Fridley	Big Jim
Joe Gallagher	Muscles
Billy Gardner	Shotgun
Jim Gentile	Diamond Jim
Thomas George	Lefty
Wally Gerber	Spooks
Al Gerheauser	Lefty
Joe Giard	Peco
Paul Gilliford	Gorilla
Joe Glenn	Gabber
Leon Goslin	Goose
Sam Gray	Sad Sam
Harvey Haddix	The Kitten
Irving Hadley	Bump
Tom Hafey	The Arm
Fred Haney	Pudge
Roy Hansen	Snipe
William Hargrave	Pinky
Bill Harper	Blue Sleeve
Grover Hartley	Slick
Frankie Hayes	Blimp
Myron Hayworth	Red
Wally Hebert	Preacher
Don Heffner	Jeep
John Heidrick	Snags
Mel Held	Country
Charlie Hemphill	Eagle Eye
George Hennessey	Three Star
Frank Henry	Dutch
Dorrel Herzog	Whitey
Willie Hogan	Happy
Elon Hogsett	Chief
Al Hollingsworth	Boots
Alva Holloman	Bobo
Rogers Hornsby	Rajah
Byron Houck	Duke
Harry Howell	Handsome Harry
Dan Howley	Dapper Dan
Willis Hudlin	Ace
Hal Hudson	Lefty
Roy Hughes	Jeep
Clarence Iott	Hooks
Grant Jackson	Buck
Albert Jacobson	Beany
William Jacobson	Baby Doll

Sig Jakucki	Jack
Tom Jenkins	Tut
Fred Johnson	Cactus
Charlie Jones	Casey
Davy Jones	Kangaroo
Earl Jones	Lefty
Sam Jones	Toothpick, Sad Sam
Sam Jones	Sad Sam
Harry Kane	Klondike
Bill Kennedy	Lefty
William Kenworthy	Duke
Bill Killefer	Reindeer Bill
Ellis Kinder	Old Folks
Ed Kinsella	Rube
John Kloza	Nap
Wayne Krenchicki	Chick
Ralph Kress	Red
John Lavan	Doc
Alfred Lawson	Roxie
Paul Lehner	Gulliver
Albert Leifield	Lefty
Don Lenhardt	Footsie
Don Leppert	Tiger
Walt Leverenz	Tiny
Glenn Liebhardt	Sandy
Fred Linke	Laddie
Johnny Lipon	Skids
Gerard Lipscomb	Nig
Carroll Lockman	Whitey
Ed Lopat	Steady Eddie
Grover Lowdermilk	Slim
Bill McGill	Parson
Frank McGowan	Beauty
Archie McKain	Happy
Norm McMillan	Bub
Glenn McQuillen	Red
Roy Mahaffey	Popeye
Fritz Maisel	Flash
Hank Majeski	Heeney
Clyde Manion	Pete
Rolla Mapel	Lefty
Cliff Mapes	Tiger
Johnny Marcum	Footsie
Marty Marion	Slats, The Octopus
Roger Marquis	Noonie
Clarence Marshall	Cuddles
Boris Martin	Babe
Elwood Martin	Speed
Joe Martin	Silent Joe
Felix Martinez	Tippy
Charlie Maxwell	Smokey
Lee May	Mo, The Big Bopper

Tommy Mee	Judge
Oscar Melillo	Spinach, Ski
Paul Meloan	Mollie
Bill Miller	Wild Bill
Bill Miller	Hooks
John Miller	Ox
Ward Miller	Windy
Howard Mills	Lefty
Al Milnar	Happy
Ron Moeller	The Kid
Gene Moore	Rowdy
Ray Moore	Farmer
William Moore	Scrappy
Clarence Mueller	Heinie
Ray Murray	Deacon
Ralph Myers	Hap
William Nance	Doc, Kid
Skelton Napier	Buddy
Leslie Narum	Buster
Albert Nelson	Red
Maurice Newlin	Mickey
Norman Newsom	Bobo, Buck
Jack O'Connor	Peace Pie
Billy O'Dell	Digger
Chuck Oertel	Ducky
Frank O'Rourke	Blackie
John Orsino	Horse
Joe Ostrowski	Professor
Frank Overmire	Stubby
Leroy Paige	Satchel
Milt Pappas	Gimpy
George Pennington	Kewpie
Russell Peters	Rusty
Carl Peterson	Buddy
Eddie Plank	Gettysburg Eddie
Mizell Platt	Whitey
Lou Polli	Crip
John Powell	Boog
Carl Powis	Jug
Earl Pruess	Gibby
Hubert Pruett	Hub, Shucks
George Puccinelli	Count
Ewald Pyle	Lefty
Raymond Radcliff	Rip
Frank Raney	Ribs
Robert Ray	Farmer
Ray Richmond	Bud
Branch Rickey	The Mahatma
Jim Rivera	Jungle Jim

Tom Rogers	Shotgun
Charlie Root	Chinski
Herold Ruel	Muddy
Roy Sanders	Simon
Art Scharein	Scoop
Harry Schirick	Dutch
George Schmees	Rocky
Johnny Schmitz	Bear Tracks
Joe Schultz	Dode
Ralph Schwamb	Blackie
Al Schweitzer	Cheese
Ken Sears	Ziggy
Alvis Shirley	Tex
Burt Shotton	Barney
Al Smith	Fuzzy
Julius Solters	Moose
Edward Spencer	Tubby
Paul Speraw	Polly, Birdie
Don Stanhouse	Stan the Man Unusual, Full Pack
George Stanton	Buck
Jim Stephens	Little Nemo
Vern Stephens	Junior, Buster
Walter Stewart	Lefty
George Stirnweiss	Snuffy
George Stovall	Firebrand
Alan Strange	Inky
Charles Street	Gabby, Old Sarge
Willie Sudhoff	Wee Willie
George Susce	Good Kid
Edward Swander	Pinky
Sherwin Swartz	Bud
Fay Thomas	Scow
John Thomas	Bud
Bobby Thomson	The Staten Island Scot
Hollis Thurston	Sloppy
Les Tietje	Toots
Paul Trout	Dizzy
Bob Turley	Bullet Bob
Roy Upright	Dixie
Tom Upton	Muscles
Fred Valentine	Squeaky
Russ Van Atta	Sheriff
Jake Wade	Whistlin' Jake
Clarence Walker	Tilly
Bobby Wallace	Rhody
Thomas Walsh	Dee
Clyde Wares	Buzzy
Earl Weaver	Spanky
Jim Weaver	Big Jim
Bob Weiland	Lefty

Nicknames (continued)

Carl Weilman	Zeke
Weldon West	Lefty
Franklin Wetzel	Buzz
Albert White	Fuzz
John Whitehead	Silent John
Bill Wight	Lefty
Gus Williams	Gloomy Gus
Jimmy Williams	Buttons
Frank Wilson	Squash
Hal Wiltse	Whitey
Wayne Wright	Rasty
Al Zarilla	Zeke
Sam Zoldak	Sad Sam
Frank Zupo	Noodles

ALL-TIME ROSTERS

Milwaukee Brewers 1901

Anderson, John, INF-OF, 1901

Bone, George, INF, 1901
Bruyette, Ed, OF-INF, 1901
Burke, Jimmy, INF, 1901

Connor, Joe, C-INF-OF, 1901
Conroy, Wid, INF, 1901

Donahue, Jiggs, C-INF, 1901
Dowling, Pete, P, 1901
Duffy, Hugh, OF, 1901

Friel, Bill, INF-OF, 1901

Garvin, Ned, P, 1901
Geier, Phil, OF-INF, 1901
Gertenrich, Lou, OF, 1901
Gilbert, Billy, INF, 1901

Hallman, Bill, OF, 1901
Hawley, Pink, P, 1901
Hogriever, George, OF, 1901
Husting, Bert, P, 1901

Jones, Davy, OF, 1901

King, Fred, C, 1901

Leahy, Tom, C-OF-INF, 1901

Maloney, Billy, C-OF, 1901
McBride, George, INF, 1901

Reidy, Bill, P, 1901

Sparks, Tully, P, 1901

Waldron, Irv, OF, 1901

St. Louis Browns 1902-53

Ables, Harry, P, 1905
Abstein, Bill, INF, 1910
Adams, Spencer, INF, 1927
Adams, Willie, P, 1912-13
Agnew, Sam, C, 1913-15
Albrecht, Ed, P, 1949-50
Alexander, Walt, C, 1912-13, 1915
Allen, Ethan, OF, 1937-38

Allen, Johnny, P, 1941
Allen, Sled, C-INF, 1910
Allison, Mack, P, 1911-13
Almada, Mel, OF, 1938-39
Alton, George, OF, 1912
Anderson, Andy, INF, 1948-49
Anderson, John, INF-OF, 1902-3
Andrews, Ivy, P, 1934-36

116

Appleton, Pete, P, 1942
Archie, George, INF, 1941
Arft, Hank, INF, 1948-52
Auker, Eldon, P, 1940-42
Austin, Jimmy, INF, 1911-23, 1925-26, 1929

Bader, Art, OF, 1904
Badgro, Red, OF, 1929-30
Baecht, Ed, P, 1937
Baichley, Grover, P, 1914
Bailey, Bill, P, 1907-12
Baker, Floyd, INF, 1943-44
Balenti, Mike, INF-OF, 1913
Ballou, Win, P, 1926-27
Barkley, Red, INF, 1937
Barnhart, Ed, P, 1924
Batts, Matt, C, 1951
Bauers, Russ, P, 1950
Baumgardner, George, P, 1912-16
Bayne, Bill, P, 1919-24
Bearden, Gene, P, 1952
Beck, Boom-Boom, P, 1924, 1927-28
Bejma, Ollie, INF, 1934-36
Bell, Beau, OF, 1935-39
Bengough, Benny, C, 1931-32
Bennett, Bugs, P, 1918
Bennett, Fred, OF, 1928
Bennett, Herschel, OF, 1923-27
Berardino, Johnny, INF, 1939-42, 1946-47, 1951
Bero, Johnny, INF, 1951
Berry, Neil, INF, 1953
Bettencourt, Larry, OF, 1928, 1931-32
Bilbrey, Jim, P, 1949
Bildilli, Emil, P, 1937-41
Billings, Josh, C, 1919-23
Binks, George, OF-INF, 1948
Biscan, Frank, P, 1942, 1946
Bisland, Rivington, INF, 1913
Black, John, INF, 1911
Blaeholder, George, P, 1925, 1927-35
Blake, Sheriff, P, 1937
Blue, Bert, C, 1908
Blue, Lu, INF, 1928-30
Blyzka, Mike, P, 1953
Boehler, George, P, 1920-21
Boland, Bernie, P, 1921
Bold, Charlie, INF, 1914
Bolen, Stew, P, 1926-27
Bonetti, Julio, P, 1937-38
Bonin, Luther, OF, 1913
Borton, Babe, INF, 1916
Bottomley, Jim, INF, 1936-37
Bowcock, Ben, INF, 1903

Bowden, Tim, OF, 1914
Boyd, Ray, P, 1910
Bradley, George, OF, 1946
Brannan, Otis, INF, 1928-29
Braxton, Garland, P, 1931
Brecheen, Harry, P, 1953
Brief, Bunny, INF-OF, 1912-13
Bronkie, Herman, INF, 1919
Brown, Bill, OF, 1912
Brown, Curly, P, 1911-13
Brown, Elmer, P, 1911-12
Brown, Lloyd, P, 1933
Brown, Walter, P, 1947
Brown, Willard, OF, 1947
Bruner, Jack, P, 1950
Buchanan, Jim, P, 1905
Buelow, Fritz, C, 1907
Burkam, Bob, PH, 1915
Burke, Pat, INF, 1924
Burkett, Jesse, OF, 1902-4
Burnett, Johnny, INF, 1935
Burns, Jack, INF, 1930-36
Burwell, Bill, P, 1920-21
Bush, Joe, P, 1925
Butler, Kid, INF, 1907
Byrne, Tommy, P, 1951-52
Byrnes, Milt, OF, 1943-45

Cafego, Tom, OF, 1937
Cain, Bob, P, 1952-53
Cain, Sugar, P, 1935-36
Caldwell, Earl, P, 1935-37
Campbell, Bruce, OF, 1932-34
Carey, Tom, INF, 1935-37
Caster, George, P, 1941-45
Chapman, Harry, C, 1916
Chartak, Mike, INF-OF, 1942-44
Christman, Mark, INF, 1939, 1943-46
Clancy, Al, INF, 1911
Clark, Earl, OF, 1934
Clarke, Nig, C-INF, 1911
Clary, Ellis, INF, 1943-45
Clemons, Bob, OF, 1914
Clemons, Verne, C, 1916
Clift, Harlond, INF, 1934-43
Cobb, Herb, P, 1929
Coffman, Dick, P, 1928-35
Coffman, Slick, P, 1940
Cole, Ed, P, 1938-39
Coleman, Ed, OF, 1935-36
Coleman, Ray, OF, 1947-48, 1950-52
Collins, Pat, C-INF, 1919-24
Collins, Rip, P, 1929-31
Compton, Pete, OF, 1911-13
Cook, Rollin, P, 1915

117

Cooney, Bob, P, 1931–32
Corriden, Red, INF, 1910
Courtney, Clint, C, 1952–53
Covington, Tex, INF, 1913
Cox, Bill, P, 1938–40
Crandall, Doc, P, 1916
Crawford, Rufus, OF, 1952
Criger, Lou, C, 1909
Criscola, Tony, OF, 1942–43
Crisp, Joe, C, 1910–11
Criss, Dode, P, 1908–11
Crompton, Ned, OF, 1909
Crossin, Frank, C, 1912–14
Crouch, Bill, P, 1910
Crouch, Jack, C, 1930–31, 1933
Crowder, General, P, 1927–30
Cullenbine, Roy, OF, 1940–42
Cullop, Nick, P, 1921
Currin, Perry, INF, 1947
Curry, George, P, 1911

Dahlgren, Babe, INF, 1942, 1946
Daley, John, INF, 1912
Dalrymple, Mike, INF, 1915
Danforth, Dave, P, 1922–25
Danning, Ike, C, 1928
Davenport, Dave, P, 1916–19
Davis, Dixie, P, 1920–26
Davis, Harry, INF, 1937
Deal, Charlie, INF, 1916
Dean, Dizzy, P, 1947
Dean, Paul, P, 1943
DeBarry, Joe, P, 1920–21
Dee, Shorty, INF, 1915
Delahanty, Jim, INF-OF, 1907
Delsing, Jim, OF, 1950–52
DeMaestri, Joe, INF, 1952
Demaree, Frank, OF, 1944
DeMars, Billy, INF, 1950–51
Demmitt, Ray, OF, 1910, 1917–19
DeMontreville, Gene, INF, 1904
Dente, Sam, INF, 1948
Devoy, Walt, OF-INF, 1909
Dillinger, Bob, INF, 1946–49
Dinneen, Bill, P, 1907–9
Dixon, Leo, C, 1925–27
Donahue, Jiggs, C-INF, 1902
Donahue, Red, P, 1902–3
Dondero, Len, INF, 1929
Dorish, Harry, P, 1950
Doyle, Jess, P, 1931
Dreisewerd, Clem, P, 1948
Drews, Karl, P, 1948–49

Duggan, Jim, INF, 1911
Durst, Cedric, OF, 1922–23, 1926
Dyck, Jim, INF-OF, 1951–53

Early, Jake, C, 1947
East, Carl, P, 1915
Edwards, Hank, OF, 1953
Elder, George, OF, 1949
Ellerbe, Frank, INF, 1921–24
Elliott, Bob, INF, 1953
Elliott, Jumbo, P, 1923
Elmore, Verdo, OF, 1924
Embree, Red, P, 1949
Enzenroth, Jack, C, 1914
Epps, Hal, OF, 1943–44
Estalella, Bobby, OF, 1941
Estrada, Oscar, P, 1929
Evans, Joe, OF, 1924–25
Evans, LeRoy, P, 1903
Ezzell, Homer, INF, 1923

Falk, Chet, P, 1925–27
Fannin, Cliff, P, 1945–52
Ferens, Stan, P, 1942
Ferrell, Rick, C, 1929–33, 1941–43
Ferrick, Tom, P, 1946, 1949–50
Ferris, Hobe, INF, 1908–9
Fincher, Bill, P, 1916
Fine, Tom, P, 1950
Finney, Lou, OF-INF, 1945–46
Fischer, Carl, P, 1932
Fisher, Red, OF, 1910
Fisher, Showboat, OF, 1932
Flanagan, Charlie, OF-INF, 1913
Foster, Eddie, INF, 1922–23
Friel, Bill, INF-OF-C-P, 1902–3
Friend, Owen, INF, 1949–50
Frill, John, P, 1912
Frisk, Emil, OF, 1905
Fuchs, Charlie, P, 1943

Gaedel, Eddie, PH, 1951
Galehouse, Denny, P, 1941–44, 1946–47
Gallagher, Joe, OF, 1939–40
Gallia, Bert, P, 1918–20
Garms, Debs, OF, 1932–35
Garver, Ned, P, 1948–52
Gaston, Milt, P, 1925–27
Gedeon, Joe, INF, 1918–20
George, Lefty, P, 1911
Gerber, Wally, INF, 1917–28
Gerheauser, Al, P, 1948
Giard, Joe, P, 1925–26

Gibson, Charlie, C, 1905
Gill, George, P, 1939
Gilligan, Jack, P, 1909-10
Giuliani, Tony, C, 1936-37
Glade, Fred, P, 1904-7
Gleason, Bill, INF, 1921
Gleason, Harry, INF, 1904-5
Glenn, Joe, C, 1939
Goldsberry, Gordon, INF, 1952
Goliat, Mike, INF, 1951-52
Gonzzle, Claude, INF, 1903
Goslin, Goose, OF, 1930-32
Grace, Joe, OF, 1938-41, 1946
Graff, Fred, INF, 1913
Graham, Bert, INF, 1910
Graham, Bill, P, 1908-10
Graham, Jack, INF, 1949
Grant, George, P, 1923-25
Gray, Pete, OF, 1945
Gray, Sam, P, 1928-33
Gregory, Howie, P, 1911
Griggs, Art, INF-OF, 1909-10
Grimes, Ed, INF, 1931-32
Groom, Bob, P, 1916-17
Groth, Johnny, OF, 1953
Grube, Frank, C, 1934-35, 1941
Gryska, Sig, INF, 1938-39
Gullic, Ted, OF-INF, 1930
Gust, Ernie, INF, 1911
Gustine, Frankie, INF, 1950
Gutteridge, Don, INF, 1942-45

Habenicht, Bob, P, 1953
Hadley, Bump, P, 1932-34
Hafey, Tom, OF-INF, 1944
Haid, Hal, P, 1919
Hale, George, C, 1914, 1916-18
Hale, Sammy, INF, 1930
Hall, Marc, P, 1910
Hallinan, Ed, INF, 1911-12
Hamilton, Earl, P, 1911-17
Hanning, Loy, P, 1939
Hansen, Snipe, P, 1935
Hargrave, Pinky, C, 1925-26
Harper, Bill, P, 1911
Harper, Jack, P, 1902
Harris, Bob, P, 1939-42
Harrist, Earl, P, 1952
Harshaney, Sam, C, 1937-40
Hartley, Grover, C, 1916-17, 1934
Hartzell, Roy, INF-OF, 1906-10
Hassler, Joe, INF, 1930
Hawk, Ed, P, 1911
Hayes, Frankie, C, 1942-43
Hayworth, Ray, C, 1942

Hayworth, Red, C, 1944-45
Heath, Jeff, OF, 1946-47
Heath, Tommy, C, 1935, 1937-38
Hebert, Wally, P, 1931-33
Heffner, Don, INF, 1938-43
Heidrick, John, OF-C, 1902-4, 1908
Helf, Hank, C, 1946
Hemingway, Ed, INF, 1914
Hemphill, Charlie, OF, 1902-4, 1906-7
Hemsley, Rollie, C-OF, 1933-37
Hendryx, Tim, OF, 1918
Hennessey, George, P, 1937
Henry, Dutch, P, 1921-22
Herrera, Tito, P, 1951
Hetki, Johnny, P, 1952
Heving, Johnnie, C, 1920
Hildebrand, Oral, P, 1937-38
Hill, Hunter, INF, 1903-4
Hitchcock, Billy, INF, 1947
Hoag, Myril, OF, 1939-41
Hoch, Harry, P, 1914-15
Hoff, Red, P, 1915
Hoffman, Danny, OF, 1908-11
Hogan, Happy, OF-INF, 1911-12
Hogsett, Chief, P, 1936-37
Hogue, Bobby, P, 1951-52
Holcombe, Ken, P, 1952
Hollingsworth, Al, P, 1942-46
Holloman, Bobo, P, 1953
Holshauser, Herm, P, 1930
Hopkins, Paul, P, 1929
Hornsby, Rogers, INF-OF, 1933-37
Houck, Byron, P, 1918
Howard, Ivan, INF-OF, 1914-15
Howell, Harry, P, 1904-10
Hudlin, Willis, P, 1940
Hudson, Hal, P, 1952
Huelsman, Frank, OF, 1904
Huffman, Ben, C, 1937
Hughes, Roy, INF, 1938-39
Hungling, Bernie, C, 1930
Hunter, Billy, INF, 1953
Hynes, Pat, P, 1904

Iott, Hooks, P, 1941

Jacobson, Baby Doll, OF, 1915, 1917, 1919-26
Jacobson, Beany, P, 1906-7
Jakucki, Sig, P, 1936, 1944-45
James, Bill, P, 1914-15
Jansen, Ray, INF, 1910
Jantzen, Heinie, OF, 1912
Jenkins, Joe, C, 1914
Jenkins, Tom, OF, 1929-32

Jennings, Bill, INF, 1951
Johns, Pete, INF-OF, 1918
Johnson, Chet, P, 1946
Johnson, Darrell, C, 1952
Johnson, Don, P, 1950-51
Johnson, Ernie, INF, 1916-18
Johnson, Fred, P, 1938-39
Johnston, Johnny, OF, 1913
Jones, Charlie, OF, 1908
Jones, Davy, OF, 1902
Jones, Earl, P, 1945
Jones, Sad Sam, P, 1927
Jones, Tom, INF, 1904-9
Jonnard, Claude, P, 1926
Jordan, Tom, C, 1948
Judnich, Walt, OF, 1940-42, 1946-47

Kahoe, Mike, C-OF, 1902-4
Kane, Harry, P, 1902
Kauffman, Dick, INF-OF, 1914-15
Kellert, Frank, INF, 1953
Kennedy, Bill, P, 1948-51
Kennedy, Ray, PH, 1916
Kennedy, Vern, P, 1939-41
Kenworthy, Duke, INF, 1917
Ketter, Phil, C, 1912
Killefer, Bill, C, 1909-10
Kimberlin, Harry, P, 1936-39
Kimsey, Chad, P, 1929-32
Kinder, Ellis, P, 1946-47
Kinsella, Ed, P, 1910
Kloza, Nap, OF, 1931-32
Kluttz, Clyde, C, 1951
Knickerbocker, Bill, INF, 1937
Knott, Jack, P, 1933-38
Koehler, Ben, OF-INF, 1905-6
Kokos, Dick, OF, 1948-50, 1953
Kolp, Ray, P, 1921-24
Koob, Ernie, P, 1915-17, 1919
Koupal, Lou, P, 1937
Kramer, Jack, P, 1939-41, 1943-47
Kreevich, Mike, OF, 1943-45
Kress, Red, INF, 1927-32, 1938-39
Kretlow, Lou, P, 1950
Krichell, Paul, C, 1911-12
Kryhoski, Dick, INF, 1952-53
Kusel, Ed, P, 1909
Kutina, Joe, INF, 1911-12

Laabs, Chet, OF, 1939-46
Lake, Joe, P, 1910-12
LaMacchia, Al, P, 1943, 1945-46
Lamb, Lyman, OF, 1920-21

LaMotte, Bobby, INF, 1925-26
Lanier, Max, P, 1953
LaPorte, Frank, INF, 1911-12
Larsen, Don, P, 1953
Lary, Lyn, INF, 1935-36, 1940
Lasley, Bill, P, 1924
Lavan, Doc, INF, 1913-17
Lawson, Roxie, P, 1939-40
Layden, Pete, OF, 1948
Leary, John, INF-C, 1914-15
Lee, Bill, OF-INF, 1915-16
Lee, Dud, INF, 1920-21
Lehner, Paul, OF, 1946-49, 1951
Leifield, Lefty, P, 1918-20
Lenhardt, Don, OF, 1950-53
Leverenz, Walt, P, 1913-15
Leverette, Hod, P, 1920
Levey, Jim, INF, 1930-33
Liebhardt, Glenn, P, 1936
Linke, Ed, P, 1938
Linke, Fred, P, 1910
Lipon, Johnny, INF, 1953
Lipscomb, Nig, P, 1937
Littlefield, Dick, P, 1952-53
Lollar, Sherm, C, 1949-51
Long, Dale, INF-OF, 1951
Lowdermilk, Grover, P, 1915, 1917-19
Lucadello, Johnny, INF, 1938-41, 1946
Lund, Don, OF, 1948
Lutz, Joe, INF, 1951
Lynch, Adrian, P, 1920
Lyons, George, P, 1924

Madison, Dave, P, 1952
Magee, Lee, INF-OF, 1917
Maguire, Jack, OF-INF, 1951
Mahaffey, Roy, P, 1936
Mahoney, Bob, P, 1951-52
Maisel, Fritz, INF-OF, 1918
Maisel, George, OF, 1913
Malloy, Alex, P, 1910
Malloy, Bob, P, 1949
Maloney, Billy, OF-C, 1902
Mancuso, Frank, C, 1944-46
Manion, Clyde, C, 1928-30
Manning, Ernie, P, 1914
Manush, Heinie, OF, 1928-30
Mapel, Rolla, P, 1919
Mapes, Cliff, OF, 1951
Marcum, Johnny, P, 1939
Marion, Marty, INF, 1952-53
Markell, Duke, P, 1951
Marsans, Armando, OF, 1916-17

Marsh, Freddie, INF, 1951–52
Marshall, Cuddles, P, 1950
Martin, Babe, OF-INF-C, 1944–46, 1953
Martin, Joe, OF-INF, 1903
Martin, Speed, P, 1917
Mayer, Wally, C, 1919
Mazzera, Mel, OF, 1935, 1937–39
McAfee, Bill, P, 1934
McAleer, Jimmy, OF, 1902, 1907
McAleese, John, OF-INF, 1909
McAllester, Bill, C, 1913
McCabe, Tim, P, 1915–18
McCarthy, Jerry, INF, 1948
McCormick, Barry, INF-OF, 1902–3
McCorry, Bill, P, 1909
McDonald, Hank, P, 1933
McDonald, Jim, P, 1951
McDonald, Joe, INF, 1910
McGill, Bill, P, 1907
McGowan, Beauty, OF, 1928–29
McKain, Archie, P, 1941
McKay, Reeves, P, 1915
McLaughlin, Jim, INF, 1932
McManus, Marty, INF, 1920–26
McMillan, Norm, INF, 1924
McNeely, Earl, OF, 1928–31
McQuillen, Glenn, OF, 1938, 1941–42, 1946–47
McQuinn, George, INF, 1938–45
Medlinger, Irv, P, 1949
Mee, Tommy, INF, 1910
Meine, Heinie, P, 1922
Meinert, Walt, OF, 1913
Melillo, Oscar, INF, 1926–35
Meloan, Paul, OF, 1911
Meola, Mike, P, 1936
Messenger, Bobby, OF, 1914
Metzler, Alex, OF, 1930
Michaels, Cass, INF, 1952
Mickelson, Ed, INF, 1953
Miller, Bill, P, 1937
Miller, Bing, OF, 1926–27
Miller, C., INF, 1912
Miller, Ed, INF, 1912
Miller, Otto, INF, 1927
Miller, Ox, P, 1943, 1945–46
Miller, Ward, OF, 1916–17
Mills, Buster, OF, 1938
Mills, Lefty, P, 1934, 1937–40
Milnar, Al, P, 1943
Miranda, Willie, INF, 1952–53
Mitchell, Roy, P, 1910–14
Mizeur, Bill, PH, 1923–24
Mogridge, George, P, 1925

Molyneaux, Vince, P, 1917
Moore, Gene, OF, 1944–45
Moore, Scrappy, INF, 1917
Moran, Charlie, INF, 1904–5
Morgan, Cy, P, 1903–5, 1907
Moser, Walter, P, 1911
Moss, Les, C, 1946–53
Moulder, Glen, P, 1947
Moulton, Ollie, INF, 1911
Mueller, Heinie, INF-OF, 1935
Mullen, Billy, INF, 1920–21, 1928
Muncrief, Bob, P, 1937, 1939, 1941–47
Murray, Ed, INF, 1917
Murray, Jim, OF, 1911
Myers, Hap, INF, 1911

Nance, Doc, OF, 1904
Napier, Buddy, P, 1912
Naples, Al, INF, 1949
Neighbors, Bob, INF, 1939
Nelson, Red, P, 1910–12
Nevers, Ernie, P, 1926–28
Newlin, Maury, P, 1940–41
Newnam, Pat, INF, 1910–11
Newsom, Bobo, P, 1934–35, 1938–39, 1943
Nieman, Bob, OF, 1951–52
Niggeling, Johnny, P, 1940–43
Niles, Harry, INF, 1906–7
Noroyke, Lou, INF, 1906
Northen, Hub, OF, 1910
Nunamaker, Les, C-INF-OF, 1918
Nye, Otto, INF, 1917

O'Brien, George, C, 1915
O'Brien, Pete, INF, 1906
O'Connor, Jack, C, 1904, 1906–7, 1910
Ogden, Jack, P, 1928–29
O'Leary, Charley, PH, 1934
O'Neill, Steve, C, 1927–28
O'Rourke, Frank, INF, 1927–31
Ostermueller, Fritz, P, 1941–43
Ostrowski, Joe, P, 1948–50
Overmire, Stubby, P, 1950–52

Pack, Frankie, PH, 1949
Padden, Dick, INF, 1902–5
Paige, Satchel, P, 1951–53
Palmero, Emilio, P, 1921
Papai, Al, P, 1949
Park, Jim, P, 1915–17
Parker, Pat, OF, 1915
Partee, Roy, C, 1948
Patterson, Ham, INF-OF, 1909
Paulette, Gene, INF, 1916–17

Pellagrini, Eddie, INF, 1948-49
Pelty, Barney, P, 1903-12
Pennington, Kewpie, P, 1917
Pepper, Ray, OF, 1934-36
Perry, Scott, P, 1915
Perryman, Parson, P, 1915
Peters, Rusty, INF, 1947
Peterson, Sid, P, 1943
Pfeffer, Jeff, P, 1911
Phillips, Tom, P, 1915
Pickering, Ollie, OF, 1907
Pillette, Duane, P, 1950-53
Pisoni, Jim, OF, 1953
Plank, Eddie, P, 1916-17
Platt, Whitey, OF, 1948-49
Polli, Lou, P, 1932
Porter, J. W., OF-INF, 1952
Poser, Bob, P, 1935
Potter, Nels, P, 1943-48
Powell, Jack, P, 1902-3, 1905-12
Powell, Sam, P, 1913
Pratt, Del, INF, 1912-17
Priddy, Jerry, INF, 1948-49
Proctor, Lou, PH, 1912
Pruess, Earl, OF, 1920
Pruett, Hub, P, 1922-24
Puccinelli, George, OF, 1934
Pyle, Ewald, P, 1939

Radcliff, Rip, OF-INF, 1940-41
Raney, Ribs, P, 1949-50
Rapp, Earl, OF, 1951-52
Ray, Farmer, P, 1910
Rego, Tony, C, 1924-25
Reidy, Bill, P, 1902-3
Remneas, Alex, P, 1915
Reynolds, Carl, OF, 1933
Rice, Harry, OF-INF-C, 1923-27
Richardson, Tom, PH, 1917
Richmond, Ray, P, 1920-21
Rickey, Branch, C-OF, 1905-6, 1914
Riley, Jim, INF, 1921
Rivera, Jim, OF, 1952
Robertson, Charlie, P, 1926
Robertson, Gene, INF, 1919, 1922-26
Rockenfeld, Ike, INF, 1905-6
Roetz, Ed, INF, 1929
Rogers, Tom, P, 1917-19
Rojek, Stan, INF, 1952
Root, Charlie, P, 1923
Rose, Chuck, P, 1909
Rossman, Claude, OF, 1909
Roth, Frank, C, 1905

Rowan, Dave, INF, 1911
Ruel, Muddy, C, 1915
Rumler, Bill, C, 1914, 1916-17

Sanders, Dee, P, 1945
Sanders, Roy, P, 1920
Sanford, Fred, P, 1943, 1946-48, 1951
Saucier, Frank, OF, 1951
Savage, Bob, P, 1949
Sax, Ollie, INF, 1928
Schacht, Sid, P, 1950-51
Schang, Wally, C-OF, 1926-29
Scharien, Art, INF, 1932-34
Scheneberg, John, P, 1920
Schepner, Joe, INF, 1919
Schirick, Dutch, PH, 1914
Schliebner, Dutch, INF, 1923
Schmandt, Ray, INF, 1915
Schmees, George, OF-INF, 1952
Schmidt, Pete P, 1913
Schmulbach, Hank, PR, 1943
Schulte, Fred, OF, 1927-32
Schulte, Johnny, INF-C, 1923
Schulte, Len, INF, 1944-46
Schultz, Joe, C, 1943-48
Schwamb, Blackie, P, 1948
Schweitzer, Al, OF, 1908-11
Schwenk, Hal, P, 1913
Sears, Ken, C, 1946
Severeid, Hank, C, 1915-25
Sewell, Luke, C, 1942
Shanley, Doc, INF, 1912
Shannon, Owen, C-INF, 1903
Shea, Merv, C, 1933
Shields, Charlie, P, 1902
Shirley, Tex, P, 1944-46
Shocker, Urban, P, 1918-24
Shore, Ray, P, 1946, 1948-49
Shorten, Chick, OF, 1922
Shotton, Burt, OF, 1909, 1911-17
Shovlin, John, INF, 1919-20
Siever, Ed, P, 1903-4
Sievers, Roy, OF-INF, 1949-53
Silber, Eddie, OF, 1937
Simon, Syl, INF, 1923-24
Sims, Pete, P, 1915
Sisler, George, INF-OF-P, 1915-22, 1924-27
Sleater, Lou, P, 1950-52
Sloan, Tod, OF, 1913, 1917
Smith, Earl, OF, 1917-21
Smith, Ed, P, 1906
Smith, Syd, C, 1908

Smith, Wib, C-INF, 1909
Smoyer, Henry, INF, 1912
Snell, Charlie, C, 1912
Solters, Moose, OF, 1935-36, 1939
Sommers, Bill, INF, 1950
Sothoron, Allen, P, 1914-15, 1917-21
Southwick, Clyde, C, 1911
Spade, Bob, P, 1910
Spence, Stan, OF-INF, 1949
Spencer, Frank, P, 1912
Spencer, Tubby, C, 1905-8
Speraw, Paul, INF, 1920
Spindel, Hal, C, 1939
Springer, Brad, P, 1925
Stanton, Buck, OF, 1931
Starr, Charlie, INF, 1905
Starr, Dick, P, 1949-51
Stauffer, Ed, P, 1925
Stephens, Bryan, P, 1948
Stephens, Jim, C, 1907-12
Stephens, Vern, INF-OF, 1941-47, 1953
Stevens, Chuck, INF, 1941, 1946
Stewart, Lefty, P, 1927-32
Stiely, Fred, P, 1929-31
Stiles, Rollie, P, 1930-31, 1933
Stirnweiss, Snuffy, INF, 1950
Stone, Dwight, P, 1913
Stone, George, OF, 1905-10
Storti, Lin, INF, 1930-33
Stovall, George, INF, 1912-13
Strange, Alan, INF, 1934-35, 1940-42
Strelecki, Ed, P, 1928-29
Stremmel, Phil, P, 1909-10
Strickland, Bill, P, 1937
Stuart, Luke, INF, 1921
Stuart, Marlin, P, 1952-53
Sturdy, Guy, INF, 1927-28
Suchecki, Jim, P, 1951
Sudhoff, Willie, P, 1902-5
Sugden, Joe, C-INF, 1902-5
Sullivan, Billy, C-INF, 1938-39
Sullivan, John, INF, 1949
Sundra, Steve, P, 1942-44, 1946
Susce, George, C, 1940
Swander, Pinky, OF, 1903-4
Swartz, Bud, P, 1947
Swift, Bob, C, 1940-42

Tamulis, Vito, P, 1938
Taylor, Bennie, INF, 1951
Taylor, Pete, P, 1952
Taylor, Wiley, P, 1913-14
Tennant, Tom, PH, 1912
Terry, John, P, 1903
Thomas, Bud, INF, 1951

Thomas, Fay, P, 1935
Thomas, Leo, INF, 1950
Thomas, Tommy, P, 1936-37
Thompson, Frank, INF, 1920
Thompson, Hank, INF, 1947
Thompson, Tommy, OF, 1939
Thurston, Sloppy, P, 1923
Tietje, Les, P, 1936-38
Tillman, Johnny, P, 1915
Tobin, Jack, OF, 1916, 1918-25
Tomer, George, PH, 1913
Trotter, Bill, P, 1937-42
Trucks, Virgil, P, 1953
Truesdale, Frank, INF, 1910-11
Turley, Bob, P, 1951
Turner, Tom, C, 1944

Upright, Dixie, PH, 1953
Upton, Tom, INF, 1950-51

Vahrenhorst, Howard, PH, 1904
Van Atta, Russ, P, 1935-39
Vangilder, Elam, P, 1919-27
Van Zandt, Ike, P, 1905
Voigt, Ollie, P, 1924
Vosmik, Joe, OF, 1937

Waddell, Rube, P, 1908-10
Waddey, Frank, OF, 1931
Wade, Jake, P, 1939
Wahl, Kermit, INF, 1951
Walden, Fred, C, 1912
Walker, Ernie, OF, 1913-15
Walker, Tilly, OF, 1913-15
Walkup, Jim, P, 1934-39
Wallace, Bobby, INF-OF-P, 1902-16
Walsh, Dee, INF, 1913-15
Wares, Buzzy, INF, 1913-14
Warnock, Hal, OF, 1935
Weaver, Art, C, 1905
Weaver, Jim, P, 1934
Weiland, Bob, P, 1935
Weilman, Carl, P, 1912-17, 1919-20
Wells, Ed, P, 1933-34
Wertz, Vic, OF, 1952-53
West, Lefty, P, 1944-45
West, Sammy, OF, 1933-38
Wetzel, Buzz, OF, 1920-21
Whaley, Bill, OF, 1923
White, Fuzz, PH, 1940
White, Hal, P, 1953
Whitehead, John, P, 1939-40, 1942
Widmar, Al, P, 1948, 1950-51
Williams, Gus, OF, 1911-15
Williams, Jimmy, INF, 1908-9

St. Louis Browns All-Time Roster (continued)

Williams, Ken, OF, 1918-27
Willis, Joe, P, 1911
Wilson, Frank, OF, 1928
Wilson, Jim, P, 1948
Wiltse, Hal, P, 1928
Winegarner, Ralph, P, 1949
Wingard, Ernie, P, 1924-27
Witte, Jerry, INF, 1946-47
Wood, Ken, OF, 1948-51
Wright, Clarence, P, 1903-4
Wright, Jim, P, 1927-28

Wright, Rasty, P, 1917-19, 1922-23
Wright, Tom, OF, 1952

Yeager, Joe, INF, 1907-8
Young, Bobby, INF, 1951-53
Young, Russ, C, 1931

Zachary, Tom, P, 1926-27
Zarilla, Al, OF, 1943-44, 1946-49, 1952
Zoldak, Sam, P, 1944-48

Baltimore Orioles 1954-82

Abrams, Cal, OF, 1954-55
Adair, Jerry, INF, 1958-66
Adams, Bobby, INF, 1956
Adamson, Mike, P, 1967-69
Alexander, Bob, P, 1955
Alexander, Doyle, P, 1972-76
Anderson, John, P, 1960
Anderson, Mike, OF, 1978
Aparicio, Luis, INF, 1963-67
Avila, Bobby, INF, 1959
Ayala, Benny, OF-DH, 1979-82

Bailor, Bob, INF-DH, 1975-76
Baker, Frank, INF, 1973-74
Bamberger, George, P, 1959
Barber, Steve, P, 1960-67
Barker, Ray, OF, 1960
Barnowski, Ed, P, 1965-66
Baylor, Don, OF-INF-DH, 1970-75
Beamon, Charlie, P, 1956-58
Beene, Fred, P, 1968-70
Belanger, Mark, INF, 1965-81
Berry, Connie, INF, 1954
Bertaina, Frank, P, 1964-67, 1969
Besana, Fred, P, 1956
Bickford, Vern, P, 1954
Birrer, Babe, P, 1956
Blair, Paul, OF, 1964-76
Blefary, Curt, OF-INF-C, 1965-68
Blyzka, Mike P, 1954
Boddicker, Mike, P, 1980-82
Bonner, Bob, INF, 1980-82
Boswell, Dave, P, 1971
Bowens, Sam, OF, 1963-67
Boyd, Bob, INF-OF, 1956-60
Brabender, Gene, P, 1966-68
Brandt, Jackie, OF, 1960-65
Breeding Marv, INF, 1960-62

Brideweser, Jim, INF, 1954-57
Briles, Nelson, P, 1977-78
Brown, Dick, C, 1963-65
Brown, Hal, P, 1955-62
Brown, Larry, INF, 1973
Brunet, George, P, 1963
Buford, Don, OF-INF, 1968-72
Bumbry, Al, OF-DH, 1972-82
Bunker, Wally, P, 1963-68
Burke, Leo, INF-OF, 1958-59
Burnside, Pete, P, 1963
Busby, Jim, OF, 1957-58, 1960-61
Buzhardt, John, P, 1967
Byrd, Harry, P, 1955

Cabell, Enos, INF-OF, 1972-74
Carrasquel, Chico, INF, 1959
Carreon, Camilo, C, 1966
Castleman, Foster, INF, 1958
Causey, Wayne, INF, 1955-57
Ceccarelli, Art, P, 1957
Chakales, Bob, P, 1954
Chevez, Tony, P, 1977
Chism, Tom, INF, 1979
Cimoli, Gino, OF, 1964
Coan, Gil, OF, 1954-55
Coggins, Rich, OF-DH, 1972-74
Coleman, Joe, P, 1954-55
Coleman, Rip, P, 1959-60
Consuegra, Sandy, P, 1956-57
Corey, Mark, OF, 1979-81
Courtney, Clint, C, 1954, 1960-61
Cox, Billy, INF, 1955
Criscione, Dave, C, 1977
Crowley, Terry, OF-INF-DH, 1969-73, 1976-82
Cuellar, Mike, P, 1969-76

Dagres, Angelo, OF, 1955

Dalrymple, Clay, C, 1969–71
Dauer, Rich, INF, 1976–82
DaVanon, Jerry, INF, 1971
Davis, Storm, P, 1982
Davis, Tommy, DH-OF-INF, 1972–75
DeCinces, Doug, INF, 1973–81
Delock, Ike, P, 1963
Dempsey, Rich, C, 1976–82
Diering, Chuck, OF, 1954–56
Dillman, Bill, P, 1967
Dimmel, Mike, OF, 1977–78
Dobson, Pat, P, 1971–72
Dorish, Harry, P, 1955–56
Drabowsky, Moe, P, 1966–68, 1970
Drago, Dick, P, 1977
Dropo, Walt, INF, 1959–61
Dukes, Tom, P, 1971
Duncan, Dave, C, 1975–76
Duren, Ryne, P, 1954
Durham, Joe, OF, 1954, 1957
Dwyer, Jim. DH-OF-INF, 1982
Dyck, Jim OF-INF, 1955–56

Epstein, Mike, INF, 1966–67
Essegian, Chuck, OF, 1961
Estrada, Chuck, P, 1960–64
Etchebarren, Andy, C, 1962, 1965–75
Evers, Hoot, OF, 1955–56

Farmer, Ed, P, 1977
Fernandez, Chico, INF, 1968
Ferrarese, Don, P, 1955–57
Finigan, Jim, INF, 1959
Fiore, Mike, INF-OF, 1968
Fisher, Eddie, P, 1966–67
Fisher, Jack, P, 1959–62
Fisher, Tom, P, 1967
Flanagan, Mike, P, 1975–82
Flinn, John, P, 1978–79, 82
Floyd, Bob, INF, 1968–70
Foiles, Hank, C, 1961
Ford, Dan, OF, 1982
Ford, Dave, P, 1978–81
Fornieles, Mike, P, 1956–57
Fox, Howie, P, 1954
Francona, Tito, OF-INF, 1956–57
Frazier, Joe, OF, 1956
Freed, Roger, INF-OF, 1970
Fridley, Jim, OF, 1954
Fuller, Jim, OF-INF-DH, 1973–74

Gaines, Joe, OF, 1963–64
Garcia, Kiko, INF, 1976–80
Garcia, Vinicio, INF, 1954
Gardner, Billy, INF, 1956–59
Garland, Wayne, P, 1973–76
Gastall, Tom, C, 1955–56

Gentile, Jim, INF, 1960–63
Gilliford, Paul, P, 1967
Ginsberg, Joe, C, 1956–60
Goodman, Billy, INF-OF, 1957
Graham, Dan, C, 1980–81
Gray, Ted, P, 1955
Green, Gene, OF, 1960
Green, Lenny, OF, 1957–59, 1964
Grich, Bobby, INF, 1970–76
Grimsley, Ross, P, 1974–77, 82
Gulliver, Glenn, IF, 1982

Haddix, Harvey, P, 1964–65
Hale, Bob, INF, 1955–59
Hall, Dick, P, 1961–66, 1969–71
Hamric, Bert, OF, 1958
Haney, Larry, C, 1966–68
Hansen, Ron, INF, 1958–62
Hardin, Jim, P, 1967–71
Harlow, Larry, OF, 1975, 1977–79
Harper, Tommy, DH-OF-INF, 1976
Harrison, Bob, P, 1955–56
Harrison, Roric, P, 1972
Harshman, Jack, P, 1958–59
Hartzell, Paul, P, 1980
Hatton, Grady, INF, 1956
Hazewood, Drungo, OF, 1980
Heard, Jehosie, P, 1954
Held, Mel, P, 1956
Held, Woodie, OF-INF, 1966–67
Hendricks, Elrod, C, 1968–76, 1978–79
Hernandez, Leo, PH, 1982
Herzog, Whitey, OF, 1961–62
Hoeft, Billy, P, 1959–62
Holdsworth, Fred, P, 1976–77
Holtzman, Ken, P, 1976
Hood, Don, P, 1973–74
Houtteman, Art, P, 1957
Howard, Bruce, P, 1968
Hunter, Billy, INF, 1954
Hutto, Jim, C, 1975
Hyde, Dick, P, 1961

Jackson, Grant, P, 1971–76
Jackson, Lou, OF, 1964
Jackson, Reggie, OF-DH, 1976
Jefferson, Jesse, P, 1973–75
Johnson, Bob, INF, 1963–67
Johnson, Connie, P, 1956–58
Johnson, Darrell, C, 1962
Johnson, Dave, INF, 1965–72
Johnson, David, P, 1974–75
Johnson, Don, P, 1955
Johnson, Ernie, P, 1959
Jones, Gordon, P, 1960–61
Jones, Sam, P, 1964

Kell, George, INF, 1956-57
Kellert, Frank, INF, 1954
Kelly, Pat, OF-DH, 1977-80
Kennedy, Bob, INF-OF, 1954-55
Kerrigan, Joe, P, 1978, 1980
Kirkland, Willie, OF, 1964
Klaus, Billy, INF, 1959-60
Knowles, Darold, P, 1965
Kokos, Dick, OF, 1954
Koslo, Dave, P, 1954
Krenchicki, Wayne, INF, 1979-81
Kretlow, Lou, P, 1954-55
Kryhoski, Dick, INF, 1954
Kuzava, Bob, P, 1954-55

Landrith, Hobie, C, 1962-63
Larsen, Don, P, 1954, 1965
Lau, Charlie, C, 1961-67
Lehew, Jim, P, 1961-62
Lehman, Ken, P, 1957-58
Lenhardt, Don, OF, 1954
Leonhard, Dave, P, 1967-72
Leppert, Don, INF, 1955
Littlefield, Dick, P, 1954
Locke, Charlie, P, 1955
Lockman, Whitey, INF-OF, 1959
Loes, Billy, P, 1956-59
Lopat, Eddie, P, 1955
Lopez, Carlos, OF, 1978
Lopez, Marcelino, P, 1967, 1969-70
Lowenstein, John, OH-DH-INF,
    1979-82
Luebber, Steve, P, 1981
Luebke, Dick, P, 1962

Mabe, Bobbie, P, 1960
Maddox, Elliott, OF-INF, 1977
Majeski, Hank, INF, 1955
Marquis, Roger, OF, 1955
Marsh, Freddie, INF, 1955-56
Marshall, Jim, INF-OF, 1958
Martin, Morrie, P, 1956
Martinez, Dennis, P, 1976-82
Martinez, Tippy, P, 1976-82
Matchick, Tom, INF, 1972
Maxwell, Charlie, OF, 1955
May, Dave, OF, 1967-70
May, Lee, INF-DH, 1975-80
May, Rudy, P, 1976-77
McCormick, Mike, P, 1963-64
McDonald, Jim, P, 1955
McGregor, Scott, P, 1976-82
McGuire, Mickey, INF, 1962, 1967

McNally, Dave, P, 1962-74
Mele, Sam, OF, 1954
Miksis, Eddie, OF, 1957-58
Miller, Bill, P, 1955
Miller, Dyar, P, 1975-77
Miller, John, P, 1962-63, 1965-67
Miller, Randy, P, 1977
Miller, Stu, P, 1963-67
Miranda, Willie, INF, 1955-59
Mitchell, Paul, P, 1975
Moeller, Ron, P, 1956, 1958
Molinaro, Bob, OF, 1979
Moore, Ray, P, 1955-57
Mora, Andres, OF-DH-INF, 1976-78
Morales, Jose, DH-INF, 1982
Morris, John, P, 1968
Moss, Les, C, 1954-55
Motton, Curt, OF-DH, 1967-71, 1973-74
Murray, Eddie, INF-DH, 1977-82
Murray, Ray, C, 1954
Muser, Tony, INF-OF-DH, 1975-77

Narum, Buster, P, 1963
Nelson, Bob, OF, 1955-57
Nelson, Roger, P, 1968
Nicholson, Dave, OF, 1960, 1962
Nieman, Bob, OF, 1956-59
Nolan, Joe, C, 1982
Nordbrook, Tim, INF, 1974-76
Northrup, Jim, OF-DH, 1974-75

Oates, Johnny, C, 1970-72
O'Dell, Billy, P, 1954, 1956-59
O'Donoghue, John, P, 1968
Oertel, Chuck, OF, 1958
Oliver, Bob, INF-DH, 1974
Orsino, John, C, 1963-65

Pagan, Dave, P, 1976
Palica, Erv, P, 1955-56
Palmer, Jim, P, 1965-67, 1969-82
Papa, John, P, 1961-62
Pappas, Milt, P, 1957-65
Parrott, Mike, P, 1977
Patton, Tom, C, 1957
Pearson, Albie, OF, 1959-60
Pena, Orlando, P, 1971, 1973
Peterson, Buddy, INF, 1957
Philley, Dave, OF-INF, 1955-56, 1960-61
Phoebus, Tom, P, 1966-70
Pilarcik, Al, OF, 1957-60
Pillette, Duane, P, 1954-55
Piniella, Lou, OF, 1964

Pope, Dave, OF, 1955-56
Portocarrero, Arnold, P, 1958-60
Powell, Boog, INF-OF-DH, 1961-74
Powers, John, OF, 1960
Powis, Carl, OF, 1957
Pyburn, Jim, OF-INF-C, 1955-57

Quirk, Art, P, 1962

Rayford, Floyd, INF-DH, 1980, 82
Reinbach, Mike, OF-DH, 1974
Rettenmund, Merv, OF, 1968-73
Reynolds, Bob, P, 1972-75
Rice, Del, C, 1960
Richert, Pete, P, 1967-71
Rineer, Jeff, P, 1979
Ripken, Cal, INF, 1981-2
Roberts, Robin, P, 1962-65
Robinson, Brooks, INF, 1955-77
Robinson, Earl, OF, 1961-62, 1964
Robinson, Eddie, INF, 1957
Robinson, Frank, OF-INF, 1966-71
Robles, Sergio, C, 1972-73
Roenicke, Gary, OF-DH, 1978-82
Rogovin, Saul, P, 1955
Rowe, Ken, P, 1964-65
Royster, Willie, C, 1981
Roznovsky, Vic, C, 1966-67
Rudolph, Ken, C, 1977

Sakata, Lenn, INF, 1980-82
Salmon, Chico, INF-OF, 1969-72
Saverine, Bob, OF-INF, 1959, 1962-64
Schallock, Art, P, 1955
Schmitz, Johnny, P, 1956
Schneider, Jeff, P, 1981
Scott, Mickey, P, 1972-73
Segrist, Kal, INF, 1955
Severinsen, Al, P, 1969
Shelby, John, OF, 1981-82
Shetrone, Barry, OF, 1959-60, 1962
Shopay, Tom, OF-DH-C, 1971-72, 1975-77
Short, Billy, P, 1962, 1966
Siebern, Norm, INF, 1964-65
Singleton, Ken, OF-DH, 1972-82
Skaggs, Dave, C, 1977-80
Sleater, Lou, P, 1958
Smith, Al, OF, 1963
Smith, Billy, INF, 1977-79
Smith, Hal, C, 1955-56
Smith, Nate, C, 1962

Snyder, Russ, OF, 1961-67
Stanhouse, Don, P, 1978-79, 82
Starrette, Herm, P, 1963-65
Stephens, Gene, OF, 1960-61
Stephens, Vern, INF, 1954-55
Stephenson, Earl, P, 1977-78
Stewart, Sammy, P, 1978-82
Stillman, Royle, INF-OF-DH, 1975-76
Stock, Wes, P, 1959-64
Stoddard, Tim, P, 1978-82
Stone, Dean, P, 1963
Stone, Steve, P, 1979-81
Stuart, Marlin, P, 1954
Sundin, Gordon, P, 1956

Tasby, Willie, OF, 1958-60
Taylor, Joe, OF, 1958-59
Temple, John, INF, 1962
Thomas, Valmy, C, 1960
Thomson, Bobby, OF, 1960
Throneberry, Marv, OF-INF, 1961-62
Torrez, Mike, P, 1975
Triandos, Gus, C-INF, 1955-62
Trout, Dizzy, P, 1957
Turley, Bob, P, 1954

Valentine, Fred, OF, 1959, 1963, 1968
Vineyard, Dave, P, 1964
Virgil, Ozzie, PH, 1962

Waitkus, Eddie, INF, 1954-55
Walker, Jerry, P, 1957-60
Ward, Pete, OF, 1962
Warwick, Carl, OF, 1965
Watt, Eddie, P, 1966-73
Welchel, Don, P, 1982
Werley, George, P, 1956
Wertz, Vic, OF, 1954
Westlake, Wally, OF, 1955
Wight, Bill, P, 1955-57
Wilhelm, Hoyt, P, 1958-62
Williams, Dallas, OF, 1981
Williams, Dick, OF-INF, 1956-58, 1961-62
Williams, Earl, C-INF-DH, 1973-75
Wilson, Jim, P, 1955-56
Woodling, Gene, OF, 1955, 1958-60

Young, Bobby, INF, 1954-55
Young, Mike, OF, 1982

Zupo, Frank, C, 1957-58, 1961
Zuverink, George, P, 1955-59

THE FRANCHISE YEAR-BY-YEAR

Year	Position	W–L	Pct.	Games Behind	Manager
1901	Eighth	48–89	.350	35½	Hugh Duffy
1902	Second	78–58	.574	5	Jimmy McAleer
1903	Sixth	65–74	.468	26½	Jimmy McAleer
1904	Sixth	65–87	.428	29	Jimmy McAleer
1905	Eighth	54–99	.353	40½	Jimmy McAleer
1906	Fifth	76–73	.510	16	Jimmy McAleer
1907	Sixth	69–83	.454	24	Jimmy McAleer
1908	Fourth	83–69	.546	6½	Jimmy McAleer
1909	Seventh	61–89	.407	36	Jimmy McAleer
1910	Eighth	47–107	.305	57	Jack O'Connor
1911	Eighth	45–107	.296	56½	Bobby Wallace
1912	Seventh	53–101	.344	53	Bobby Wallace (12–27) George Stovall (41–74)
1913	Eighth	57–96	.373	39	George Stovall (50–84) Jimmy Austin (2–6) Branch Rickey (5–6)
1914	Fifth	71–82	.464	28½	Branch Rickey
1915	Sixth	63–91	.409	39½	Branch Rickey
1916	Fifth	79–75	.513	12	Fielder Jones
1917	Seventh	57–97	.370	43	Fielder Jones
1918	Fifth	58–64	.475	15	Fielder Jones (23–24) Jimmy Austin (6–8) Jimmy Burke (29–32)
1919	Fifth (tie)	67–72	.482	20½	Jimmy Burke
1920	Fourth	76–77	.497	21½	Jimmy Burke
1921	Third	81–73	.526	17½	Lee Fohl
1922	Second	93–61	.604	1	Lee Fohl
1923	Fifth	74–78	.487	24	Lee Fohl (51–49) Jimmy Austin (23–29)
1924	Fourth	74–78	.487	17	George Sisler
1925	Third	82–71	.536	15	George Sisler
1926	Seventh	62–92	.403	29	George Sisler
1927	Seventh	59–94	.386	50½	Dan Howley
1928	Third	82–72	.532	19	Dan Howley
1929	Fourth	79–73	.520	26	Dan Howley
1930	Sixth	64–90	.416	38	Bill Killefer
1931	Fifth	63–91	.409	45	Bill Killefer
1932	Sixth	63–91	.409	44	Bill Killefer
1933	Eighth	55–96	.364	43½	Bill Killefer (34–59) Allen Sothoron (1–3) Rogers Hornsby (20–39)
1934	Sixth	67–85	.441	33	Rogers Hornsby
1935	Seventh	65–87	.428	28½	Rogers Hornsby
1936	Seventh	57–95	.375	44½	Rogers Hornsby
1937	Eighth	46–108	.299	56	Rogers Hornsby (25–50) Jim Bottomley (21–58)
1938	Seventh	55–97	.362	44	Gabby Street
1939	Eighth	43–111	.279	64½	Fred Haney
1940	Sixth	67–87	.435	23	Fred Haney
1941	Sixth (tie)	70–84	.455	31	Fred Haney (15–29) Luke Sewell (55–55)

1942	Third	82–69	.543	19½	Luke Sewell
1943	Sixth	72–80	.474	25	Luke Sewell
1944	First	89–65	.578	—	Luke Sewell
1945	Third	81–70	.536	6	Luke Sewell
1946	Seventh	66–88	.429	38	Luke Sewell (53–71)
					Zack Taylor (13–17)
1947	Eighth	59–95	.383	38	Muddy Ruel
1948	Sixth	59–94	.386	37	Zack Taylor
1949	Seventh	53–101	.344	44	Zack Taylor
1950	Seventh	58–96	.377	40	Zack Taylor
1951	Eighth	52–102	.338	46	Zack Taylor
1952	Seventh	64–90	.416	31	Rogers Hornsby (22–28)
					Marty Marion (42–62)
1953	Eighth	54–100	.351	46½	Marty Marion
1954*	Seventh	54–100	.351	57	Jimmy Dykes
1955	Seventh	57–97	.370	39	Paul Richards
1956	Sixth	69–85	.448	28	Paul Richards
1957	Fifth	76–76	.500	21	Paul Richards
1958	Sixth	74–79	.484	17½	Paul Richards
1959	Sixth	74–80	.481	20	Paul Richards
1960	Second	89–65	.578	8	Paul Richards
1961	Third	95–67	.586	14	Paul Richards (84–47)
					Luman Harris (11–20)
1962	Seventh (tie)	77–85	.475	19	Billy Hitchcock
1963	Fourth	86–76	.531	18½	Billy Hitchcock
1964	Third	97–65	.599	2	Hank Bauer
1965	Third	94–68	.580	8	Hank Bauer
1966	First	97–63	.606	—	Hank Bauer
1967	Sixth (tie)	76–85	.472	15½	Hank Bauer
1968	Second	91–71	.562	12	Hank Bauer (43–37)
					Earl Weaver (48–34)
1969	First	109–53	.673	—	Earl Weaver
1970	First	108–54	.567	—	Earl Weaver
1971	First	101–57	.639	—	Earl Weaver
1972	Third	80–74	.519	5	Earl Weaver
1973	First	97–65	.599	—	Earl Weaver
1974	First	91–71	.562	—	Earl Weaver
1975	Second	90–69	.566	4½	Earl Weaver
1976	Second	88–74	.543	10½	Earl Weaver
1977	Second (tie)	97–64	.602	2½	Earl Weaver
1978	Fourth	90–71	.559	8½	Earl Weaver
1979	First	102–57	.642	—	Earl Weaver
1980	Second	100–62	.617	3	Earl Weaver
1981**	Second	59–46	.562	1	Earl Weaver
1982	Second	94–96	.580	1	Earl Weaver

* First season in Baltimore.
** Combined figures for the first and second halves of season.

MANAGERS AND THEIR RECORDS

Manager	Years	Wins	Losses	Percentage
Hugh Duffy	1901	48	89	.350
Jimmy McAleer	1902–9	551	622	.470
Jack O'Connor	1910	47	107	.305
Bobby Wallace	1911–12	57	134	.298
George Stovall	1912–13	91	158	.365
Jimmy Austin	1913, 1918, 1923	31	43	.419
Branch Rickey	1913–15	139	179	.437
Fielder Jones	1916–18	159	198	.445
Jimmy Burke	1918–20	172	181	.487
Lee Fohl	1921–23	225	183	.551
George Sisler	1924–26	218	241	.475
Dan Howley	1927–29	220	239	.475
Bill Killefer	1930–33	224	331	.404
Allen Sothoron	1933	1	3	.250
Rogers Hornsby	1933–37, 1952	256	384	.400
Jim Bottomley	1937	21	58	.266
Gabby Street	1938	55	97	.362
Fred Haney	1939–41	125	227	.355
Luke Sewell	1941–46	432	410	.513
Zack Taylor	1946, 1948–51	235	410	.364
Muddy Ruel	1947	59	95	.383
Marty Marion	1952–53	96	162	.372
Jimmy Dykes	1954	54	100	.351
Paul Richards	1955–61	523	529	.497
Luman Harris	1961	11	20	.355
Billy Hitchcock	1962–63	163	161	.503
Hank Bauer	1964–68	407	318	.561
Earl Weaver	1968–82	1354	919	.596

1954 BALTIMORE ORIOLES

Front row: unidentified, Diering, Mele, Murray, Courtney, Hunter, Moss, Stephens, *batboy.*
Middle row: trainer, Kennedy, Abrams, *unidentified*, Oliver *(coach)*, Brecheen *(coach)*, Dykes *(manager)*, Skaff *(coach)*, Pillette, Chakales, Coan.
Back row: Coleman, Turley, Kryhoski, Kretlow, Fox, Larsen, Fridley, Blyzka, Stuart, *unidentified*, Young, O'Dell.

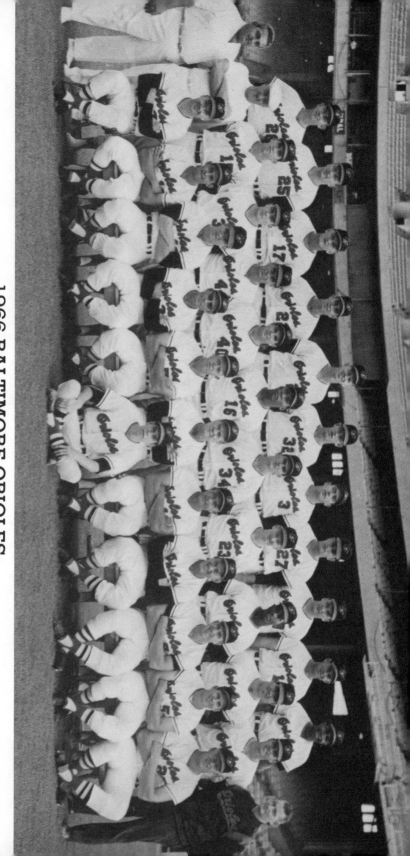

1966 BALTIMORE ORIOLES

Front row: S. Miller, Aparicio, McNally, Brecheen (*coach*), Hunter (*coach*), Bauer (*manager*), Woodling (*coach*), Lollar (*coach*), Snyder, B. Robinson, Powell.

Middle row: Salvon (*trainer*), Weidner (*trainer*), D. Johnson, Watt, Lau, Bertaina, Bowens, Haney, Roznovsky, Blair, Etchebarren, B. Johnson, Reid (*equipment mgr.*)

Back row: Fisher, Drabowsky, J. Miller, Palmer, Hall, Brabender, Blefary, Bunker, Barber, Held, F. Robinson.

Batboy: Sherr.

1969 BALTIMORE ORIOLES

Front row: Watt, Lau *(coach)*, Staller *(coach)*, Hunter *(coach)*, Weaver *(manager)*, Bamberger *(coach)*, Phoebus, Hardin, Salmon.
Middle row: Reid *(equipment mgr.)*, Buford, Palmer, Johnson, McNally, Hendricks, Belanger, Cuellar, Rettenmund, May, Dalrymple, Salvon *(trainer)*.
Back row: Powell, Lopez, Hall, B. Robinson, Etchebarren, F. Robinson, Floyd, Richert, Motton, Blair. *Batboy:* Mazzone.

1970 BALTIMORE ORIOLES

Front row: Phoebus, Buford, Frey (*coach*), Hunter (*coach*), Weaver (*manager*), Bamberger (*coach*), Staller (*coach*), McNally, Salmon. *Middle row:* Reid (*equipment mgr.*), Etchebarren, Powell, Richert, Belanger, Leonhard, B. Robinson, Hendricks, Rettenmund, Johnson, Watt, Salvon (*trainer*). *Back row:* Lopez, Palmer, Drabowsky, F. Robinson, Cuellar, Hall, Grich, Motton, Crowley, Blair. *Batboy:* Mazzone.

1971 BALTIMORE ORIOLES

Front row: Shopay, Buford, Frey *(coach)*, Hunter *(coach)*, Weaver *(manager)*, Bamberger *(coach)*, Staller *(coach)*, Salmon, Rettenmund.
Middle row: Reid *(equipment mgr.)*, Dukes, Davanon, Belanger, Etchebarren, Motton, Cuellar, B. Robinson, Hendricks, Powell, Watt, Salvon *(trainer)*.
Back row: Jackson, McNally, Richert, Dobson, Palmer, Hall, F. Robinson, Hardin, Johnson, Dalrymple, Blair. *Batboy:* Mazzone.

1973 BALTIMORE ORIOLES

Front row: Davis, Rettenmund, B. Robinson, Frey *(coach)*, Hunter *(coach)*, Weaver *(manager)*, Staller *(coach)*, Bamberger *(coach)*, Brown, Watt, Cashen *(batboy)*.

Middle row: Bumbry, Palmer, Crowley, Belanger, Grich, Pena, Alexander, Powell, Baker, Hendricks, Salvon *(trainer)*.

Back row: Cuellar, Williams, Reynolds, Etchebarren, Coggins, Scott, Baylor, Jackson, McNally, Blair, Reid *(equipment mgr.)*.

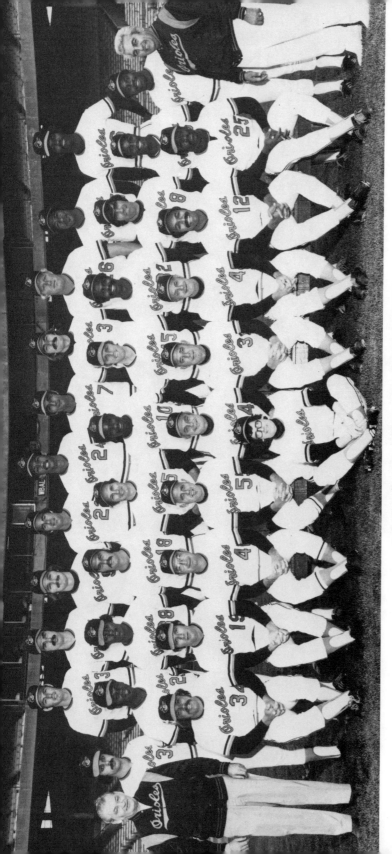

1974 BALTIMORE ORIOLES

Front row: Reynolds, McNally, Frey *(coach)*, Hunter *(coach)*, Weaver *(manager)*, Bamberger *(coach)*, Staller *(coach)*, Davis, Baylor.
Middle row: Reid *(equipment mgr.)*, Grimsley, Jackson, Jefferson, Fuller, Robinson, Hendricks, Baker, Williams, Etchebarren, Coggins, Bumbry, Salvon *(trainer)*.
Back row: Alexander, Hood, Reinbach, Palmer, Cabell, Belanger, Grich, Powell, Cuellar. Blair.
Batboy: Cashen.

1979 BALTIMORE ORIOLES

Front row: Tyler (equipment mgr.), Kelly, Singleton, Hendricks (player-coach), Frey (coach), Weaver (manager), Miller (coach), Ripken (coach), Robinson (coach), Bumbry, Salvon (trainer).
Middle row: Stoddard, Lowenstein, Belanger, Stewart, Ayala, T. Martinez, Murray, Skaggs, Flanagan, Roenicke, Palmer, Stanhouse.
Back row: McGregor, Smith, Garcia, Crowley, Dempsey, May, Dauer, De Cinces, D. Martinez, Stone. *Batboy:* Cashen.

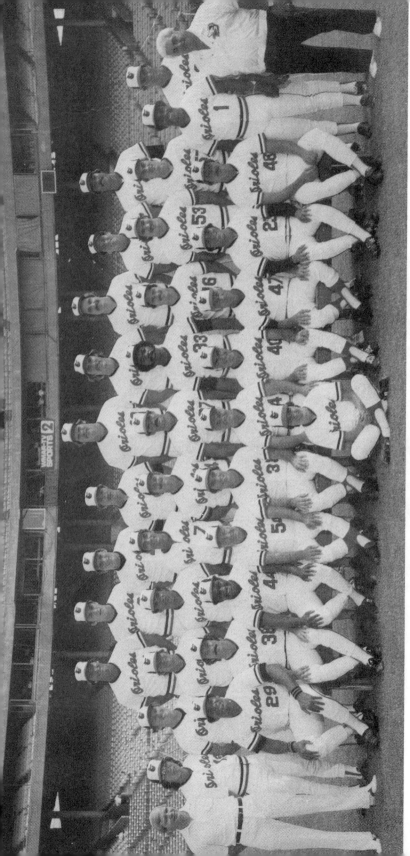

1981 BALTIMORE ORIOLES

Front row: Singleton, Lowenstein, Hendricks *(coach),* Rowe *(coach),* Miller *(coach),* Weaver *(manager),* Williams *(coach),* Ripken *(coach),* T. Martinez, Flanagan.
Middle row: Tyler *(equipment mgr.),* Sakata, Crowley, Dwyer, Morales, Belanger, Dempsey, Ayala, Murray, McGregor, Stewart, Schneider, Bumbry, Palmer, Salvon *(trainer).*
Back row: DeCinces, Ripken, Graham, Dauer, Stoddard, Roenicke, Ford, Stone, D. Martinez.
Batboy: Deaton.

Gorgeous George Sisler, the greatest Brown and first baseman of all time. A .340 lifetime hitter, this southpaw was originally signed out of college as a pitcher. He was a slick fielder and leading base stealer.

By the time he came to the Browns as a playing manager, Rogers Hornsby had seen his best days. His time in St. Louis in the Thirties and once more in the Fifties was marked by fiery confrontations with owners and players alike.

His one year in baseball during wartime caused a sensation across the league. He was one-armed Pete Gray, an outfielder who inspired Browns fans with his courage and determination. In his only year with the team in 1945, Gray hit .218.

Judged by many to be the greatest pitcher of all time, Satchel Paige fought the color line most of his career, breaking into the big leagues only at the age of 41. He proved to be an ace reliever for the Browns in his three seasons with the club and was named to the American League All-Star team twice.

Oriole Fan Favorites

Center fielder Paul Blair was the premier fielder of his time and a dependable clutch hitter.

First baseman Bob Boyd was the first black star for Baltimore, hitting over .300 in four different seasons.

Second baseman Jerry Adair gave Oriole fans solid fielding during the early Sixties.

One of the game's original flakes, center fielder Jackie Brandt played with a nonchalance that drove manager Paul Richards up a wall.

Catcher Gus Triandos was named to the Orioles Hall of Fame in 1981, in recognition of the fact that he was the team's first bonafide star and long-ball threat. He was a fan favorite from 1955 to 1962.

Birds of a Feather

Milt Pappas won 110 games for the Orioles before going to Cincinnati in 1965.

Hall-of-Famer Robin Roberts enjoyed three good seasons in Baltimore at the tail end of his career.

Tom Phoebus was a local boy who made good, hurling a no-hitter in 1968 against the Red Sox.

Bonus baby Steve Barber paid off handsomely, winning 95 games for the Birds in seven and a half seasons.

Hank Bauer will hold a special place in Orioles fans' hearts as the first manager to lead the team to a pennant and a World's Championship. His 1966 club won 97 games and swept the Dodgers in the Series in four straight games.

Keys to a Pennant

Left fielder Russ Snyder hit .306 during the 1966 pennant chase.

Right fielder Frank Robinson won the Triple Crown in 1966, leading the O's to the World's Championship.

Little Looie Aparicio held the infield together with his slick glove at shortstop.

Third sacker Brooks Robinson drove in 100 runs for Hank Bauer's pennant-bound Birds.

Barons of the Bird Bullpen

Grant Jackson provided crucial southpaw relief during the early to mid-Seventies.

Stu Miller's 88 career saves lead the Orioles. His 71 appearances in 1963 set a new record at the time.

Dick Hall notched 51 saves during two stints with the Orioles in the early and late Sixties.

For eight seasons, righthander Eddie Watt was a mainstay in the Birds' bullpen.

Dave McNally ranks as the greatest southpaw in Oriole history, notching 181 wins and 33 shutouts with the Birds. His best seasons coincided with the team's pennant drives of 1969-70-71.

(right) John Wesley Powell, better known as Boog, played a key role as a power-hitting outfielder and first baseman in the Oriole winning teams of 1966, 1969, 1970, 1971, 1973 and 1974. In all, he slugged 303 home runs as the all-time Oriole home run leader.

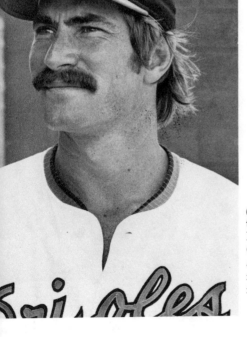

(left) Oriole fans in the early Seventies thrilled to the slick fielding and clutch hitting of second baseman Bobby Grich. He since has gone on via free agency to the Angels, where he remains the premier second baseman in the American League.

Stars of the Seventies

Lee May provided power as first baseman and designated hitter for the Birds, driving in many clutch runs.

Southpaw Mike Cuellar from Cuba won 24 games in 1970 and 20 the following year as a mainstay in the pitching rotation.

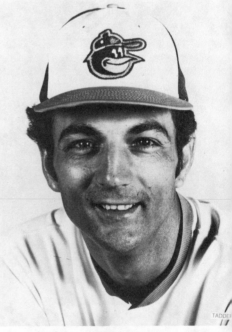

Doug DeCinces admirably followed in Brooks Robinson's footsteps at third base, with great fielding and clutch hitting in the '79 pennant drive.

Mark Belanger rewrote the record book as one of the slickest fielding shortstops in baseball history. He won eight Gold Gloves for the Birds.

A filled stadium on a sunny afternoon in Baltimore is the goal of the Orioles' front office. Until something is decided about a new stadium, Memorial Stadium will remain the home of Oriole fans.

(left) New owner Edward Bennett Williams has pledged to keep the team competitive during the Eighties.

(right) General manager Hank Peters is responsible for the day-to-day operation of the team and all trades.

The Resident Genius

With 1,354 career wins as a manager, Earl Weaver ranks 17th on the all-time list. He ranks as the dean of current managers, having bossed the Birds since 1968. During his tenure, which he claims will end after the '82 season, Weaver had led the team to six division titles and one world's championship.

Pitching coach Ray Miller

Third-base coach Cal Ripken Sr.

The Oriole Braintrust

Batting coach Ralph Rowe

First-base coach Jimmy Williams

Hard-hitting first baseman Eddie Murray is destined to be one of the game's great stars. He led the league in home runs in 1981 during the strike-shortened season and appears to be just approaching his potential as a hitter.

Shortstop Lenn Sakata

Second baseman Rich Dauer

First baseman Eddie Murray

Third baseman Cal Ripken Jr.

The Oriole Infield

Right fielder Ken Singleton has been consistently one of the finest players in the game since his acquisition from Montreal in 1974. This switch-hitter is a solid .300 hitter and a team leader well respected throughout the league.

Al Bumbry

Gary Roenicke

John Lowenstein

Ken Singleton

Manning the O's Outfield

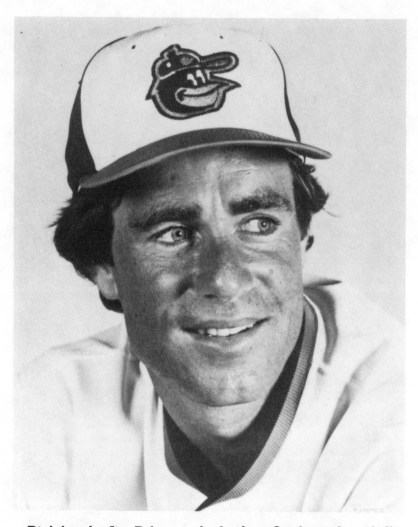

Righthander Jim Palmer is the leading Oriole pitcher of all time, with 263 wins, 3,853 innings pitched, 211 complete games, and 53 shutouts going into the 1983 season. A certain Hall-of-Famer, Palmer has an outside shot at 300 career wins if he stays healthy.

Steve Stone

Scott McGregor

Bird Starting Pitchers

Dennis Martinez

Mike Flanagan

Sammy Stewart

The Bird Bullpen

Tim Stoddard

Tippy Martinez

Dave Ford

Terry Crowley

Jose Morales

Benny Ayala

Jim Dwyer

The Valuable Bird Bench

Current
Oriole
Fan
Favorites

The Bird!

Ellie Hendricks
Bullpen coach

Dan Graham
Catcher

Rick Dempsey
Catcher

TADDER

Frank Robinson (shown here as a coach in 1979) today manages the San Francisco Giants. Many fans are wondering if Frank ultimately will return to Baltimore as Earl Weaver's replacement.

TADDER

Brooks Robinson can look forward to a certain Hall of Fame induction in 1983 after a 23-season career that saw him rewrite the record books for third baseman. Brooks remains active as an Oriole broadcaster.

THE BALLPARKS

Sportsman's Park

Organized baseball enjoys a rich history in St. Louis—and much of it is linked to the Grand Avenue Grounds, which later evolved into Sportsman's Park.

The Browns made Sportsman's Park their home for their entire stay in St. Louis. But the site had been used much earlier by St. Louis teams in the old National Association and American Association. When Ralph T. Orthwein obtained the Milwaukee Brewers and brought them to St. Louis for the 1902 season, he moved the team into Sportsman's Park.

Several years later, a new owner named Robert Hedges decided to erect a permanent double-deck stand from first to third with pavilions adjacent to the grandstand and bleachers in the outfield. The project included the use of concrete and steel in the main stand. The new stands were opened on April 14, 1909, and were only the second of their kind in the majors. The expanded facility had a capacity of 18,500.

The next expansion came under a new owner, Phil Ball, in 1926 when the double-deck grandstand was extended into the left and right field corners and a roof was put on the right-field pavilion. This $500,000 project nearly doubled the capacity of Sportsman's Park, to 30,000.

During the years that the Browns enjoyed less than sterling attendance, the facility kept its owners afloat by serving as the home for another tenant, the National League Cardinals. So it was that the 1944 World Series between the Browns and Redbirds became known as the "Trolley Series," since all the games were played at Sportsman's Park.

When the Browns were sold in 1953 to Baltimore, the park already had been sold to Cardinal owner Gussie Busch as part of Bill Veeck's last-ditch effort to keep the team in St. Louis by raising sorely needed cash.

The park then became Busch Stadium and remained in active use until 1966, when the new Busch Memorial Stadium opened.

Memorial Stadium

In 1949, a new 30,000-seat Memorial Stadium opened in Baltimore to house the International League Orioles and football. When the purchase of the Browns was announced on October 29, 1953, work began to virtually reconstruct the park, expanding the capacity by more than 50 percent with a second deck.

A crowd of 46,354 showed up for the Orioles' debut on April 15, 1954, and the park has been humming ever since. The park was the first in the big leagues with an open-air upper deck. Memorial Stadium remains pretty much the same way it was when it opened in 1954, with the exception of some new box seats and the elimination of the center field hedge.

The field's configurations are only 309 feet down the right and left field lines, while the power alleys in left and right center break sharply open to 385 feet. Dead center field stands 410 feet from home plate.

Since Edward Bennett Williams acquired the club in 1979, there has been considerable discussion about construction of a new facility either downtown near the Harborplace development or out on one of the freeways between Washington and Baltimore. Until firm plans are agreed to, however, the fans will continue to enjoy the open-air, relaxed atmosphere of the old ballyard called Memorial Stadium.

ATTENDANCE

Brown Attendance

1902 — 272,283	1928 — 339,497
1903 — 380,405	1929 — 280,697
1904 — 318,108	1930 — 152,088
1905 — 339,112	1931 — 179,126
1906 — 389,157	1932 — 112,558
1907 — 419,025	1933 — 88,113
1908 — 618,947	1934 — 115,305
1909 — 366,274	1935 — 80,922
1910 — 249,889	1936 — 93,267
1911 — 207,984	1937 — 123,121
1912 — 214,070	1938 — 130,417
1913 — 250,330	1939 — 109,159
1914 — 244,714	1940 — 239,591
1915 — 150,358	1941 — 176,240
1916 — 335,740	1942 — 255,617
1917 — 210,486	1943 — 214,392
1918 — 122,076	1944 — 508,644
1919 — 349,350	1945 — 482,986
1920 — 419,311	1946 — 526,435
1921 — 355,978	1947 — 320,474
1922 — 712,918	1948 — 335,564
1923 — 430,296	1949 — 270,936
1924 — 533,349	1950 — 247,131
1925 — 462,898	1951 — 293,790
1926 — 283,986	1952 — 518,796
1927 — 247,879	1953 — 297,238

Oriole Attendance

1954 — 1,060,910	1968 — 868,709
1955 — 852,039	1969 — 1,062,094
1956 — 901,201	1970 — 1,057,069
1957 — 1,029,581	1971 — 1,023,037
1958 — 829,991	1972 — 899,950
1959 — 891,926	1973 — 960,303
1960 — 1,187,849	1974 — 962,572
1961 — 951,089	1975 — 1,002,157
1962 — 790,254	1976 — 1,058,609
1963 — 774,343	1977 — 1,195,769
1964 — 1,116,215	1978 — 1,051,724
1965 — 781,649	1979 — 1,681,009
1966 — 1,203,366	1980 — 1,797,438
1967 — 860,390	1981 — 1,024,153

Brown Attendance Records

Highest Season — 1922, 712,918
Lowest Season — 1935, 80,922
Largest Crowd, World Series Game — 36,568, vs. St. Louis, October 8, 1944
Largest Crowd, Day Game — 34,625 vs. New York, October 1, 1944
Largest Crowd, Doubleheader — 31,932 vs. New York, June 17, 1928

Largest Crowd, Night Game — 22,847 vs. Cleveland, May 24, 1940
Largest Crowd, Opening Day — 19,561 vs. Detroit, April 18, 1923

Oriole Attendance Records

Highest Season — 1980, 1,797,438
Lowest Season — 1963, 781,649
Largest Crowd, World Series Game — 54,458 vs. Los Angeles, October 9, 1966
Largest Crowd, Day Game — 51,798 vs. Boston, September 18, 1977
Largest Crowd, Night Game — 51,649 vs. New York, August 16, 1980
Largest Crowd, Day Doubleheader — 46,796 vs. New York, May 16, 1954
Largest Crowd, Night Doubleheader — 45,814 vs. Detroit, June 23, 1979
Largest Crowd, Opening Day — 50,244 vs. Kansas City, April 15, 1980
Smallest Crowd — 655 vs. Chicago, August 17, 1972

BROWNS WHO SERVED IN WORLD WAR II

Pitchers	Full Seasons Missed
Pete Appleton	1943-44
Frank Biscan	1943-44-45
Denny Galehouse	1945
Hooks Iott	1943-44-45
Al Milnar	1944-45
Maury Newlin	1942-43-44-45
Fred Sanford	1944-45
Steve Sundra	1945

Catchers	
Hank Helf	1944-45
Tom Turner	1945

Infielders	
George Archie	1942-43-44-45
Johnny Berardino	1943-44-45
Johnny Lucadello	1942-43-44-45
Hank Schmulbach	1944-45-46
Chuck Stevens	1943-44-45

Outfielders	
Joe Grace	1942-43-44-45
Walt Judnich	1943-44-45
Glenn McQuillen	1943-44-45
Al Zarilla	1945

1953 BROWNS/1954 ORIOLES

A total of 17 members of the final 1953 Browns' team opened the season in 1954 with the fledgling Baltimore Orioles. In addition, two team outfielders, J. W. Porter and Frank Saucier, were in military service but credited against both teams' rosters. Neither ever played for the Orioles.

The 17 original Browns/Orioles were:

Catchers — Clint Courtney, Les Moss
First Base — Dick Kryhoski, Frank Kellert
Second Base — Bobby Young

Third Base — Vern Stephens
Shortstop — Billy Hunter
Outfielders — Dick Kokos, Don Lenhardt, Vic Wertz
Pitchers — Mike Blyzka, Lou Kretlow, Don Larsen, Dick Littlefield,
 Duane Pillette, Marlin Stuart, Bob Turley
The Browns' farm system also produced a number of players who made the Orioles in subsequent years. These big leaguers included: pitchers Ryne Duren, Bob Harrison, and Mel Held; first baseman Bob Hale; outfielders Joe Durham, Tito Francona, and Lenny Green.

ORIOLE MAJOR LEAGUE DRAFT SELECTIONS

1953 — Chuck Diering, OF ($15,000)
 Vinicio Garcia, INF ($7,500)
1955 — Bob Boyd, 1B ($10,000)
1956 — Tommy Patton, C ($10,000)
1957 — Bert Hamric, OF ($15,000)
1960 — Hank Foiles, C ($25,000)
 Dave Massarelli, C ($12,000)
1961 — Billy Short, P ($25,000)
 Ozzie Virgil, C ($25,000)
 Steve Cosgrove, P ($12,000)
1962 — Dave May, OF ($12,000)
 Paul Blair, OF ($12,000)
 Roger Sorenson, OF ($8,000)
1963 — Lou Jackson, OF ($25,000)
 Mike Fiore, 1B ($8,000)

Jim Jankow, P ($8,000)
Bill McMahon, P ($8,000)
1964 — Byron Randolph, P ($8,000)
 Ted Miller, P ($8,000)
 John Jeter, OF ($8,000)
1965 — Moe Drabowsky, P ($25,000)
 Gene Brabender, P ($25,000)
1966 — Owen John, C ($25,000)
1967 — Elrod Hendricks, C ($25,000)
1968 — Larry Miller, P ($25,000)
1969 — Tom Shopay, OF ($25,000)
1972 — Mike Johnson, P ($25,000)
1976 — Mike Dimmel, OF ($25,000)
1977 — Andy Replogle, P ($25,000)

ORIOLE EXPANSION DRAFT LOSSES

December 1960

Los Angeles Angels — Pitchers Dean Chance and Ron Moeller and infielder Don Ross, each for $75,000. Outfielder Albie Pearson selected from Rochester roster for $25,000.
Washington Senators — Catcher Gene Green, infielder Billy Klaus, and outfielders Chuck Hinton and Gene Woodling, each for $75,000. Infielder Leo Burke selected from Rochester roster for $25,000.

October 1968

Kansas City Royals — Pitcher Roger Nelson (first player chosen in draft), and pitchers Moe Drabowsky and Wally Bunker, and first baseman Mike Fiore, each for $175,000.
Seattle Pilots — Catcher Larry Haney and pitcher John Morris, each for $175,000.

November 1976

Toronto Blue Jays — Infielder Bob Bailor and pitchers Mike Darr and Mike Willis, each for $175,000.
Seattle Mariners — Pitchers Dave Pagan and Bob Galasso, each for $175,000.

ORIOLES AND THE RE-ENTRY DRAFT

Year	Players Eligible	Signed With
1976	Bobby Grich, 2B	California
	Reggie Jackson, OF	New York (AL)
	Royle Stillman, OF	Chicago (AL)
	Wayne Garland, P	Cleveland
1977	Elliott Maddox, OF	New York (NL)
	Ross Grimsley, P	Montreal
	Dick Drago, P	Boston
1978	Al Bumbry, OF	Baltimore
1979	Don Stanhouse, P	Los Angeles
1981	Mark Belanger, SS	Los Angeles

Year	Players Signed	Previous Team
1976	Billy Smith, 2B-SS	California
1978	Al Bumbry, OF	Baltimore
	Steve Stone, P	Chicago (AL)
1980	Jose Morales, C-DH	Minnesota
	Jim Dwyer, OF	Boston

IT'S A FACT

Baseball fans love nothing better than hard-core trivia about their favorites. And baseball has a singularly rich lore of unusual and amusing facts that is enriched by the treasure trove of statistics that trivia thrives on. Here is just a sample of the wealth of trivial information that exists on the Browns and Orioles:

- Outfielder Johnny Groth scored the Browns' last run on a single by Ed Mickelson.
- Barry Shetrone of Southern High School was the first Baltimore city native to play for the Orioles.
- Despite three catchers on the roster in 1968 (Etchebarren, Hendricks, and Haney), Curt Blefary was behind the plate for Tom Phoebus' no-hitter.
- Carl Powis was the Birds' Opening Day right fielder in 1957. He appeared in 15 games, batted .195, and shortly after disappeared into the minors.
- Second baseman Del Pratt holds the Browns' iron-man record by playing in 367 consecutive games.
- In a series of spring and fall exhibition games between the Browns and Cardinals, the Browns held the edge with 136 wins, 112 losses, and 10 ties.
- Oriole bonus baby Bob Nelson was known as the "Babe Ruth of Texas," but he never did anything in the majors to live up to his billing.
- Including his days in both the National and the American Leagues, Frank Robinson slugged home runs in 33 different ballparks.
- The 1922 Browns had a team batting average of .313 to lead the league. Among the hot hitters were: George Sisler, .420; Ken Williams, .332; Jack Tobin, .331; Hank Severeid, .321; Baby Doll Jacobson, .317; Marty McManus, .312; and Eddie Foster, .306.
- Among the nine American League pitchers permitted to use the spitball after its ban in 1920 were two St. Louis Browns, Urban Shocker and Allen Sothoron.
- Outfielder Albie Pearson was the smallest Oriole ever, standing 5'5" and weighing 140 pounds.

It's a Fact (continued)

- In the Orioles' first season in Baltimore, a total of six players saw duty at first base (Vic Wertz, Eddie Waitkus, Dick Kryhoski, Frank Kellert, Don Lenhardt, and Sam Mele).
- Brown outfielder Mike Kreevich had only four fingers on one of his hands.
- Two members of pro football's Hall of Fame, Red Badgro and Ernie Nevers, played for the Browns. In the late Twenties, Badgro played in the outfield and Nevers was a pitcher.
- The first black ball players for the Browns and Orioles were second baseman Hank Thompson in 1947 and pitcher Jehosie Heard in 1954.
- Boog Powell was the first player to appear in both the Little League World Series and the major league World Series.
- Oriole hurler Jack Harshman holds the club record for the most home runs by a pitcher in a season with six in 1958.
- Bird bonus baby Bruce Swango was so shy that he couldn't pitch in front of big crowds. Signed in May of 1955, the Oklahoma farm boy was released just a few weeks later in July.
- Steve Dalkowski, believed to have been the fastest pitcher ever, never made it to the big leagues with the Orioles because of a terminal case of wildness and an inability to control his off-the-field activities.
- Browns' manager Luke Sewell had a superstition about keeping his infielders' gloves in the third-base coaching box while his team hit.
- The Browns' bid for a pennant in 1922 was foiled by one game when Connie Mack sent a rookie pitcher, Otto Rettig, to the mound for his Athletics and he won. The Browns' crucial loss to Rettig was his only major league win.
- When it came time for the 1913 Browns to break training camp in Montgomery, Alabama, the team was unable to pay its rent for the field. So rookie infielder Buzzy Wares was given to the Montgomery minor league team in payment.
- Oriole players Bobby Grich and Don Baylor were among the first interracial roommates in the game.
- In 1976, Oriole pitcher Dennis Martinez became the first native of Nicaragua ever to play in the major leagues.

AWARD WINNERS

Major Browns Award Winners

Most Valuable Player, American League (Baseball Writers Association)
    George Sisler, 1B, 1922
Major League Executive of the Year (*The Sporting News*)
    William O. DeWitt, 1944
Major League Manager of the Year (*The Sporting News*)
    Luke Sewell, 1944
American League Rookie of the Year (Baseball Writers Association)
    Roy Sievers, OF, 1949
American League Rookie of the Year (*The Sporting News*)
    Roy Sievers, OF, 1949
    Clint Courtney, C, 1952

Major Orioles Award Winners

Most Valuable Player, American League (Baseball Writers Association)
    Brooks Robinson, 3B, 1964
    Frank Robinson, RF, 1966
    Boog Powell, 1B, 1970
Player of the Year, American League (*The Sporting News*)
    Brooks Robinson, 3B, 1964
    Frank Robinson, RF, 1966
Player of the Year, Major Leagues (*The Sporting News*)
    Frank Robinson, RF, 1966
Pitcher of the Year, American League (*The Sporting News*)
    Chuck Estrada, 1960
    Jim Palmer, 1973, 1975, 1976
    Mike Flanagan, 1979
    Steve Stone, 1980
Cy Young Award, American League (Baseball Writers Association)
    Mike Cuellar, 1969 (tie with Denny McLain)
    Jim Palmer, 1973, 1975, 1976
    Mike Flanagan, 1979
    Steve Stone, 1980
Rookie of the Year, American League (Baseball Writers Association)
    Ron Hansen, SS, 1960
    Curt Blefary, LF, 1965
    Al Bumbry, OF, 1973
    Eddie Murray, DH, 1977
Rookie of the Year, American League (*The Sporting News*)
    Ron Hansen, SS, 1960
    Curt Blefary, LF, 1965
    Al Bumbry, OF, 1973
Rookie Pitcher of the Year, American League (*The Sporting News*)
    Wally Bunker, 1964
    Tom Phoebus, 1967
Executive of the Year, Major League (*The Sporting News*)
    Harry Dalton, 1970
    Hank Peters, 1979
Executive of the Year, Major League (United Press International)
    Hank Peters, 1979
Manager of the Year, Major League (*The Sporting News*)
    Hank Bauer, 1966
    Earl Weaver, 1977, 1979
Manager of the Year, American League (Associated Press)
    Paul Richards, 1960
    Hank Bauer, 1964, 1966
    Earl Weaver, 1973, 1977, 1979
Manager of the Year, American League (United Press International)
    Earl Weaver, 1979
Most Valuable Player, World Series (*Sport Magazine*)
    Frank Robinson, 1966
    Brooks Robinson, 1970
Most Valuable Player, All-Star Game (Arch Ward Trophy awarded by Commissioner's Office)
    Billy O'Dell, 1958
    Brooks Robinson, 1966
    Frank Robinson, 1971

Major Orioles Award Winners (continued)

Roberto Clemente Award (Commissioner's Office: given to player who best typifies the game of baseball, both on and off the field)
    Brooks Robinson, 1972
Joe Cronin Award (American League Office: given to American League player for significant achievement)
    Jim Palmer, 1976
    Brooks Robinson, 1977

MOST VALUABLE ORIOLES

This award is given annually by the Sports Boosters of Maryland to the most valuable Oriole as determined by a vote of sportswriters and broadcasters who cover the club on a regular basis.

1954 — Chuck Diering, OF
1955 — Dave Philley, OF
1956 — Bob Nieman, OF
1957 — Billy Gardner, 2B
1958 — Gus Triandos, C
1959 — Gene Woodling, OF
1960 — Brooks Robinson, 3B
1961 — Jim Gentile, 1B
1962 — Brooks Robinson, 3B
1963 — Stu Miller, P
1964 — Brooks Robinson, 3B
1965 — Stu Miller, P
1966 — Frank Robinson, OF
1967 — Frank Robinson, OF
1968 — Dave McNally, P

1969 — Boog Powell, 1B
1970 — Boog Powell, 1B
1971 — Brooks Robinson, 3B
    Frank Robinson, OF
1972 — Jim Palmer, P
1973 — Jim Palmer, P
1974 — Paul Blair, OF
    Mike Cuellar, P
1975 — Ken Singleton, OF
1976 — Lee May, 1B
1977 — Ken Singleton, OF
1978 — Eddie Murray, 1B
1979 — Ken Singleton, OF
1980 — Al Bumbry, OF
1981 — Eddie Murray, 1B
1982 — Eddie Murray, 1B

ORIOLE GOLDEN GLOVE AWARD WINNERS

1960 — Brooks Robinson, 3B
1961 — Brooks Robinson, 3B
1962 — Brooks Robinson, 3B
1963 — Brooks Robinson, 3B
1964 — Brooks Robinson, 3B
    Luis Aparicio, SS
1965 — Brooks Robinson, 3B
1966 — Brooks Robinson, 3B
    Luis Aparicio, SS
1967 — Brooks Robinson, 3B
    Paul Blair, CF
1968 — Brooks Robinson, 3B
1969 — Dave Johnson, 2B
    Brooks Robinson, 3B
    Mark Belanger, SS
    Paul Blair, CF
1970 — Dave Johnson, 2B
    Brooks Robinson, 3B
    Paul Blair, CF
1971 — Dave Johnson, 2B
    Brooks Robinson, 3B
    Mark Belanger, SS
    Paul Blair, CF

1972 — Brooks Robinson, 3B
    Paul Blair, CF
1973 — Bobby Grich, 2B
    Brooks Robinson, 3B
    Mark Belanger, SS
    Paul Blair, CF
1974 — Bobby Grich, 2B
    Brooks Robinson, 3B
    Mark Belanger, SS
    Paul Blair, CF
1975 — Bobby Grich, 2B
    Brooks Robinson, 3B
    Mark Belanger, SS
    Paul Blair, CF
1976 — Bobby Grich, 2B
    Mark Belanger, SS
    Jim Palmer, P
1977 — Mark Belanger, SS
    Jim Palmer, P
1978 — Mark Belanger, SS
    Jim Palmer, P
1979 — Jim Palmer, P

ALL-STAR GAME SELECTIONS

Brown All-Star Game Selections

1933
Sammy West

1934
Sammy West

1935
Rollie Hemsley (ST)*
Sammy West

1936
Rollie Hemsley

1937
Sammy West (ST)
Harlond Clift
Beau Bell

1938
Bobo Newsom

1939
George McQuinn
Myril Hoag

1940
George McQuinn

1941
Roy Cullenbine

1942
George McQuinn

1943
Vern Stephens (ST)
Chet Laabs (ST)

1944
George McQuinn (ST)
Vern Stephens (ST)
Bob Muncrief

1945
No All-Star game

1946
Vern Stephens (ST)
Jack Kramer

1947
Jack Kramer

1948
Al Zarilla

1949
Bob Dillinger
Bob Muncrief

1950
Sherm Lollar

1951
Ned Garver (ST)

1952
Satchel Paige

1953
Billy Hunter
Satchel Paige

_____

*ST = Starting lineup.

Oriole All-Star Game Selections

1954
Bob Turley

1955
Jim Wilson

1956
George Kell (ST)

1957
George Kell (ST)
Gus Triandos
Billy Loes

1958
Gus Triandos (ST)
Billy O'Dell

Oriole All-Star Game Selections (continued)

1959
Gus Triandos (ST)*
Jerry Walker (ST)
Gene Woodling
Hoyt Wilhelm
Billy O'Dell

1960
Ron Hansen (ST)
Jim Gentile
Brooks Robinson
Chuck Estrada

1961
Brooks Robinson (ST)
Jim Gentile
Jackie Brandt
Hoyt Wilhelm

1962
Jim Gentile
Brooks Robinson
Milt Pappas
Hoyt Wilhelm

1963
Brooks Robinson
Luis Aparicio

1964
Brooks Robinson (ST)
Norm Siebern
Luis Aparicio

1965
Brooks Robinson (ST)
Milt Pappas (ST)

1966
Brooks Robinson (ST)
Frank Robinson (ST)
Andy Etchebarren
Steve Barber

1967
Brooks Robinson (ST)
Andy Etchebarren
Frank Robinson

1968
Brooks Robinson (ST)
Dave Johnson
Boog Powell

1969
Boog Powell (ST)
Frank Robinson (ST)
Dave Johnson
Brooks Robinson
Paul Blair
Dave McNally

1970
Boog Powell (ST)
Dave Johnson (ST)
Frank Robinson (ST)
Jim Palmer (ST)
Brooks Robinson
Mike Cuellar
Dave McNally

1971
Brooks Robinson (ST)
Frank Robinson (ST)
Boog Powell
Don Buford
Jim Palmer
Mike Cuellar

1972
Bobby Grich (ST)
Brooks Robinson (ST)
Jim Palmer (ST)
Dave McNally
Pat Dobson

1973
Brooks Robinson (ST)
Paul Blair

1974
Brooks Robinson (ST)
Bobby Grich
Mike Cuellar

1975
Jim Palmer

1976
Bobby Grich (ST)
Mark Belanger

1977
Jim Palmer (ST)
Ken Singleton

-----
*ST = Starting lineup

140

1978
Jim Palmer (ST)
Eddie Murray
Mike Flanagan

1979
Ken Singleton
Don Stanhouse

1980
Steve Stone (ST)
Al Bumbry

1981
Ken Singleton (ST)
Eddie Murray
Scott McGregor

1982
Eddie Murray

ALL-TIME TEAMS
(as selected by the author)

St. Louis Browns

First Team		Second Team	
1B	George Sisler	1B	George McQuinn
2B	Marty McManus	2B	Del Pratt
3B	Harland Clift	3B	Jimmy Austin
SS	Bobby Wallace	SS	Vern Stephens
LF	Ken Williams	LF	George Stone
CF	Baby Doll Jacobson	CF	Sammy West
RF	Jack Tobin	RF	Beau Bell
C	Hank Severeid	C	Rollie Hemsley

All-Time Browns' Pitching Staff

Jack Powell
Carl Weilman
Elam Vangilder
Urban Shocker
Allen Sothoron

Lefty Stewart
Bobo Newsom
Nelson Potter
Ned Garver
Satchel Paige

Baltimore Orioles

First Team		Second Team	
1B	Boog Powell	1B	Eddie Murray
2B	Dave Johnson	2B	Bobby Grich
3B	Brooks Robinson	3B	Doug DeCinces
SS	Mark Belanger	SS	Luis Aparicio
LF	Don Buford	LF	Don Baylor
CF	Paul Blair	CF	Al Bumbry
RF	Frank Robinson	RF	Ken Singleton
C	Gus Triandos	C	Andy Etchebarren

All-Time Orioles' Pitching Staff

Steve Barber
Milt Pappas
Stu Miller
Dick Hall
Dave McNally

Mike Cuellar
Eddie Watt
Jim Palmer
Mike Flanagan
Dennis Martinez

All-Time Combined Brown/Oriole Franchise Team

	First Team		Second Team
1B	George Sisler	1B	Boog Powell
2B	Dave Johnson	2B	Marty McManus
3B	Brooks Robinson	3B	Harland Clift
SS	Bobby Wallace	SS	Vern Stephens
LF	Ken Williams	LF	George Stone
CF	Baby Doll Jacobson	CF	Paul Blair
RF	Frank Robinson	RF	Ken Singleton
C	Hank Severeid	C	Gus Triandos

All-Time Pitching Staff

Jack Powell	Stu Miller
Urban Shocker	Dave McNally
Bobo Newsom	Mike Cuellar
Satchel Paige	Eddie Watt
Milt Pappas	Jim Palmer

GEORGE SISLER

He is judged by many to be the greatest first baseman of them all. Certainly, there can be no argument that George Sisler was the greatest Brown of all time.

Ty Cobb once described Sisler as being the "nearest thing to a perfect ball player." Gorgeous George was a slick fielder, superb base runner, accomplished pitcher, and, most of all, a great lefthanded hitter who compiled a .340 lifetime average in 16 major league seasons.

A graduate of the University of Michigan, he joined the Browns in 1915 as a pitcher. The Pirates also claimed him at the time, and the dispute nearly caused a war between the leagues. Although a fine southpaw, Sisler proved to be too valuable not to play every day.

His greatest years came in 1920-22, when he hit .407, .371, and .420 and won batting titles with his .400 seasons. Eye trouble forced him to sit out the 1923 season, but he came back strong in 1924 as a playing manager. Sisler guided the team as field boss for three seasons, but then gave up and returned to full-time playing.

Sisler holds the major league record for the most hits in a season—257 in 1920—and was named Most Valuable Player in the American League following the exciting pennant chase of 1922.

Two of George's sons, Dick and Dave, followed in his footsteps as big leaguers, and another son, George Jr., is a successful minor league baseball executive in Columbus.

He was inducted into the Hall of Fame in 1939.

Sisler's Career Record

Year	Team	G	AB	R	H	2B	3B	HR	RBI	Avg.	StB
1915	St.L	81	274	28	78	10	2	3	29	.285	10
1916	St.L	151	580	83	177	21	11	4	76	.305	34
1917	St.L	135	539	60	190	30	9	2	52	.353	37
1918	St.L	114	452	69	154	21	9	2	41	.341	45*
1919	St.L	132	511	96	180	31	15	10	83	.352	28
1920	St.L	154#	631*	137	257*	49	18	19	122	.407*	42
1921	St.L	138	582	125	216	38	18	12	104	.371	35*
1922	St.L	142	586	134*	246*	42	18*	8	105	.420*	51*
1923	St.L				(Did not play due to eye trouble)						
1924	St.L	151	636	94	194	27	10	9	74	.305	19
1925	St.L	150	649	100	224	21	15	12	105	.345	11
1926	St.L	150	613	78	178	21	12	7	71	.289	12
1927	St.L	149	614	87	201	32	8	5	97	.327	27*
1928	Wash	20	49	1	12	1	0	0	2	.245	0
1928	Bos (N)	118	491	71	167	26	4	4	68	.340	11
1929	Bos	154	629	67	205	40	8	2	79	.326	6
1930	Bos	116	431	54	133	15	7	3	67	.309	7
Totals		2055	8267	1284	2812	425	164	102	1175	.340	375

Year	Team	Wins	Losses	ERA	G	GS	CG	IP	H	BB	SO	ShO
1915	St.L	4	4	2.83	15	8	6	70	62	38	41	0
1916	St.L	1	2	1.00	3	3	3	27	18	6	12	1
1918	St.L	0	0	4.50	2	1	0	8	10	4	4	0
1920	St.L	0	0	0.00	1	0	0	1	0	0	2	0
1925	St.L	0	0	0.00	1	0	0	2	1	1	1	0
1926	St.L	0	0	0.00	1	0	0	2	0	2	3	0
1928	Bos	0	0	0.00	1	0	0	1	0	1	0	0
Totals		5	6	2.35	24	12	9	111	91	52	63	1

* Led league.
# Tied for league lead.

KEN WILLIAMS

Like many other great players, Ken Williams had the misfortune of playing in the shadow of George Sisler. As a result, he has been ignored in the Hall of Fame voting, despite the fact that he compiled a .319 career batting average in 14 seasons and was one of the game's foremost sluggers in his day.

He enjoyed his greatest season during the Browns' run for the pennant in 1922. He led the league in home runs with 39 and RBIs with 155, but with a .332 batting average trailed far behind batting title winner George Sisler, who hit .420.

The left fielder for the Browns for eight straight seasons, Williams did not match his offensive skills in the field. He led the league in errors in 1921, but also compiled some credible assist totals during his career.

He is best known for his home run power and during the '22 season, he accomplished the following feats:
- hit three home runs in one game, April 22, 1922;
- hit two home runs in the sixth inning, August 7, 1922;
- hit home runs in six consecutive games, July 28–August 2, 1922.

Williams' Career Record

Year	Team	G	AB	R	H	2B	3B	HR	RBI	Avg.	StB
1915	Cin	71	219	22	53	10	4	0	16	.242	4
1916	Cin	10	27	1	3	0	0	0	1	.111	1
1918	St.L	2	1	0	0	0	0	0	1	.000	0
1919	St.L	65	227	32	68	10	5	6	35	.300	7
1920	St.L	141	521	90	160	34	13	10	72	.307	18
1921	St.L	146	547	115	190	31	7	24	117	.347	20
1922	St.L	153	585	128	194	34	11	39*	155*	.332	37
1923	St.L	147	555	106	198	37	12	29	91	.357	18
1924	St.L	114	398	78	129	21	4	18	84	.324	20
1925	St.L	102	411	83	136	31	5	25	105	.331	10
1926	St.L	108	347	55	97	15	7	17	74	.280	5
1927	St.L	131	421	70	136	23	6	17	74	.323	9
1928	Bos	133	462	59	140	25	1	8	67	.303	4
1929	Bos	74	139	21	48	14	2	3	21	.345	1
Totals		1397	4860	860	1552	285	77	196	913	.319	154

* Led league.

SATCHEL PAIGE

This lanky righthander broke into the major leagues in 1948 with Cleveland at the advanced age of 41—the victim of baseball's unconscionable ban on blacks.

By the time he reached the "Big Show" his best years were behind him. But he had spent them well as the biggest star in the Negro leagues. Most experts credit Satch with being the greatest pitcher of all time—not because of his fastball, but his pinpoint control. On many occasions, he would call in his outfielders to sit down on the pitching mound while he would proceed to strike out the side on nine pitches. In exhibition games with big league stars, Paige demonstrated his skills as their peer and satisfied his own mind that he ranked with the best—black or white.

When Bill Veeck brought him to St. Louis in 1951, Satchel gave the Browns sterling relief pitching. In 1952 and 1953, he was named to the American League All-Star team. During the 1952 season, he won 12 games, including eight in relief, saved 10 others and pitched two shutouts—all at the age of 48! He made the Hall of Fame in 1971.

Paige's Career Record

Year	Team	Wins	Losses	ERA	G	GS	CG	IP	H	BB	SO	ShO	Saves
1948	Clev	6	1	2.48	21	7	3	73	61	25	45	2	1
1949	Clev	4	7	3.04	31	5	1	83	70	33	54	0	5
1951	St.L	3	4	4.79	23	3	0	62	67	29	48	0	5
1952	St.L	12	10	3.07	46	6	3	138	116	57	91	2	10
1953	St.L	3	9	3.53	57	4	0	117	114	39	51	0	11
1965	K.C.	0	0	0.00	1	1	0	3	1	0	1	0	0
Totals		28	31	3.29	179	26	7	476	429	183	290	4	32

FRANK ROBINSON

A 1982 member of the Hall of Fame and the second Oriole to be elected he is very much on the baseball scene as the manager of the San Francisco Giants. And, if the Earl of Weaver does retire, Frank certainly would find his name on the list of possible replacements.

During his six seasons with the Birds the club won four American League pennants and two World's Championships, thanks in no small part to Robby's contributions.

His first season with the team, 1966, was his best. He became only the 10th player in history to win a Triple Crown as he hit .316, belted 49 homers, and drove in 122 runs. Cincinnati had given up on Frank, declaring him an old 30 and shipping him to Baltimore in December of 1965.

Robinson might have reached his career goals of 600 home runs and 3,000 hits had he not become the first black manager in history with Cleveland in 1975. He tried to be a playing manager, but soon devoted most of his energies to his duties as field boss. As it is, he ranks in the top ten in the number of games played, home runs, runs scored, and strikeouts.

An intense competitor, Robinson played hurt when he had to and remained aggressive throughout his career. His feistiness as a player has carried over into his managerial career, but he appears to have mellowed a bit in his second stint as the boss.

Frank Robinson's Career Record

Year	Team	G	AB	R	H	2B	3B	HR	RBI	Avg.	StB
1956	Cin	152	572	122*	166	27	6	38	83	.290	8
1957	Cin	150	611	97	197	29	5	29	75	.322	10
1958	Cin	148	554	90	149	25	6	31	83	.269	10
1959	Cin	146	540	106	168	31	4	36	125	.311	18
1960	Cin	139	464	86	138	33	6	31	83	.297	13
1961	Cin	153	545	117	176	32	7	37	124	.323	22
1962	Cin	162	609	134*	208	51*	2	39	136	.342	18
1963	Cin	140	482	79	125	19	3	21	91	.259	26
1964	Cin	156	568	103	174	38	6	29	96	.306	23
1965	Cin	156	582	109	172	33	5	33	113	.296	13
1966	Balt	155	576	122*	182	34	2	49*	122*	.316*	8
1967	Balt	129	479	83	149	23	7	30	94	.311	2
1968	Balt	130	421	69	113	27	1	15	52	.268	11
1969	Balt	148	539	111	166	19	5	32	100	.308	9
1970	Balt	132	471	88	144	24	1	25	78	.306	2
1971	Balt	133	455	82	128	16	2	28	99	.281	3
1972	LA	103	342	41	86	6	1	19	59	.251	2
1973	Cal	147	534	85	142	29	0	30	97	.266	1
1974	Cal-Clev	144	477	81	117	27	3	22	68	.245	5
1975	Clev	49	118	19	28	5	0	9	24	.237	0
1976	Clev	36	67	5	15	0	0	3	10	.224	0
Totals		2808	10,006	1829	2943	528	72	586	1812	.294	204

* Led league.

BROOKS ROBINSON

Mr. Oriole. The most beloved player in Baltimore history and a shoo-in in the 1983 Hall of Fame election. Brooks Robinson minded the hot corner with more skill and flair than any player in his generation and possibly in the history of the game.

Brooks Robinson (continued)

Over the course of a 23-year big-league career, Brooks thrilled the fans with his "vacuum cleaner" plays at third.

Although recognized primarily for his defense, Brooks also made a major contribution at the plate. He was a .267 lifetime hitter, but a great clutch hitter who hammered 268 home runs and banged out 2,848 hits. Not bad for a glove man.

Robinson remains highly visible as a broadcaster for the Orioles today. His career achievements will keep him fresh in the fans' minds for many years to come as they ponder these amazing accomplishments:

- 16 straight Gold Glove awards;
- second highest number of games played in American League history (only Ty Cobb played more);
- started 20 consecutive Opening Days at third base (1957-76);
- nine major league records for a third baseman;
- led the league in fielding for 11 seasons.

As long as there is a World Series, fans will relive his superhuman exploits at third during the '70 classic.

Brooks Robinson's Career Record

Year	Team	G	AB	R	H	2B	3B	HR	RBI	Avg.	StB
1955	Balt	6	22	0	2	0	0	0	1	.091	0
1956	Balt	15	44	5	10	4	0	1	1	.227	0
1957	Balt	50	117	13	28	6	1	2	14	.239	1
1958	Balt	145	463	31	110	16	3	3	32	.238	1
1959	Balt	88	313	29	89	15	2	4	24	.284	2
1960	Balt	152	595	74	175	27	9	14	88	.294	2
1961	Balt	163	668*	89	192	38	7	7	61	.287	1
1962	Balt	162	634	77	192	29	9	23	86	.303	3
1963	Balt	161	589	67	148	26	4	11	67	.251	2
1964	Balt	163	612	82	194	35	3	28	118*	.317	1
1965	Balt	144	559	81	166	25	2	18	80	.297	3
1966	Balt	157	620	91	167	35	2	23	100	.269	2
1967	Balt	158	610	88	164	25	5	22	77	.269	1
1968	Balt	162	608	65	154	36	6	17	75	.253	1
1969	Balt	156	598	73	140	21	3	23	84	.234	2
1970	Balt	158	608	84	168	31	4	18	94	.276	1
1971	Balt	156	589	67	160	21	1	20	92	.272	0
1972	Balt	153	556	48	139	23	2	8	64	.250	1
1973	Balt	155	549	54	141	17	2	9	72	.267	2
1974	Balt	153	553	46	159	27	0	7	59	.288	2
1975	Balt	144	482	50	97	15	1	6	53	.201	0
1976	Balt	71	218	16	46	8	2	3	11	.211	0
1977	Balt	24	47	3	7	2	0	1	4	.149	0
Totals		2896	10,654	1233	2848	482	68	268	1357	.267	28

* Led league.

HALL OF FAME PROFILES

JIM BOTTOMLEY — A graceful fielder at first and an excellent clutch hitter, "Sunny Jim" joined the Browns at the end of a great career. He joined the club in a trade in the spring of 1936 and in the middle of the next season, took over as a playing manager. He hit .298 as a starter in '36, but at age 36 was clearly not the same as the great first baseman for the hometown rival Cardinals he was during the Twenties. (Inducted 1974)

JESSE BURKETT — This slight (5'8", 155 lbs.) outfielder earned a reputation as one of the greatest bunters ever during his sterling career. He joined the Browns in their 1902 debut in St. Louis and played four seasons before moving on to the Red Sox. "Crab," as he was known by his teammates, hit .306 in his first year with the Browns. (Inducted 1946)

DIZZY DEAN — The great Cardinal righthander managed 150 wins in a career cut short by injury. His only appearance with the Browns came after on-the-air remarks that he could pitch better than anyone on the team. So, on the last day of the 1947 season, Dean started and pitched four shutout innings, giving up three hits and walking one. (Inducted 1953)

HUGH DUFFY — As manager of the 1901 Milwaukee Brewers, Duffy also played 78 games in the outfield and hit .308. The diminutive Duffy was known as a brilliant outfielder and compiled a lofty lifetime average of .330, with his best years coming in the 1890s with Boston in the National League. (Inducted 1945)

GOOSE GOSLIN — After being a key part of the Senators' best teams in the Twenties, this hard-hitting flyhawk joined the Browns in 1930 in a trade involving another Hall-of-Famer, Heinie Manush. He spent two full seasons with the Browns before moving on to Detroit in 1934, in time to help lead them to two pennants. His best season in St. Louis was 1931, when he hit 24 home runs, drove in 105 runs and hit .328. (Inducted 1968)

ROGERS HORNSBY — Regarded as perhaps the greatest righthanded hitter ever, Rajah played sparingly for the Browns in his first stint as manager in the 1930s. His glory years came with the Cardinals in the Twenties, when he averaged better than .400 during a five-season span (1921–25). His success on the diamond, however, was never matched as a field boss. (Inducted 1942)

HEINIE MANUSH — In two and a half seasons with the Browns, this line drive hitter banged out averages of .378, .355, and .328. Small wonder his nickname was "The Tuscumbia Thumper," so-named for his birthplace in Alabama. He left St. Louis in a trade with Washington for Goose Goslin. (Inducted 1964)

EDDIE PLANK — "Gettysburg Eddie" ended his major league career in St. Louis after a distinguished stint with the Philadelphia Athletics. The southpaw Plank racked up 305 wins, the last 21 coming with the Browns. His next-to-last season, 1916, Plank won 16 games as a starter for St. Louis. (Inducted 1946)

BRANCH RICKEY — A mediocre catcher and manager, "The Mahatma" is remembered for his considerable skills as an executive. He is credited with inventing the farm system of player development and breaking baseball's shameful color line by signing Jackie Robinson. He managed the Browns with little distinction from 1913 to 1915 before beginning his front-office career with them in 1916. He enjoyed his greatest success with the Cardinals and Dodgers. (Inducted 1967)

ROBIN ROBERTS — The fireballing righthander is the first Oriole to make the Hall of Fame. But his great years came with the Phillies in the Fifties. He came to Baltimore in 1962 and pitched well for four seasons before being dealt to Houston. His best year with the O's came in 1964 when he was 13-7 with a 2.91 ERA. (Inducted 1976)

RUBE WADDELL — A typically eccentric lefthander, Waddell starred for Connie Mack's Athletics from 1902 to 1907. He then was sold to the Browns where he won 19 games and set a single-game strikeout record of 16. He pitched two more seasons before ending his career. (Inducted 1946)

BOBBY WALLACE — His brilliant glove work earned him the title of "Mr. Short-stop" during his 15 seasons with the Browns. A lifetime .267 hitter, he managed to get above .300 only twice with the Cardinals before joining the Browns. He served as a playing manager in 1911 and part of 1912, but could not get the club out of last place. (Inducted 1953)

BATTING LEADERS, BY YEARS

By Certain Categories

Year	Leader in Hits		Leader in HRs		Leader in RBIs		Leader in Avg.	
	Name	No.	Name	No.	Name	No.	Name	No.
1901	Anderson	190	Anderson	8	Anderson	99	Anderson	.330
1902	Burkett	168	Hemphill	6	Anderson	85	Hemphill	.317
1903	Anderson	156	Burkett	3	Anderson	78	Burkett	.296
			Hemphill	3				
1904	Burkett	157	Burkett	2	Wallace	69	Burkett	.273
			Hemphill	2			Heidrick	.273
			Jones	2			Wallace	.273
			Wallace	2				
1905	Stone	187*	Stone	7	Wallace	59	Stone	.296
1906	Stone	208	Stone	6	Stone	71	Stone	.358*
1907	Stone	191	Stone	4	Wallace	70	Stone	.320
1908	Stone	165	Stone	5	Ferris	74	Stone	.281
1909	Hartzell	161	Ferris	3	Ferris	58	Stone	.287
			Stephens	3				
1910	Stone	144	Griggs	2	Stone	40	Wallace	.258
			Hartzell	2				
			Newnam	2				
			Schweitzer	2				
1911	LaPorte	159	Kutina	3	LaPorte	82	LaPorte	.314
			Meloan	3				
			Murray	3				
1912	Pratt	172	Pratt	5	Pratt	69	Pratt	.302
1913	Pratt	175	Williams	5	Pratt	87	Shotton	.297
1914	Pratt	165	Walker	6	Walker	78	Walker	.298
1915	Pratt	175	Walker	5	Pratt	78	Pratt	.291
1916	Sisler	177	Pratt	5	Pratt	103*	Sisler	.305
1917	Sisler	190	Jacobson	4	Severeid	57	Sisler	.353
1918	Sisler	154	Sisler	2	Demmitt	61	Sisler	.341
1919	Sisler	180	Sisler	10	Sisler	83	Sisler	.352
1920	Sisler	257*	Sisler	19	Jacobson	122	Sisler	.407*
					Sisler	122		
1921	Tobin	236	Williams	24	Williams	117	Sisler	.371
1922	Sisler	246*	Williams	39*	Williams	155*	Sisler	.420*
1923	Tobin	202	Williams	29	McManus	94	Williams	.357
1924	Sisler	194	Jacobson	19	Jacobson	97	McManus	.333
1925	Sisler	224	Williams	25	Sisler	105	Rice	.359
					Williams	105		
1926	Rice	181	Williams	17	Williams	74	Miller	.331
1927	Sisler	201	Williams	17	Sisler	97	Sisler	.327
1928	Manush	241*	Blue	14	Manush	108	Manush	.378
1929	Manush	204	Kress	9	Kress	107	Manush	.355
1930	Kress	192	Goslin	30	Kress	112	Goslin	.326
1931	Goslin	194	Goslin	24	Kress	114	Goslin	.328
1932	Burns	188	Goslin	17	Goslin	104	Ferrell	.315
1933	Burns	160	Campbell	16	Campbell	106	West	.300
1934	Pepper	168	Clift	14	Pepper	101	West	.326
1935	Solters	182	Solters	18	Solters	104	Solters	.330
1936	Bell	212	Clift	20	Solters	134	Bell	.344

Year	Leader in Hits		Leader in HRs		Leader in RBIs		Leader in Avg.	
	Name	No.	Name	No.	Name	No.	Name	No.
1937	Bell	218*	Clift	29	Clift	118	Bell	.340
1938	McQuinn	195	Clift	34	Clift	118	Almada	.342
1939	McQuinn	195	McQuinn	20	McQuinn	94	McQuinn	.316
1940	Radcliff	200#	Judnich	24	Judnich	89	Radcliff	.342
1941	Cullenbine	159	McQuinn	18	Cullenbine	98	Cullenbine	.317
1942	Stephens	169	Laabs	27	Laabs	99	Judnich	.313
1943	Stephens	148	Stephens	22	Stephens	91	Stephens	.289
1944	Stephens	164	Stephens	20	Stephens	109*	Kreevich	.301
1945	Stephens	165	Stephens	24*	Stephens	89	Stephens	.289
1946	Berardino	154	Laabs	16	Judnich	72	Stephens	.307
1947	Dillinger	168	Heath	27	Heath	85	Dillinger	.294
1948	Dillinger	207*	Moss	14	Platt	82	Zarilla	.329
1949	Dillinger	176	Graham	24	Sievers	91	Dillinger	.324
1950	Lenhardt	131	Lenhardt	22	Lenhardt	81	Lollar	.280
1951	Young	159	Wood	15	Coleman	55	Coleman	.282
1952	Young	142	Nieman	18	Nieman	74	Nieman	.289
1953	Groth	141	Wertz	19	Wertz	70	Kryhoski	.278
1954	Abrams	124	Stephens	8	Stephens	46	Abrams	.293
1955	Triandos	133	Triandos	12	Triandos	65	Triandos	.277
1956	Triandos	126	Triandos	21	Triandos	88	Nieman	.322
1957	Gardner	169	Triandos	19	Triandos	72	Boyd	.318
1958	Gardner	126	Triandos	30	Triandos	79	Nieman	.325
1958	Woodling	132	Triandos	25	Woodling	77	Woodling	.300
1960	Robinson	175	Hansen	22	Gentile	98	Robinson	.294
1961	Robinson	192	Gentile	46	Gentile	141	Gentile	.302
1962	Robinson	192	Gentile	33	Gentile	87	Snyder	.305
1963	Aparicio	150	Powell	25	Powell	82	Orsino	.272
							Smith	.272
1964	Robinson	194	Powell	39	Robinson	118*	Robinson	.317
1965	Robinson	166	Blefary	22	Robinson	80	Robinson	.297
1966	Aparicio	182	F. R'bnsn.	49*	F. R'bnsn.	122*	F. R'bnsn.	.316*
	F. R'bnsn.	182						
1967	Robinson	164	F. R'bnsn.	30	F. R'bnsn.	94	F. R'bnsn.	.311
1968	Robinson	154	Powell	22	Powell	85	Buford	.282
1969	Blair	178	Powell	37	Powell	121	F. R'bnsn.	.308
1970	Robinson	168	Powell	35	Powell	114	F. R'bnsn.	.306
1971	Robinson	160	F. R'bnsn.	28	F. R'bnsn.	99	Rett'nmd.	.318
1972	Robinson	139	Powell	21	Powell	81	Grich	.278
1973	Grich	146	Williams	22	Davis	89	Bumbry	.337
1974	Davis	181	Grich	19	Davis	84	Davis	.289
1975	Singleton	176	Baylor	25	May	99	Singleton	.300
1976	Singleton	151	Jackson	27	May	109*	Singleton	.278
1977	Singleton	176	May	27	May	27	Singleton	.328
			Murray	27	Singleton	99		
1978	Murray	174	DeCinces	28	Murray	95	Singleton	.293
1979	Murray	179	Singleton	35	Singleton	111	Murray	.295
							Singleton	.295
1980	Bumbry	205	Murray	32	Murray	116	Bumbry	.318
1981	Murray	111	Murray	22#	Murray	78*	Murray	.294
1982	Murray	174	Murray	32	Murray	110	Murray	.316

149

Batting Leaders, by Years (cont.)

By Additional Categories

Year	Leader in Runs		Leader in 2B		Leader in 3B		Leader in StB	
	Name	No.	Name	No.	Name	No.	Name	No.
1901	Anderson	90	Anderson	46	Duffy	8	Anderson	35
1902	Burkett	99	Wallace	33	Hemphill	11	Hemphill	23
1903	Burkett	74	Anderson	34	Wallace	17	Heidrick	19
1904	Burkett	72	Wallace	28	Heidrick	10	Heidrick	35
					Jones	10		
1905	Stone	76	Wallace	29	Stone	13	Stone	26
1906	Stone	91	Stone	24	Stone	19	Stone	35
			Wallace	24				
1907	Stone	77	Yeager	21	Stone	13	Jones	24
1908	Stone	89	Ferris	26	Stone	8	Hartzell	24
1909	Hartzell	64	Ferris	18	Hoffman	7	Hoffman	24
1910	Stone	60	Griggs	22	Stone	12	Truesdale	29
1911	Shotton	85	LaPorte	37	LaPorte	12	Austin	26
							Shotton	26
1912	Shotton	87	Pratt	26	Pratt	15	Shotton	35
1913	Shotton	105	Pratt	31	Williams	16	Shotton	43
1914	Pratt	85	Pratt	34	Walker	16	Shotton	40
1915	Shotton	93	Pratt	31	Pratt	11	Shotton	43
					Shotton	11		
1916	Shotton	97	Pratt	35	Pratt	12	Marsans	46
1917	Austin	61	Sisler	30	Sisler	9	Sisler	37
1918	Sisler	69	Demmitt	23	Sisler	9	Sisler	45*
1919	Sisler	96	Jacobson	31	Sisler	15	Sisler	28
			Sisler	31				
1920	Sisler	137	Sisler	49	Sisler	18	Sisler	42
1921	Tobin	132	Jacobson	38	Sisler	18	Sisler	35*
			Sisler	38	Tobin	18		
1922	Sisler	134*	Sisler	42	Sisler	18*	Sisler	51*
1923	Williams	106	Williams	37	Tobin	15	Williams	18
1924	Jacobson	103	Jacobson	41	Jacobson	12	Williams	20
1925	McManus	108	McManus	44*	Sisler	15	Sisler	11
1926	McManus	102	McManus	30	Sisler	12	Sisler	12
1927	Rice	90	Miller	32	Gerber	9	Sisler	27*
			Sisler	32	Rice	9		
1928	Blue	116	Manush	47#	Manush	20	Manush	17
1929	Blue	111	Manush	45#	Blue	10	O'Rourke	14
					Manush	10		
					Melillo	10		
1930	Kress	94	Kress	43	Melillo	10	Melillo	15
1931	Goslin	114	Kress	46	Melillo	11	Burns	19
1932	Burns	111	Campbell	35	Campbell	11	Burns	17
			Schulte	35	Melillo	11		
1933	West	93	Burns	43	Reynolds	14	Melillo	12
1934	Clift	104	Hemsley	31	Clift	10	Burns	9
					West	10		
1935	Clift	101	Solters	39	Coleman	9	Lary	25
1936	Clift	145	Solters	45	Bell	12	Lary	37*

Year	Leader in Runs		Leader in 2B		Leader in 3B		Leader in StB	
	Name	No.	Name	No.	Name	No.	Name	No.
1937	Clift	103	Bell	51*	Vosmik	9	Clift	8
1938	Clift	119	McQuinn	42	Clift	7	Clift	10
					McQuinn	7		
1939	McQuinn	101	McQuinn	37	McQuinn	13	Hoag	9
1940	Judnich	97	McQuinn	39	McQuinn	10	Clift	9
1941	Clift	108	Judnich	40	Clift	9	Clift	6
					Cullenbine	9	Cullenbine	6
1942	Clift	108	Clift	39	McQuillen	12	Gutteridge	16
1943	Laabs	83	Gutteridge	35	Byrnes	7	Gutteridge	10
					Laabs	7		
1944	Stephens	91	Stephens	32	Gutteridge	11	Gutteridge	20
1945	Stephens	90	McQuinn	31	Byrnes	4	Gutteridge	9
					Christman	4		
					Finney	4		
1946	Berardino	70	Berardino	29	Zarilla	9	Dillinger	8
1947	Heath	81	Lehner	25	Lehner	9	Dillinger	34*
1948	Dillinger	110	Priddy	40	Dillinger	10	Dillinger	28*
					Platt	10		
1949	Sievers	84	Kokos	28	Dillinger	13	Dillinger	20*
			Sievers	28				
1950	Kokos	77	Kokos	27	Coleman	6	Kokos	8
					Lenhardt	6		
					Upton	6		
1951	Young	75	Lollar	21	Young	9	Young	8
			Marsh	21				
1952	Nieman	66	Courtney	24	Young	9	Rivera	8
1953	Groth	65	Groth	27	Wertz	6	Groth	5
1954	Abrams	67	Abrams	22	Abrams	7	Coan	9
1955	Abrams	56	Smith	23	Miranda	6	Diering	5
							Pope	5
1956	Francona	62	Nieman	20	Nieman	6	Francona	11
1957	Gardner	79	Gardner	36#	Boyd	8	Pilarcik	14
1958	Triandos	59	Gardner	28	Boyd	5	Pilarcik	7
1959	Tasby	69	Woodling	22	Tasby	5	Pilarcik	9
1960	Robinson	74	Robinson	27	Robinson	9	Breeding	10
1961	Gentile	96	Robinson	38	Robinson	7	Brandt	10
1962	Gentile	80	Adair	29	Robinson	9	Brandt	9
			Brandt	29				
			Robinson	29				
1963	Aparicio	73	Robinson	26	Aparicio	8	Aparicio	40*
1964	Aparicio	93	Robinson	35	Adair	3	Aparicio	57*
					Aparicio	3		
					Robinson	3		
1965	Robinson	81	Adair	26	Aparicio	10	Aparicio	26
1966	F. R'bnsn.	122*	Robinson	35	Aparicio	8	Aparicio	25
1967	Robinson	88	Johnson	30	Blair	12*	Aparicio	18
1968	F. R'bnsn.	69	Robinson	36	Robinson	6	Buford	27
1969	F. R'bnsn.	111	Johnson	34	Blair	5	Blair	20
					F. R'bnsn.	5		
1970	Buford	99	Robinson	31	Belanger	5	Blair	24
1971	Buford	99*	Johnson	26	Blair	8	Buford	15
							Rett'nmd.	15

By Additional Categories (cont.)

Year	Leader in Runs		Leader in 2B		Leader in 3B		Leader in StB	
	Name	No.	Name	No.	Name	No.	Name	No.
1972	Grich	66	Robinson	23	Blair	8	Baylor	24
1973	Grich	82	Grich	29	Bumbry	11#	Baylor	32
1974	Grich	92	Grich	29	Grich	6	Baylor	29
1975	Singleton	88	Singleton	37	Baylor	6	Baylor	32
1976	Grich	93	Grich	31	Bumbry	7	Bumbry	42
1977	Singleton	90	Bumbry	31	Belanger	4	Kelly	25
					Dempsey	4		
1978	Murray	85	DeCinces	37	Garcia	4	Harlow	14
1979	Singleton	93	Murray	30	Garcia	9	Bumbry	37
1980	Bumbry	118	Murray	36	Bumbry	9	Bumbry	44
1981	Bumbry	61	Dauer	27	Belanger	2	Bumbry	22
					Bumbry	2		
					DeCinces	2		
					Murray	2		
1982	Ripkin	90	Ripken	32	Ripken	5	Bumbry	10

CAREER BATTING LEADERS

Browns, 1902–53

GAMES
George Sisler 1,647
Bobby Wallace 1,566
Harlond Clift 1,443

AT-BATS
George Sisler 6,667
Bobby Wallace 5,547
Harlond Clift 5,281

HITS
George Sisler 2,295
Baby Doll Jacobson 1,503
Harlond Clift 1,463

RUNS
George Sisler 1,091
Harlond Clift 1,013
Ken Williams 757

BATTING AVERAGE
Heinie Manush .... .362
George Sisler .... .344
Ken Williams .... .326

SINGLES
George Sisler 1,716
Oscar Melillo 1,224
Jimmy Austin 1,221

DOUBLES
George Sisler 343
Harlond Clift 294
Baby Doll Jacobson 270

TRIPLES
George Sisler 145
Baby Doll Jacobson 89
Bobby Wallace 75

HOME RUNS
Ken Williams 185
Harlond Clift 170
Vern Stephens 113

RUNS BATTED IN
George Sisler 964
Ken Williams 807
Harlond Clift 769

CAREER BATTING LEADERS

Orioles, 1954–82

GAMES
Brooks Robinson 2,896
Mark Belanger 1,962
Boog Powell 1,763
Paul Blair 1,700
Al Bumbry 1,185
Ken Singleton................ 1,184
Dave Johnson 995
Gus Triandos 953
Eddie Murray................. 888
Doug DeCinces 858

AT-BATS
Brooks Robinson 10,654
Boog Powell 5,912
Mark Belanger 5,734
Paul Blair 5,606
Ken Singleton................ 4,245
Al Bumbry 4,236
Dave Johnson 3,489
Eddie Murray................ 3,376
Gus Triandos 3,186
Luis Aparicio 2,948

HITS
Brooks Robinson 2,848
Boog Powell 1,574
Paul Blair 1,426
Mark Belanger 1,304
Ken Singleton................ 1,237
Al Bumbry 1,206
Eddie Murray................. 997
Dave Johnson 904
Frank Robinson 882
Gus Triandos 794

RUNS
Brooks Robinson 1,232
Boog Powell 796
Paul Blair 737
Mark Belanger 670
Al Bumbry 662
Ken Singleton 604
Frank Robinson 555
Eddie Murray 500
Bobby Grich 432
Don Buford 408

DOUBLES
Brooks Robinson 482
Paul Blair 269
Boog Powell 243
Ken Singleton 207
Dave Johnson 186
Al Bumbry 191
Mark Belanger 174
Eddie Murray................ 178
Doug DeCinces 161
Eddie Murray................ 148

TRIPLES
Brooks Robinson 68
Paul Blair 51
Al Bumbry 47
Luis Aparicio 34
Mark Belanger 33
Bobby Grich 27
Jackie Brandt 22
Bob Boyd 20
Russ Snyder 20
Frank Robinson 18

HOME RUNS
Boog Powell 303
Brooks Robinson 268
Frank Robinson 179
Eddie Murray 165
Ken Singleton 158
Gus Triandos 142
Paul Blair 126
Jim Gentile 124
Lee May 123
Doug DeCinces 107

RUNS BATTED IN
Brooks Robinson 1,357
Boog Powell 1,063
Ken Singleton 646
Eddie Murray 586
Paul Blair 567
Frank Robinson 545
Gus Triandos 517
Lee May 487
Jim Gentile 398
Doug DeCinces 397

TOTAL BASES

Brooks Robinson	4,270
Boog Powell	2,748
Paul Blair	2,175
Ken Singleton	1,948
Mark Belanger	1,604
Frank Robinson	1,598
Al Bumbry	1,632
Eddie Murray	1,694
Gus Triandos	1,351
Dave Johnson	1,320

EXTRA BASE HITS

Brooks Robinson	818
Boog Powell	557
Paul Blair	446
Frank Robinson	340
Ken Singleton	380
Eddie Murray	355
Doug DeCinces	282
Dave Johnson	268
Gus Triandos	267
Al Bumbry	285

BATTING AVERAGE

Bob Nieman	.303
Bob Boyd	.301
Frank Robinson	.300
Ken Singleton	.291
Tommy Davis	.291
Eddie Murray	.295
Al Bumbry	.285
Merv Rettenmund	.284
Russ Snyder	.280
Gene Woodling	.280

STOLEN BASES

Al Bumbry	231
Paul Blair	167
Luis Aparicio	166
Mark Belanger	166
Don Baylor	118
Don Buford	85
Bobby Grich	77
Pat Kelly	55
Merv Rettenmund	52
Rich Coggins	43

BATTERS HITTING 20 HOME RUNS OR MORE

Browns

1921 — Ken Williams	24	1940 — Walt Judnich	24	
1922 — Ken Williams	39	Harland Clift	20	
1923 — Ken Williams	29	1942 — Chet Laabs	37	
1925 — Ken Williams	25	1943 — Vern Stephens	22	
1930 — Goose Goslin	30	1944 — Vern Stephens	20	
1931 — Goose Goslin	24	1945 — Vern Stephens	24	
1936 — Harlond Clift	20	1947 — Jeff Heath	27	
1937 — Harlond Clift	29	1949 — Jack Graham	24	
1938 — Harlond Clift	34	Dick Kokos	23	
1939 — George McQuinn	20	1950 — Don Lenhardt	22	

Orioles

1956 — Gus Triandos	21	1964 — Boog Powell	39
1958 — Gus Triandos	30	Brooks Robinson	28
1959 — Gus Triandos	25	Sam Bowens	22
Bob Nieman	21	1965 — Curt Blefary	22
1960 — Ron Hansen	22	1966 — Frank Robinson	49
Jim Gentile	21	Boog Powell	34
1961 — Jim Gentile	46	Brooks Robinson	23
1962 — Jim Gentile	33	Curt Blefary	23
Brooks Robinson	23	1967 — Frank Robinson	30
1963 — Boog Powell	25	Brooks Robinson	22
Jim Gentile	24	Curt Blefary	22

1968 — Boog Powell	22	Lee May	25
1969 — Boog Powell	37	1977 — Eddie Murray	27
Frank Robinson	32	Lee May	27
Paul Blair	26	Ken Singleton	24
Brooks Robinson	23	1978 — Doug DeCinces	28
1970 — Boog Powell	35	Eddie Murray	27
Frank Robinson	25	Lee May	25
1971 — Boog Powell	22	Ken Singleton	20
Brooks Robinson	20	1979 — Ken Singleton	35
1972 — Boog Powell	21	Eddie Murray	25
1973 — Earl Williams	22	Gary Roenicke	25
1975 — Don Baylor	25	1980 — Eddie Murray	32
Lee May	20	Ken Singleton	24
1976 — Reggie Jackson	27	1981 — Eddie Murray	22
		1982 — Eddie Murray	32
		Cal Ripken	28
		John Lowenstein	24
		Gary Roenicke	21

Orioles

1961 — Jim Gentile	141	Frank Robinson	100
1964 — Brooks Robinson	118	1970 — Boog Powell	114
1966 — Frank Robinson	122	1976 — Lee May	109
Boog Powell	109	1979 — Ken Singleton	111
Brooks Robinson	100	1980 — Eddie Murray	116
1969 — Boog Powell	121	Ken Singleton	104
		1982 — Eddie Murray	110

BATTERS STEALING 20 BASES OR MORE

Brewers

1901 — John Anderson	35
Wid Conroy	21

BATTERS WITH 100 RBIs OR MORE

Browns

1916 — Del Pratt	103	Goose Goslin	100
1920 — George Sisler	122	1931 — Red Kress	114
Baby Doll Jacobson	122	Goose Goslin	105
1921 — Ken Williams	117	1932 — Goose Goslin	104
George Sisler	104	1933 — Bruce Campbell	106
1922 — Ken Williams	155	1934 — Ray Pepper	101
Marty McManus	109	1935 — Moose Solters	104
George Sisler	105	1936 — Moose Solters	134
Baby Doll Jacobson	102	Beau Bell	123
1925 — George Sisler	105	1937 — Harlond Clift	118
Ken Williams	105	Beau Bell	117
1928 — Heinie Manush	108	1938 — Harlond Clift	118
1929 — Red Kress	107	1944 — Vern Stephens	109
1930 — Red Kress	112		

Browns

1902 — Charlie Hemphill 23
Jesse Burkett 22
1904 — Snags Heidrick 35
Charlie Hemphill 23
Dick Padden 23
1905 — George Stone 26
Harry Gleason 23
Ben Koehler 22
1906 — George Stone 35
Charlie Hemphill 33
Harry Niles 30
Tom Jones 27
Pete O'Brien 25
Bobby Wallace 24
Roy Hartzell 21
1907 — Tom Jones 24
George Stone 23
1908 — Roy Hartzell 24
George Stone 20
1909 — Denny Hoffman 24
1910 — Frank Truesdale 29
Al Scheitzer 26
George Stone 20
1911 — Burt Shotton 26
Jimmy Austin 26
1912 — Burt Shotton 35
Jimmy Austin 28
Del Pratt 24
1913 — Burt Shotton 43
Jimmy Austin 37
Del Pratt 37
Gus Williams 31

1914 — Burt Shotton 40
Del Pratt 37
Gus Williams 35
Tilly Walker 29
Jimmy Austin 20
1915 — Burt Shotton 43
Del Pratt 32
Ivon Howard 29
Tilly Walker 20
1916 — Armando Marsans 46
Burt Shotton 41
George Sisler 34
Del Pratt 26
Ward Miller 25
1917 — George Sisler 37
1918 — George Sisler 45
1919 — George Sisler 28
1920 — George Sisler 42
Jack Tobin 21
1921 — George Sisler 35
Ken Williams 20
1922 — George Sisler 51
Ken Williams 37
1924 — Ken Williams 20
1927 — George Sisler 27
1935 — Lyn Lary 25
1936 — Lyn Lary 37
1944 — Don Gutteridge 20
1947 — Bob Dillinger 34
1948 — Bob Dillinger 28
1949 — Bob Dillinger 20

Orioles

1963 — Luis Aparicio 40
1964 — Luis Aparicio 57
1965 — Luis Aparicio 26
1966 — Luis Aparicio 25
1968 — Don Buford 27
1969 — Paul Blair 20
1970 — Paul Blair 24
1972 — Don Baylor 24
1973 — Don Baylor 32
Al Bumbry 23
1974 — Don Baylor 29

Paul Blair 27
Rich Coggins 26
1975 — Don Baylor 32
1976 — Al Bumbry 42
Reggie Jackson 28
Mark Belanger 27
1977 — Pat Kelly 25
1979 — Al Bumbry 37
1980 — Al Bumbry 44
1981 — Al Bumbry 22

PITCHING LEADERS, BY YEARS

Year	Leader in Wins		Leader in Losses		Leader in IP		Leader in ERA	
	Name	No.	Name	No.	Name	No.	Name	No.
1901	Reidy	15	Garvin	21	Reidy	301	Garvin	3.47
1902	Donahue	22	Powell	17	Powell	328	Donahue	2.76
	Powell	22						
1903	Sudhoff	21	Powell	19	Powell	306	Sudhoff	2.27
1904	Glade	18	Howell	21	Pelty	301	Howell	2.19
1905	Howell	14	Glade	24*	Howell	323	Howell	1.98
1906	Pelty	17	Glade	15	Howell	277	Pelty	1.59
1907	Howell	16	Pelty	21*	Howell	316	Howell	1.94
1908	Waddell	19	Waddell	14	Howell	324	Howell	1.89
							Waddell	1.89
1909	Powell	12	Powell	16	Powell	239	Powell	2.11
1910	Lake	11	Bailey	18	Lake	261	Lake	2.21
			Lake	18				
1911	Lake	10	Powell	19*	Lake	215	Pelty	2.83
1912	B'mgrdnr.	11	B'mgrdnr.	14	Hamilton	250	Brown	3.00
	Hamilton	11	Hamilton	14				
1913	Hamilton	13	Weilman	20*	B'mgrdnr.	253	Hamilton	2.57
	Mitchell	13					Levereny	2.57
1914	Weilman	18	Hamilton	18	Hamilton	302	Weilman	2.08
1915	Weilman	18	L'wdrmlk.	19	Weilman	296	Weilman	2.34
1916	Weilman	17	Weilman	18	Davenport	291	Weilman	2.15
1917	Davenport	17	Groom	19*	Davenport	281	Plank	1.79
			Sothoron	19*				
1918	Sothoron	13	Sothoron	12	Sothoron	209	Sothoron	1.94
1919	Sothoron	20	Gallia	14	Sothoron	270	Weilman	2.07
1920	Shocker	20	Sothoron	15	Davis	269	Shocker	2.71
1921	Shocker	27*	Davis	16	Shocker	327	Shocker	3.55
1922	Shocker	24	Shocker	17	Shocker	348	Pruett	2.32
1923	Shocker	20	Vangilder	17	Vangilder	282	Vangilder	3.06
1924	Shocker	16	Davis	13	Shocker	246	Wingard	3.51
			Shocker	13				
1925	Gaston	15	Bush	14	Gaston	239	Danforth	4.36
			Gaston	14				
1926	Zachary	14	Gaston	18#	Zachary	247	Wingard	3.57
1927	Gaston	13	Gaston	17	Gaston	254	Stewart	4.27
1928	Crowder	21	Ogden	16	Gray	263	Gray	3.19
1929	Gray	18	Blaeholder	15	Gray	305*	Stewart	3.24
			Crowder	15				
			Gray	15				
1930	Stewart	20	Coffman	18	Stewart	271	Stewart	3.45
1931	Stewart	14	Gray	24#	Gray	258	Collins	3.79
					Stewart	258		
1932	Blaeholder	14	Hadley	20*	Stewart	260	Gray	4.52
	Stewart	14						
1933	Blaeholder	15	Hadley	20	Hadley	317*	Hadley	3.92
	Hadley	15						
1934	Newsom	16	Newsom	20*	Newsom	262	Newsom	4.02
1935	Andrews	13	Van Atta	16	Andrews	213	Andrews	3.55

Pitching Leaders, by Years (cont.)

Year	Leader in Wins		Leader in Losses		Leader in IP		Leader in ERA	
	Name	No.	Name	No.	Name	No.	Name	No.
1936	Hogsett	13	Knott	17	Hogsett	215	Andrews	4.85
1937	Walkup	9	Hogsett	19	H'dlebrd.	201	Knott	4.90
1938	Newsom	20	Newsom	16	Newsom	330*	Newsom	5.07
1939	Kennedy	9	Kennedy	17	Kramer	212	Lawson	5.30
	Kramer	9						
1940	Auker	16	Kennedy	17	Auker	264	Auker	3.95
1941	Auker	14	Auker	15	Auker	216	Galehouse	3.65
1942	Niggeling	15	Auker	13	Auker	249	Niggeling	2.67
1943	Sundra	15	H'llgswth.	13	Galehouse	224	Galehouse	2.77
1944	Potter	19	Kramer	13	Kramer	257	Kramer	2.49
1945	Potter	15	Kramer	15	Potter	255	Potter	2.47
1946	Kramer	13	Galehouse	12	Kramer	195	Kramer	3.18
			Muncrief	12				
			Shirley	12				
1947	Kramer	11	Kramer	16	Kramer	199	Zoldak	3.47
			Sanford	16				
1948	Sanford	12	Sanford	21*	Sanford	227	Garver	3.41
1949	Garver	12	Garver	17#	Garver	224	Ferrick	3.89
1950	Garver	13	Garver	18	Garver	260	Garver	3.39
1951	Garver	20	Pillette	14#	Garver	246	Garver	3.73
1952	Cain	12	Byrne	14	Pillette	205	Paige	3.07
	Paige	12						
1953	Stuart	8	Brecheen	13	Larsen	193	Brecheen	3.08
			Pillette	13				
1954	Turley	14	Larsen	21*	Turley	247	Pillette	3.12
1955	Wilson	12	Wilson	18*	Wilson	235	Wight	2.46
1956	Moore	12	Wight	12	Moore	185	Johnson	3.42
1957	Johnson	14	Moore	13	Johnson	242	Zuverink	2.47
1958	P'rtcrro.	15	Harshman	15	Harshman	236	Harshman	2.90
1959	Pappas	15	O'Dell	12	Wilhelm	226	Wilhelm	2.19*
	Wilhelm	15						
1960	Estrada	18#	Estrada	11	Estrada	209	Brown	3.06
			Fisher	11				
			Pappas	11				
1961	Barber	18	Fisher	13	Barber	248	Hoeft	2.02
1962	Pappas	12	Estrada	17#	Estrada	223	Hall	2.29
1963	Barber	20	Barber	13	Barber	259	Miller	2.25
			Roberts	13				
1964	Bunker	19	Barber	13	Pappas	252	Bunker	2.69
1965	Barber	15	Barber	10	Barber	221	Miller	1.89
					Pappas	221		
1966	Palmer	15	Palmer	10	McNally	213	Barber	2.30
1967	Phoebus	14	Miller	10	Phoebus	208	Watt	2.25
			Richert	10				
1968	McNally	22	Phoebus	15	McNally	273	McNally	1.95
1969	Cuellar	23	Cuellar	11	Cuellar	291	Palmer	2.34
1970	Cuellar	24#	Palmer	10	Palmer	305#	Palmer	2.71
	McNally	24#						
1971	McNally	21	Cuellar	9	Cuellar	292	Palmer	2.68
			Palmer	9				

Year	Leader in Wins		Leader in Losses		Leader in IP		Leader in ERA	
	Name	No.	Name	No.	Name	No.	Name	No.
1972	Palmer	21	Dobson	18#	Palmer	274	Palmer	2.07
1973	Palmer	22	McNally	17	Palmer	296	Palmer	2.40*
1974	Cuellar	22	Crimsley	13	Grimsley	296	Grimsley	3.07
1975	Palmer	23#	Grimsley	13	Palmer	323	Palmer	2.09*
1976	Palmer	22*	Cuellar	13	Palmer	315*	Palmer	2.51
			Palmer	13				
1977	Palmer	20#	May	14	Palmer	319*	Palmer	2.91
1978	Palmer	21	Flanagan	15	Palmer	296*	Palmer	2.46
1979	Flanagan	23*	D. M'rtnz.	16	D. M'rtnz.	292*	Flanagan	3.08
1980	Stone	25*	Flanagan	13	McGregor	252	Stone	3.23
1981	D. M'rtnz.	14#	Stewart	8	D. M'rtnz.	179	Stewart	2.33
			Palmer	8				
1982	D. M'rtnz.	16	D. M'rtnz.	12	D. M'rtnz.	252	Palmer	3.13
			McGregor	12				

* League leader.
\# Tied for league lead.

PITCHING LEADERS, BY YEARS

Year	Leader in Games		Leader in CG		Leader in SO		Leader in Saves	
	Name	No.	Name	No.	Name	No.	Name	No.
1901	Reidy	37	Reidy	28	Garvin	122	Garvin	2
	Garvin						Husting	
1902	Powell	42	Powell	36	Powell	137	Powell	3*
1903	Powell	38	Powell	33	Powell	169	Powell	2
	Sudhoff							
1904	Pelty	39	Howell	32	Glade	156	Glade	1
							Pelty	
1905	Howell	38	Howell	35#	Howell	198	Buchanan	2
1906	Howell	35	Howell	30	Howell	140	Pelty	2
	Glade							
1907	Howell	42	Pelty	29	Howell	118	Dinneen	4*
1908	Waddell	43	Howell	27	Waddell	232	Waddell	3
1909	Powell	34	Powell	18	Waddell	141	Powell	3
	Graham							
1910	Lake	35	Lake	24	Lake	141	Lake	2
1911	Hamilton	32	Powell	18	Lake	69	Powell	1
			Pelty				Hamilton	
							Nelson	
1912	Hamilton	41	Powell	21	Hamilton	139	Hamilton	2
1913	Weilman	39	B'mgardner	22	Hamilton	101	Mitchell	1
							Baumgardner	
							Leverenz	
							Schmidt	
1914	Baumgardner	45	Weilman	20	Weilman	119	Mitchell	4#
			Hamilton					
1915	Weilman	47	Weilman	19	Lowdermilk	130	Weilman	4
1916	Davenport	59*	Weilman	19	Davenport	129	Plank	4
1917	Sothoron	48	Davenport	19	Davenport	100	Sothoron	4
1918	Davenport	31	Sothoron	14	Sothoron	71	Shocker	2
							Houck	
							Rogers	

PITCHING LEADERS, BY YEARS

Year	Leader in Games		Leader in CG		Leader in SO		Leader in Saves	
	Name	No.	Name	No.	Name	No.	Name	No.
1919	Sothoron	40	Sothoron	21	Sothoron	106	Sothoron	3
1920	Shocker Davis	38	Shocker Davis	22	Shocker	107	Shocker	5#
1921	Shocker Bayne	47	Shocker	31	Shocker	132	Shocker	4
1922	Shocker	48	Shocker	29	Shocker	149*	Pruett	7
1923	Shocker	43	Shocker	25	Shocker	109	Shocker	5
1924	Vangilder	43	Shocker	17	Shocker	88	Danforth	4
1925	Vangilder	52	Gaston	16	Gaston	84	Vangilder	6
1926	Ballou	43	Zachary	18	Ballou	59	Wingard	3
1927	Vangilder	44	Gaston	21	Gaston	77	Crowder	3
1928	Crowder	41	Gray	21	Gray	102	Gray Blaeholder Stewart	3
1929	Gray	43	Gray	23	Gray	109	Crowder	4
1930	Kimsey	42	Stewart	23	Stewart	79	Blaeholder	4
1931	Gray	43	Stewart	20	Stewart	89	Kimsey	7
1932	Gray	52	Stewart	18	Hadley	132	Gray	4
1933	Hadley	45	Hadley	19	Hadley	149	Gray	4
1934	Newsom	47	Newsom	15	Newsom	135	Newsom	5
1935	Walkup	55	Andrews	10	Van Atta	87	Knott	7*
1936	Van Atta	52*	Andrews	11	Hogsett	67	Knott	6
1937	Knott	38	Hildebrand	12	Hildebrand	75	Knott Hogsett	2
1938	Newsom	44	Newsom	31*	Newsom	226	Johnson Cole	3
1939	Trotter	41	Kennedy	12	Mills	103	Mills	2
1940	Auker	38	Auker	20	Niggeling	82	Lawson	4
1941	Muncrief	36	Auker Niggeling	13	Niggeling	68	Caster	3
1942	Caster	39	Auker	17	Niggeling	107	Caster	5
1943	Caster Muncrief Hollingsworth	35	Galehouse	14	Galehouse	114	Caster	8
1944	Caster	42	Kramer	18	Kramer	124	Caster	12#
1945	Potter Shirley	32	Potter	21	Potter	129	Jakucki Kramer	2
1946	Zoldak	35	Kramer	13	Galehouse	90	Ferrick	5
1947	Zoldak	35	Kinder	10	Kinder	110	Sanford	4
1948	Widmar	49	Fannin	10	Fannin	102	Garver	5
1949	Ferrick	50	Garver	16	Garver	70	Ferrick	6
1950	Garver	37	Garver	22#	Garver	85	Widmar	4
1951	Pillette	35	Garver	24*	Garver	84	Paige	5
1952	Paige	46	Byrne	14	Paige Byrne	91	Paige	10
1953	Stuart	60	Larsen	7	Littlefield	104	Paige	11
1954	Chakales Fox	38	Coleman	15	Turley	185*	Chakales	3
1955	Moore	46	Wilson	14	Wilson	96	Moore Dorish	6

Year	Leader in Games		Leader in CG		Leader in SO		Leader in Saves	
	Name	No.	Name	No.	Name	No.	Name	No.
1956	Zuverink	62*	Moore Johnson	9	Johnson	130	Zuverink	16*
1957	Zuverink	56*	Johnson	14	Johnson	177	Zuverink	9
1958	Zuverink	45	Harshman	17	Harshman	161	O'Dell	8
1959	O'Dell	38	Pappas	15	Wilhelm	139	Loes	14
1960	Wilhelm	41	Estrada	12	Estrada	144	Wilhelm	7
1961	Wilhelm	51	Barber	14	Estrada	160	Wilhelm	18
1962	Hoeft	57	Pappas	9	Estrada	165	Wilhelm	15
1963	Miller	71*	Barber Pappas	11	Barber	180	Miller	27*
1964	Miller	66	Pappas	13	Pappas	157	Miller	23
1965	Miller	67	Pappas	9	Barber	130	Miller	24
1966	Miller	51	Palmer	6	McNally	158	Miller	18
1967	Watt	49	Phoebus	7	Phoebus	179	Drabowsky	12
1968	Watt	59	McNally	18	McNally	202	Watt	11
1969	Watt	56	Cuellar	18	Cuellar	182	Watt	16
1970	Watt	53	Cuellar	21*	Palmer	199	Richert	13
1971	Dobson Cuellar	38	Cuellar	21	Dobson	187	Watt	11
1972	Harrison	39	Palmer	18	Palmer	184	Jackson	8
1973	Jackson	45	Palmer	19	Palmer	158	Jackson Reynolds	9
1974	Reynolds	54	Cuellar	20	Grimsley	158	Jackson	12
1975	Jackson	41	Palmer	25	Palmer	193	D. Miller	8
1976	D. Miller	49	Palmer	23	Palmer	159	T. Martinez	8
1977	D. Martinez	42	Palmer	22#	Palmer	193	T. Martinez	9
1978	Stanhouse	56	Palmer	19	Flanagan	167	Stanhouse	24
1979	Stanhouse	52	D. Martinez	18*	Flanagan	190	Stanhouse	21
1980	Stoddard	64	McGregor	12	Stone	149	Stoddard	26
1981	T. Martinez	37	D. Martinez	9	D. Martinez	88	T. Martinez	11
1982	T. Martinez	76	Flanagan	11	D. Martinez	111	T. Martinez	16

* Led American League.
# Tied for American League lead.

CAREER PITCHING LEADERS

Browns, 1902–53

Games — Elam Vangilder, 323
Complete Games — Jack Powell, 208
Innings Pitched — Jack Powell, 2,222
Wins — Urban Shocker, 126
Losses — Jack Powell, 142
Winning Percentage — Urban Shocker, .612
Shutouts — Jack Powell, 26
Earned Run Average — Carl Weilman, 2.68
Hits Allowed — Jack Powell, 2,093
Walks — Dixie Davis, 640
Strikeouts — Jack Powell, 879

CAREER PITCHING LEADERS

Orioles, 1954–82

GAMES

Jim Palmer	539
Dave McNally	412
Eddie Watt	363
Dick Hall	342
Tippy Martinez	316
Stu Miller	297
Mike Cuellar	290
Milt Pappas	264
Steve Barber	253
Mike Flanagan	230

INNINGS

Jim Palmer	3,853
Dave McNally	2,653
Mike Cuellar	2,028
Milt Pappas	1,632
Mike Flanagan	1,480
Steve Barber	1,415
Dennis Martinez	1,294
Scott McGregor	1,175
Hal Brown	1,032
Ross Grimsley	908

WINS

Jim Palmer	263
Dave McNally	181
Mike Cuellar	143
Milt Pappas	110
Mike Flanagan	100
Steve Barber	95
Dennis Martinez	82
Scott McGregor	78
Dick Hall	65
Hal Brown	62

LOSSES

Jim Palmer	145
Dave McNally	113
Mike Cuellar	88
Steve Barber	75
Milt Pappas	74
Mike Flanagan	70
Dennis Martinez	57
Hal Brown	48
Scott McGregor	50
Ross Grimsley	45

WON-LOSS PERCENTAGE*

Steve Stone	.656
Jim Palmer	.645
Wally Bunker	.620
Mike Cuellar	.619
Dick Hall	.619
Dave McNally	.616
Scott McGregor	.609
Milt Pappas	.598
Dennis Martinez	.590
Mike Flanagan	.588

COMPLETE GAMES

Jim Palmer	211
Mike Cuellar	133
Dave McNally	120
Milt Pappas	81
Mike Flanagan	78
Dennis Martinez	60
Steve Barber	53
Scott McGregor	48
Ross Grimsley	38
Pat Dobson	31

* Based on 50 or more decisions.

SHUTOUTS

Jim Palmer	53
Dave McNally	33
Mike Cuellar	30
Milt Pappas	26
Steve Barber	19
Mike Flanagan	14
Scott McGregor	14
Tom Phoebus	11
Hal Brown	9
Dennis Martinez	9
Pat Dobson	7
Ross Grimsley	7
Jim Hardin	7
Robin Roberts	7

STRIKEOUTS

Jim Palmer	2,174
Dave McNally	1,476
Mike Cuellar	1,011
Milt Pappas	944
Steve Barber	917
Mike Flanagan	872
Dennis Martinez	640
Tom Phoebus	578
Scott McGregor	521
Chuck Estrada	517

EARNED RUN AVERAGE*

Stu Miller	2.37
Hoyt Wilhelm	2.42
Eddie Watt	2.73
Pat Dobson	2.78
Jim Palmer	2.80
Billy O'Dell	2.87
Dick Hall	2.89
Jim Hardin	2.95
Tom Phoebus	3.06
Robin Roberts	3.09

SAVES**

Stu Miller	88
Eddie Watt	72
Tippy Martinez	62
Dick Hall	51
Tim Stoddard	48
Don Stanhouse	45
Grant Jackson	39
Hoyt Wilhelm	35
Pete Richert	29
Moe Drabowsky	23

* 500 or more innings.
** 1975 rule applied.

20-GAME WINNERS

Browns

1902 — Red Donahue	22	1923 — Urban Shocker	20
Jack Powell	22	1928 — General Crowder	21
1903 — Willie Sudhoff	21	Sam Gray	20
1919 — Allen Sothoron	20	1930 — Lefty Stewart	20
1920 — Urban Shocker	20	1938 — Bobo Newsom	20
1921 — Urban Shocker	27	1951 — Ned Garver	20
1922 — Urban Shocker	24		

Career Pitching Leaders (continued)

Orioles

1963 — Steve Barber 20
1968 — Dave McNally 22
1969 — Mike Cuellar 23
       Dave McNally 20
1970 — Mike Cuellar 24
       Dave McNally 24
       Jim Palmer 21
1971 — Dave McNally 21
       Mike Cuellar 20
       Jim Palmer 20
       Pat Dobson 20
1972 — Jim Palmer 21

1973 — Jim Palmer 22
1974 — Mike Cuellar 22
1975 — Jim Palmer 23
       Mike Torrez 20
1976 — Jim Palmer 22
       Wayne Garland 20
1977 — Jim Palmer 20
1978 — Jim Palmer 21
1979 — Mike Flanagan 23
1980 — Steve Stone 25
       Scott McGregor 20

NO-HIT GAMES

By Browns Pitchers

1912 — Earl Hamilton vs. Detroit, August 30 (at Detroit) 5-1
1917 — Ernie Koob vs. Chicago, May 5 (at St. Louis) 1-0
       Bob Groom vs. Chicago, May 6 (at St. Louis) 3-0
1934 — Bobo Newsom vs. Boston, September 18 (at St. Louis) 1-2
       no-hitter for $9\frac{2}{3}$ innings, lost in 10th on hit
1953 — Bobo Holloman vs. Philadelphia, May 6 (at St. Louis) 6-0

Versus Browns

1905 — Weldon Henley, Philadelphia, July 22 (at St. Louis) 6-0
1911 — Smokey Joe Wood, Boston, July 29 (at Boston) 5-0
1912 — George Mullin, Detroit, July 4 (at Detroit) 7-0
1916 — Dutch Leonard, Boston, August 30 (at Boston) 4-0
1917 — Ed Cicotte, Chicago, April 14 (at St. Louis) 11-0
1931 — Wes Ferrell, Cleveland, April 29 (at Cleveland) 9-0
1937 — Bill Dietrich, Chicago, June 1 (at Chicago) 8-0
1945 — Dick Fowler, Philadelphia, September 9 (at Philadelphia) 1-0

By Orioles Pitchers

1958 — Hoyt Wilhelm vs. New York, September 20 (at Baltimore) 1-0
1967 — Steve Barber & Stu Miller vs. Detroit, April 30 (at Baltimore) 1-2
1968 — Tom Phoebus vs. Boston, April 27 (at Baltimore) 6-0
1969 — Jim Palmer vs. Oakland, August 13 (at Baltimore) 8-0

Versus Orioles

1962 — Bo Belinsky, Los Angeles, May 5 (at Los Angeles) 2-0
1975 — Nolan Ryan, California, June 1 (at California) 1-0

CLUB SEASON RECORDS

Browns

HITTING

Games — Del Pratt, 159 in 1915
At-Bats — John Tobin, 671 in 1921
Runs — Harlond Clift, 145 in 1936
Hits — George Sisler, 257 in 1920*
Batting Average — George Sisler, .420 in 1922
Singles — John Tobin, 179 in 1921
Doubles — Beau Bell, 51 in 1937
Triples — Heinie Manush, 20 in 1928
Home Runs — Ken Williams, 39 in 1922
Runs Batted In — Ken Williams, 155 in 1922
Stolen Bases — George Sisler, 51 in 1922 (out of 70 attempts)
Strikeouts — Gus Williams, 143 in 1914
Walks — Bird Blue, 126 in 1929
Hit By Pitch — Frank O'Rourke, 12 in 1927

---

* Major league record for a single season.

PITCHING

Games — Marlin Stuart, 60 in 1953
Complete Games — Jack Powell, 36 in 1902
Innings Pitched — Urban Shocker, 348 in 1922
Wins — Urban Shocker, 27 in 1922
Losses — Fred Glade, 25 in 1905
Winning Percentage — General Crowder, .808 (21-5) in 1928
Shutouts — Fred Glade, 6 in 1904; Harry Howell, 6 in 1906
Earned Run Average — Carl Weilman, 2.20 in 307 innings in 1914
Walks — Bobo Newsom, 192 in 1938
Strikeouts — Rube Waddell, 232 in 1908

Orioles

HITTING

Games — Brooks Robinson, 163 in 1961 and 1964
At-Bats — Brooks Robinson, 668 in 1961
Runs — Frank Robinson, 122 in 1966
Hits — Al Bumbry, 205 in 1980
Batting Average — Al Bumbry, .337 in 1973
Singles — Al Bumbry, 158 in 1980
Doubles — Brooks Robinson, 38 in 1961
Triples — Paul Blair, 12 in 1967
Home Runs — Frank Robinson, 49 in 1966
Runs Batted In — Jim Gentile, 141 in 1961
Stolen Bases — Luis Aparicio, 57 in 1964
Strikeouts — Boog Powell, 125 in 1966
Walks — Ken Singleton, 118 in 1975
Hit By Pitch — Bobby Grich, 20 in 1974
Pinch-Hits — Dave Philley, 24 in 1961*
Sacrifice Hits — Mark Belanger, 23 in 1975
Consecutive Games Hit Safely — Doug DeCinces, 21 in 1978

---

* American League record.

PITCHING

Games — Tippy Martinez, 76 in 1982
Complete Games — Jim Palmer, 25 in 1975
Games Started — Dave McNally, 40 in 1969 and 1970
      Mike Cuellar, 40 in 1970
      Mike Flanagan, 40 in 1978
Games Finished — Stu Miller, 59 in 1963
Innings Pitched — Jim Palmer, 323 in 1975
Wins — Steve Stone, 25 in 1980
Losses — Don Larsen, 21 in 1954
Winning Percentage — Dave McNally, .808 (21-5) in 1971
Shutouts — Jim Palmer, 10 in 1975
Earned Run Average — Dave McNally, 1.95 in 1968
Walks — Bob Turley, 181 in 1954
Strikeouts — Dave McNally, 202 in 1968
Home Runs Allowed — Robin Roberts, 35 in 1963
Saves — Tim Stoddard, 26 in 1980

WORLD SERIES AND PLAYOFFS

1944 World Series

For once, the impossible dream of the Browns came true. However, the only pennant winner in the team's history was not a powerhouse like the mighty 1922 Brown lineup. It was wartime baseball at its best and worst as the Brownies fought tooth and nail down to the final day to edge out the Tigers for the crown.

The Brown win set up an unusual World Series—all the games would be played in the same park, Sportsman's Park, because the hometown rival St. Louis Cardinals nailed down the National League title for the third straight year. Clearly, the Redbirds rated their favorites' role while the Browns tugged at the heartstrings of those who loved the underdog.

The Browns were led by their power-hitting shortstop Vern Stephens while the Cards countered with league MVP shortstop Marty Marion and a young Stan Musial.

 Game 1 at St. Louis (N)— October 4   33,242
 St. Louis (A) 0 0 0   2 0 0   0 0 0—2 2 0   WP Galehouse
 St. Louis (N) 0 0 0   0 0 0   0 0 1—1 7 0   LP M. Cooper

Despite a two-hitter by Mort Cooper, the Browns managed to make the most of their safeties as Gene Moore singled and George McQuinn homered in the fourth inning. Denny Galehouse hurled a seven-hitter to hold the Redbirds at bay.

 Game 2 at St. Louis (N)— October 5   35,076
 St. Louis (A) 0 0 0   0 0 0   2 0 0   0 0—2 7 4 LP Muncrief
 St. Louis (N) 0 0 1   1 0 0   0 0 0   0 1—3 7 0 WP Donnelly

A pinch-single by Ken O'Dea in the bottom of the 11th off Bob Muncrief evened up the Series for the Cardinals as rookie reliever Blix Donnelly held the Browns for four shutout innings.

Game 3 at St. Louis (A)— October 6   34,737
St. Louis (N) 1 0 0 0 0 0 1 0 0—2 7 0   LP Wilks
St. Louis (A) 0 0 4 0 0 0 2 0 x—6 8 2   WP Kramer

A four-run third inning off Cardinal rookie Ted Wilks powered the Browns to a 6-2 win in game three of the Series. The Browns ran off five straight singles by Gene Moore, Vern Stephens, George McQuinn, Al Zarilla, and Mark Christman to chase Wilks from the mound. Jack Kramer threw a seven-hitter and struck out 10 Redbirds to lead the Browns to victory.

Game 4 at St. Louis (A)— October 7   35,455
St. Louis (N) 2 0 2 0 0 1 0 0 0—5 12 0   WP Brecheen
St. Louis (A) 0 0 0 0 0 0 0 1 0—1 9 1   LP Jakucki

The Browns suffered total frustration at the hands of Harry "The Cat" Brecheen, banging out nine hits and stranding 10 men on base while scoring only once. Card right fielder Stan Musial enjoyed a big day with three hits, including a double and homer, and two RBIs.

Game 5 at St. Louis (A)— October 8   36,568
St. Louis (N) 0 0 0 0 0 1 0 1 0—2 6 1   WP M. Cooper
St. Louis (A) 0 0 0 0 0 0 0 0 0—0 7 1   LP Galehouse

In a replay of game one, Mort Cooper pitched another fine game for the National Leaguers and this time came out on top. Denny Galehouse threw a six-hitter and struck out 10, but gave up home runs to Ray Sanders and Danny Litwhiler for the two Redbird runs.

Game 6 at St. Louis (N)— October 9   31,630
St. Louis (A) 0 1 0 0 0 0 0 0 0—1 3 2   LP Potter
St. Louis (N) 0 0 0 3 0 0 0 0 x—3 10 0   WP Lanier

A throwing error by shortstop Vern Stephens in the fourth inning opened the door to a three-run inning, giving the Cardinals the runs needed to clinch the World Championship. Dreams die hard and this one was never meant to be.

Top Brown hitter— First baseman George McQuinn, 7 for 16, 2 doubles, 1 HR, 5 RBIs, 7 walks, .438
Top Brown pitcher— Denny Galehouse, 2 complete games, 1 win, 15 strikeouts, 1.50 ERA
Top Cardinal hitter— Second baseman Emil Verban, 7 for 17, 2 RBIs, .412
Top Cardinal pitcher— Mort Cooper, 2 games, 1 complete game, 1 win, 16 strikeouts, 1.13 ERA
Winning player's share— $4,626
Losing player's share— $2,744

1966 World Series

Paced by Triple Crown winner Frank Robinson, Baltimore won its first pennant going away from the rest of the American League. Their World Series rivals, the Los Angeles Dodgers, had repeated as National League champs on the strength of a pitching staff led by the likes of Sandy Koufax and Don Drysdale.

All the experts expected Dodger pitching to tell the tale of this Fall Classic—but few, if any, dreamed that the mastery of the Oriole staff would be the order of the day.

Game 1 at Los Angeles— October 5	55,941
Baltimore 3 1 0 1 0 0 0 0 0—5 9 0	WP Drabowsky
Los Angeles 0 1 1 0 0 0 0 0 0—2 3 0	LP Drysdale

A walk to Russ Snyder and back-to-back home runs by the Robinsons (Frank and Brooks) gave the Orioles a quick 3-0 lead in the first inning of game one. But the real story of the day was the unbelievable performance of Moe Drabowsky in relief of a wild Dave McNally. Moe hurled 6⅔ innings of one-hit, shutout relief for the win, striking out 11 Dodgers, including six in a row.

Game 2 at Los Angeles— October 6	55,947
Baltimore 0 0 0 0 3 1 0 2 0—6 8 0	WP Palmer
Los Angeles 0 0 0 0 0 0 0 0 0—0 4 6	LP Koufax

Jim Palmer threw a sterling four-hitter to shackle the Dodgers in game two, 6-0. A three-run Oriole fifth inning gave the Birds all the runs they needed, thanks to three errors by center fielder Willie Davis, ordinarily a defensive standout.

Game 3 at Baltimore— October 8	54,445
Los Angeles 0 0 0 0 0 0 0 0 0—0 6 0	LP Osteen
Baltimore 0 0 0 0 1 0 0 0 x—1 3 0	WP Bunker

Down by two games, the Dodgers pinned their hopes on Claude Osteen's strong left arm—unfortunately, he threw a three-hitter only to lose on a homer to Paul Blair. The Orioles continued their shutout mastery of the Dodgers as Wally Bunker hurled a six-hit shutout.

Game 4 at Baltimore— October 9	54,458
Los Angeles 0 0 0 0 0 0 0 0 0—0 4 0	LP Drysdale
Baltimore 0 0 0 1 0 0 0 0 x—1 4 0	WP McNally

The Birds won their first World's Championship behind the brilliant pitching of southpaw Dave McNally, who outdueled Don Drysdale to win 1-0. Appropriately, a Frank Robinson home run proved the margin of difference.

The excellence of the Oriole pitching in this Series remains virtually unchallenged, as the young O's threw 33 consecutive shutout innings at the Dodgers.

Top Oriole hitter— Right fielder Frank Robinson, 2 HRs, 4 runs, 3 RBIs
Top Oriole pitcher— Moe Drabowsky, 11 strikeouts, 0.00 ERA
Top Dodger hitter— Right fielder Lou Johnson, 4 for 15, .267
Top Dodger pitcher— Claude Osteen, 1 run in 7 innings, 1.29 ERA
Winning player's share— $11,683
Losing player's share— $8,189

1969 A.L. Championship Series

Baltimore took the league's Eastern Division title to enter the first Championship Series in American League history. The O's faced a powerful Minnesota Twins club led by slugger Harmon Killebrew. The Orioles had most of the leaders from the '66 champs, with the addition of Don Buford and Mark Belanger.

Game 1 at Baltimore— October 4   39,324
Minnesota   0 0 0 0 1 0 2 0 0 0 0 0—3 4 2   LP Perranoski
Baltimore   0 0 0 1 1 0 0 0 1 0 0 1—4 10 1   WP Hall

A two-out suicide squeeze bunt by Paul Blair scored Mark Belanger in the 12th inning to beat the Twins in the league series opener. Aiding the Birds' cause were solo homers by Frank Robinson, Mark Belanger, and Boog Powell.

Game 2 at Baltimore— October 5   41,704
Minnesota   0 0 0 0 0 0 0 0 0 0 0—0 3 1   LP Boswell
Baltimore   0 0 0 0 0 0 0 0 0 0 1—1 8 0   WP McNally

Southpaw Dave McNally hung tough, going 11 innings and striking out 10 to beat the Twins 1–0 in game two. With two outs in the 11th, Curt Motton pinch-hit for catcher Elrod Hendricks and drove in Boog Powell with a line single over Twin second sacker Rod Carew's outstretched glove.

Game 3 at Minnesota— October 6   32,735
Baltimore   0 3 0 2 0 1 0 2 3—11 18 0   WP Palmer
Minnesota   1 0 0 0 1 0 0 0 0— 2 10 2   LP Miller

Baltimore swept the Championship Series, shellacking the Twins in Bloomington, 11–2. Center fielder Paul Blair led the attack with a homer and two doubles for 5 RBIs. Other big bats belonged to Don Buford, who banged out four hits, and Ellie Hendricks, who drove in three runs.

Top Oriole hitter— Center fielder Paul Blair, 6 for 15, 11 total bases, 6 RBIs, .400
Top Oriole pitcher— Dave McNally, 11 strikeouts in 11 innings, 1 win, 0.00 ERA
Top Twin hitter— Right fielder Tony Oliva, 5 for 13, 10 total bases, .385
Top Twin pitcher— Dave Boswell, 10⅔ innings, 0.84 ERA

1969 World Series

The Orioles entered the Series heavily favored to beat the surprising New York Mets, who had rushed past Chicago to take the National League Eastern Division and then beat Atlanta in three straight games for the pennant.

But the Amazin' Mets had not run out of miracles, as Earl Weaver and Company soon would find out.

Game 1 at Baltimore— October 11   50,429
New York   0 0 0 0 0 0 1 0 0—1 6 1   LP Seaver
Baltimore   1 0 0 3 0 0 0 0 x—4 6 0   WP Cuellar

The Birds got out to a quick one-game lead as Mike Cuellar hurled a six-hitter. The O's scored first when left fielder Don Buford hit Tom Seaver's second pitch over the right field fence. Singles by Mark Belanger and Mike Cuellar and a Buford double scored three runs in the fourth.

Game 2 at Baltimore—October 12   50,850
New York   0 0 0   1 0 0   0 0 1—2 6 0   WP Koosman
Baltimore   0 0 0   0 0 0   1 0 0—1 2 0   LP McNally

The Orioles could manage only two hits off Jerry Koosman; while a Donn Clendenon homer and Al Weis single gave the Mets the runs they needed to win and even up the Series.

Game 3 at New York—October 14   56,335
Baltimore   0 0 0   0 0 0   0 0 0—0 4 1   LP Palmer
New York   1 2 0   0 0 1   0 1 x—5 6 0   WP Gentry

Great fielding by center fielder Tommie Agee kept the Birds in check in game three as the Birds could not score off starter Gary Gentry and reliever Nolan Ryan. The fleet Agee saved two runs in the fourth with a one-hand running catch at the base of the wall and stopped a potential three-run rally in the seventh with a sliding catch in right center.

Game 4 at New York—October 15   57,367
Baltimore   0 0 0   0 0 0   0 0 1   0—1 6 1   LP Hall
New York   0 1 0   0 0 0   0 0 0   1—2 10 1   WP Seaver

A great pitching effort by Tom Seaver stopped the O's in game four and put them down three games to one. Seaver went 10 innings to beat Baltimore. The Orioles' chance for a big rally in the ninth died when right fielder Ron Swoboda made a spectacular diving catch to rob Brooks Robinson of a triple.

Game 5 at New York—October 16   57,397
Baltimore   0 0 3   0 0 0   0 0 0—3 5 2   LP Watt
New York   0 0 0   0 0 2   1 2 x—5 7 0   WP Koosman

The Mets completed their Impossible Dream season with a 5-3 win over Baltimore behind the five-hit pitching of Jerry Koosman. Third-inning homers by Dave McNally and Frank Robinson did not stand up to homers by Donn Clendenon and Al Weis.

Top Oriole hitter— First baseman Boog Powell, 5 for 19, .263
Top Oriole pitcher— Mike Cuellar, 13 strikeouts, 1.13 ERA
Top Met hitter— First baseman Donn Clendenon, 3 HRs, 4 RBIs, .357
Top Met pitcher— Jerry Koosman, 2 wins, 9 strikeouts, 2.04 ERA
Winning player's share— $13,260
Losing player's share— $9,350

1970 A.L. Championship Series

The year 1970 brought a repeat of the previous year's winners, as the O's and Twins squared off once more for the American League crown. The Twins were led by 24-game winner Jim Perry while the Birds boasted two 24-game winners in Mike Cuellar and Dave McNally.

```
Game 1 at Minnesota—October 3                    26,847
Baltimore    0 2 0  7 0 1  0 0 0—10 13 0         WP R. Hall
Minnesota    1 1 0  1 3 0  0 0 0— 6 11 2         LP Perry
```

The O's erupted for seven runs in the fourth inning of game one, paced by a grand slam by starting pitcher Mike Cuellar. Harmon Killebrew homered for the losing Twins.

```
Game 2 at Minnesota—October 4                    27,490
Baltimore    1 0 2  1 0 0  0 0 7—11 13 0         WP McNally
Minnesota    0 0 0  3 0 0  0 0 0— 3  6 2         LP T. Hall
```

Baltimore continued its dominance of the Twins as Dave McNally threw a six-hitter to win game two 11-3. Homers by Frank Robinson and Dave Johnson led the Oriole attack.

```
Game 3 at Baltimore—October 5                    27,608
Minnesota    0 0 0  0 1 0  0 0 0—1  7 2          LP Kaat
Baltimore    1 1 3  0 0 0  1 0 x—6 10 0          WP Palmer
```

The Birds rapped up another league pennant by sweeping the Twins three straight. Jim Palmer went the distance for the win as Brooks Robinson rapped three hits and Davy Johnson homered.

Top Oriole hitter—First baseman Boog Powell, 6 for 14, 6 RBIs, .429
Top Oriole pitcher—Jim Palmer, 1 win, 1 complete game, 1.00 ERA
Top Twin hitter—Right fielder Tony Oliva, 6 for 12, .500
Top Twin pitcher—Stan Williams, 2 games, 6 innings, 0.00 ERA

1970 World Series

Despite their easy win over the Twins, the Orioles could not take the World Series for granted. They faced the vaunted Big Red Machine, the Cincinnati Reds, who had bumped off the Pittsburgh Pirates in the National League title fight.

The Series gave Frank Robinson a chance to encounter his former team, which was now led by Johnny Bench, Pete Rose, and Tony Perez.

```
Game 1 at Cincinnati—October 10                  51,531
Baltimore    0 0 0  2 1 0  1 0 0—4 7 2           WP Palmer
Cincinnati   1 0 2  0 0 0  0 0 0—3 5 0           LP Nolan
```

Three home runs by Boog Powell, Elrod Hendricks, and Brooks Robinson gave Jim Palmer the ammunition he needed to beat the Reds in Riverfront Stadium, 4-3. The game provided the first glimpse of what would become some of the most memorable fielding ever by a third baseman—Brooks Robinson became the "Human Vacuum Cleaner," sucking up vicious shots down the third base line. The game also featured a controversial call at home plate in which Bernie Carbo was tagged out in a close one by Elrod Hendricks.

171

1970 World Series (continued)

Game 2 at Cincinnati— October 11   51,531

| Baltimore | 0 0 0 | 1 5 0 | 0 0 0—6 | 10 2 | WP Phoebus |
| Cincinnati | 3 0 1 | 0 0 1 | 0 0 0—5 | 7 0 | LP Wilcox |

For the second day in a row, the Reds squandered an early lead and lost to the O's, this time 6-5. The Birds enjoyed a five-run rally in the fifth, capped by an Elrod Hendricks double.

Game 3 at Baltimore— October 13   51,773

| Cincinnati | 0 1 0 | 0 0 0 | 2 0 0—3 | 9 0 | LP Cloninger |
| Baltimore | 2 0 1 | 0 1 4 | 1 0 x—9 | 10 1 | WP McNally |

Game three found Cincinnati on the ropes and ready for the knockout as lefty Dave McNally scattered nine hits and slugged a grand slam to left field to lead a 9-3 Oriole win. Brooks Robinson continued his sensational fielding and hit a two-run double.

Game 4 at Baltimore— October 14   53,007

| Cincinnati | 0 1 1 | 0 1 0 | 0 3 0—6 | 8 3 | WP Carroll |
| Baltimore | 0 1 3 | 0 0 1 | 0 0 0—5 | 8 0 | LP Watt |

A clutch 8th inning home run by first baseman Lee May gave the Big Red Machine its only win of the Series as the Reds beat the O's 6-5 to end a 17-game winning streak for the Birds. The Orioles had won their last 11 games of the season, three against the Twins and three versus the Reds.

Game 5 at Baltimore— October 15   45,341

| Cincinnati | 3 0 0 | 0 0 0 | 0 0 0—3 | 6 0 | LP Merritt |
| Baltimore | 2 2 2 | 0 1 0 | 0 2 x—9 | 15 0 | WP Cuellar |

Baltimore wrapped up its second World's Championship in five years, beating the Reds 9-3 to take the Series four games to one. A 15-hit Bird attack gave Mike Cuellar the offense needed to win the game. Frank Robinson and Merv Rettenmund slugged homers to aid the win.

Top Oriole hitter— Third baseman Brooks Robinson, 9 for 21, 2 HRs, 6 RBIs, .429

Top Oriole pitcher— Dave McNally, 1 win, 1 complete game, 3.00 ERA

Top Red hitter— First baseman Lee May, 2 HRs, 8 RBIs, .389

Top Red pitcher— Clay Carroll, 4 games, 1 win, 9 innings, 11 strikeouts, 0.00 ERA

Winning player's share— $18,216

Losing player's share— $13,688

1971 A.L. Championship Series

The defending World Champion Orioles breezed to another Eastern Division title, winning their last 11 regular season games. They faced Charlie Finley's upstart Oakland A's, who were led by slugger Reggie Jackson and rookie pitching sensation Vida Blue.

The O's entered the league series with more experience and depth and it quickly showed.

Game 1 at Baltimore— October 3   42,621
Oakland   0 2 0 1 0 0 0 0 0—3 9 0   LP Blue
Baltimore   0 0 0 1 0 0 4 0 x—5 7 1   WP McNally

After getting just one run off Vida Blue in the first six innings, the O's exploded in the seventh for four runs, with Paul Blair's two-run double keying the uprising. Southpaw Dave McNally survived a shaky start to get the win in game one.

Game 2 at Baltimore— October 4   35,003
Oakland   0 0 0 1 0 0 0 0 0—1 6 0   LP Hunter
Baltimore   0 1 1 0 0 0 1 2 x—5 7 0   WP Cuellar

Four Oriole home runs gave Mike Cuellar all the runs he needed in game two's duel with Catfish Hunter. First baseman Boog Powell slugged two homers for 3 RBIs while Brooks Robinson and Elrod Hendricks added solo shots.

Game 3 at Oakland— October 5   33,176
Baltimore   1 0 0 0 2 0 2 0 0—5 12 0   WP Palmer
Oakland   0 0 1 0 0 1 0 1 0—3 7 0   LP Segui

The Orioles swept the series three games to none as Brooks Robinson delivered a clutch fifth-inning single with the bases loaded to break a 1-1 tie. Brooks' hit came after an intentional walk to Elrod Hendricks to load the bases. Jim Palmer hung on for the win despite giving up three homers, two to Reggie Jackson, one to Sal Bando.

Top Oriole hitter— Third baseman Brooks Robinson, 4 for 11, 8 total bases, 3 RBIs, .364
Top Oriole pitcher— Mike Cuellar, 1 win, 1 complete game, 1.00 ERA
Top A's hitter— Right fielder Reggie Jackson, 11 total bases, 2 HRs, .333
Top A's pitcher— Mudcat Grant, 2 innings, 0 runs, 0.00 ERA

1971 World Series

The 1971 Fall Classic made history by being the first to feature night games. But even more important, it will be long remembered for becoming a personal show-case for the brilliant Pirate right fielder Roberto Clemente.

The Bucs had vanquished the Giants to get into the Series, thus dealing a double disappointment to the Bay area. In addition to the Great Roberto, Pittsburgh boasted a young slugger in Willie Stargell, who had hit 48 home runs and driven in 125 runs during the season.

But the Orioles were not intimidated. They had won their third straight pennant and had a strong lineup, featuring Brooks and Frank Robinson and Boog Powell. They also had four 20-game winners in Jim Palmer, Mike Cuellar, Dave McNally and Pat Dobson.

173

1971 World Series (continued)

Game 1 at Baltimore— October 9   53,229
Pittsburgh   0 3 0   0 0 0   0 0 0—3 3 0   LP Ellis
Baltimore   0 1 3   0 1 0   0 0 x—5 10 3   WP McNally

The Orioles came back from a three-run deficit to beat the Bucs in game one, as Dave McNally threw a three-hitter and struck out nine. A three-run homer by Merv Rettenmund and solo shots by Frank Robinson and Don Buford paced the win.

Game 2 at Baltimore— October 11   53,239
Pittsburgh   0 0 0   0 0 0   0 3 0— 3 8 1   LP R. Johnson
Baltimore   0 1 0   3 6 1   0 0 x— 11 14 1   WP Palmer

After a day's rain delay, the Series resumed, with the Orioles continuing their dominance of the Pirates. The Birds banged out 14 hits against the Pirate pitching and Brooks Robinson tied a Series record by getting on base five straight times (3 hits and 2 walks).

Game 3 at Pittsburgh— October 12   50,403
Baltimore   0 0 0   0 0 0   1 0 0—1 3 3   LP Cuellar
Pittsburgh   1 0 0   0 0 1   3 0 x—5 7 0   WP Blass

Back in their home park, the Pirates bounced back as Steve Blass threw a three-hitter and struck out eight to beat the Birds, 5-1. A three-run homer by first baseman Bob Robertson was the big blow for the Bucs.

Game 4 at Pittsburgh— October 13   51,378
Baltimore   3 0 0   0 0 0   0 0 0—3 4 1   LP Dobson
Pittsburgh   2 0 1   0 0 0   1 0 x—4 14 0   WP Kison

Game four was the historic first night game for the Series and 21-year-old Bruce Kison provided plenty of drama as he pitched 6⅓ innings of one-hit relief to beat Baltimore, 4–3. The Pirates rallied from a three-run deficit to win on Milt May's pinch-single.

Game 5 at Pittsburgh— October 14   51,377
Baltimore   0 0 0   0 0 0   0 0 0—0 2 1   LP McNally
Pittsburgh   0 2 1   0 1 0   0 0 x—4 9 0   WP Briles

The Pirates took a 3-2 edge in games after the fifth game, as Nelson Briles stymied the Birds on a two-hitter. Bob Robertson hit another homer for the Pirates and Clemente continued his World Series hitting streak to 12 games.

Game 6 at Baltimore— October 16   44,174
Pittsburgh   0 1 1   0 0 0   0 0 0   0—2 9 1   LP Miller
Baltimore   0 0 0   0 0 1   1 0 0   1—3 8 0   WP McNally

Not ready to quit, Baltimore battled the Pirates for 10 innings to win game six on Brooks Robinson's sacrifice fly that scored Frank Robinson. Dave McNally got the win in relief after pitching out of a bases-loaded jam in the top of the 10th.

Game 7 at Baltimore— October 17   47,291
Pittsburgh   0 0 0   1 0 0   0 1 0—2 6 1   WP Blass
Baltimore   0 0 0   0 0 0   0 1 0—1 4 0   LP Cuellar

Steve Blass threw a tough four-hitter to lead the Pirates to the World's Championship over the Orioles. A homer by Roberto Clemente and a double by third baseman Jose Pagan to score Willie Stargell gave Blass all the runs he needed to win.

Top Oriole hitter— Third baseman Brooks Robinson, 7 for 22, 5 RBIs, .318
Top Oriole pitcher— Dave McNally, 2 wins, 12 strikeouts, 1.98 ERA
Top Pirate hitter— Right fielder Roberto Clemente, 12 for 29, 2 HRs, 4 RBIs, .414
Top Pirate pitcher— Steve Blass, 2 wins, 2 complete games, 13 strikeouts, 1.00
                        ERA
Winning player's share— $18,165
Losing player's share— $13,906

1973 A.L. Championship Series

After a brief one-year hiatus, the Orioles won their division title by eight games, leaving Boston in the dust. They faced the defending World Champion Oakland A's for the 1973 pennant in a matchup of superb pitching.
Oakland's staff included three 20-game winners (Catfish Hunter, Ken Holtzman and Vida Blue) and relief ace Rollie Fingers. The O's countered with Jim Palmer (22 wins), Mike Cuellar (18 wins) and Dave McNally (17 wins).

Game 1 at Baltimore— October 6   41,279
Oakland   0 0 0   0 0 0   0 0 0—0   5 1   LP Blue
Baltimore   4 0 0   0 0 0   1 1 x—6 12 0   WP Palmer

A four-run first-inning explosion off Vida Blue and a five-hit shutout by Jim Palmer gave the O's a win in game one of the league series. Blue lasted only two-thirds of an inning as the Orioles took 23 minutes to bat in the bottom of the first.

Game 2 at Baltimore— October 7   48,425
Oakland   1 0 0   0 0 2   0 2 1—6 9 0   WP Hunter
Baltimore   1 0 0   0 0 1   0 1 0—3 8 0   LP McNally

Four Oakland home runs, including two by Sal Bando and one each by Joe Rudi and Bert Campaneris, gave the A's a 6-3 triumph in game two. A sensational catch high against the fence in left field by rookie Al Bumbry robbed Bando of a third homer.

Game 3 at Oakland— October 9   34,367
Baltimore   0 1 0   0 0 0   0 0 0   0 0—1 3 0   LP Cuellar
Oakland   0 0 0   0 0 0   0 1 0   0 1—2 4 3   WP Holtzman

Two southpaws, Mike Cuellar and Ken Holtzman, locked horns in an 11-inning pitchers' duel, with the A's prevailing on a Bert Campaneris homer to lead off the bottom of the 11th.

175

1973 A.L. Championship Series (continued)

```
Game 4 at Oakland—October 10                    27,497
Baltimore   0 0 0  0 0 0  4 1 0—5 8 0          WP Jackson
Oakland     0 3 0  0 0 1  0 0 0—4 7 0          LP Fingers
```

Second baseman Bobby Grich hit a home run in the eighth to break a 4-4 tie and give the Orioles a 5-4 win to deadlock the series at two games each. Catcher Andy Etchebarren added a three-run homer to the Oriole cause in inning seven.

```
Game 5 at Oakland—October 11                    24,265
Baltimore   0 0 0  0 0 0  0 0 0—0 5 2          LP Alexander
Oakland     0 0 1  2 0 0  0 0 x—3 7 0          WP Hunter
```

Catfish Hunter gave Oakland its second straight pennant by hurling a five-hit shutout over the Birds. No Oriole reached third base in the game and there was no more than one O's runner on base in any inning.

Top Oriole hitter—Catcher Andy Etchebarren, 5 for 14, 9 total bases, 1 HR, 4 RBIs, .357
Top Oriole pitcher—Jim Palmer, 3 games, 1 win, 15 strikeouts, 1.84 ERA
Top A's hitter—Shortstop Bert Campaneris, 7 for 21, 14 total bases, 2 HRs, 3 RBIs, .333
Top A's pitcher—Catfish Hunter, 2 wins, 1 complete game, 1.65 ERA

1974 A.L. Championship Series

The Birds returned the very next year to the Championship Series for a rematch with the still-reigning World Champion A's. Once more, Catfish Hunter led Oakland, this time with 25 wins. The O's staff was led by 22-game winner Mike Cuellar.

The Oriole offense was headed by second sacker Bobby Grich, with 19 home runs and 82 RBIs. Oakland's lineup featured four batters with 20 homers or better (Reggie Jackson, 29; Gene Tenace, 26; and Joe Rudi and Sal Bando with 22 each).

```
Game 1 at Oakland—October 5                     41,609
Baltimore   1 0 0  1 4 0  0 0 0—6 10 0         WP Cuellar
Oakland     0 0 1  0 1 0  0 0 1—3  9 0         LP Hunter
```

A two-run homer by Bobby Grich and solo round-trippers by Brooks Robinson and Paul Blair gave Mike Cuellar a win in game one of the title series.

```
Game 2 at Oakland—October 6                     42,810
Baltimore   0 0 0  0 0 0  0 0 0—0 5 2          LP McNally
Oakland     0 0 0  1 0 1  0 3 x—5 8 0          WP Holtzman
```

The A's evened the Series with a 5-0, five-hit shutout by Ken Holtzman. A three-run homer by catcher Roy Fosse and a bases-empty blast by Sal Bando paced the Oakland attack.

```
Game 3 at Baltimore—October 8                   32,060
Oakland     0 0 0  1 0 0  0 0 0—1 4 2          WP Blue
Baltimore   0 0 0  0 0 0  0 0 0—0 2 1          LP Palmer
```

Jim Palmer lost a heart-breaking pitchers' duel to Vida Blue in game three as his four-hitter fell victim to Blue's sterling two-hitter. A fourth-inning homer by Sal Bando provided the winning margin.

```
Game 4 at Baltimore— October 9                28,136
Oakland      0 0 0  0 1 0  1 0 0—2 1 0        WP Hunter
Baltimore    0 0 0  0 0 0  0 0 1—1 5 1        LP Cuellar
```

The O's pennant dreams crashed in game four as Oakland won 2-1 on just one hit off Mike Cuellar and Ross Grimsley. Eleven walks, including nine by Cuellar, proved Baltimore's undoing as the Cuban lefty walked Gene Tenace in the 5th inning to force in a run. The winning run came in the seventh as Reggie Jackson doubled in Sal Bando, who had been walked by Grimsley.

Top Oriole hitter—Center fielder Paul Blair, 4 for 14, 2 RBIs, .286
Top Oriole pitcher—Jim Palmer, 1 complete game, 1.00 ERA
Top A's hitter—Catcher Ray Fosse, 4 for 12, 1 HR, 3 RBIs, .333
Top A's pitcher—Vida Blue, 1 win, 1 complete game, 0.00 ERA

1979 A.L. Championship Series

After a four-year layoff, the Orioles again captured the Eastern Division crown, this time led by Cy Young Award winner Mike Flanagan, a 23-game winner, and right fielder Ken Singleton, who slugged 35 homers and drove home 111 runs.

The Birds faced a newcomer to championship play, the California Angels. Fireballing Nolan Ryan was the Angels' ace and former Oriole Don Baylor led the offense with 36 home runs and a league-leading 139 RBIs.

```
Game 1 at Baltimore— October 3               52,787
California   1 0 1  0 0 1  0 0 0  0—3 7 1     LP Montague
Baltimore    0 0 2  1 0 0  0 0 0  3—6 6 0     WP Stanhouse
```

Pinch-hitter John Lowenstein slugged a dramatic three-run home run with two out in the 10th inning to give the Birds a 6-3 win in game one. Don Stanhouse pitched a perfect 10th inning to get the win.

```
Game 2 at Baltimore— October 4               52,108
California   1 0 0  0 0 1  1 3 2—8 10 1       LP Frost
Baltimore    4 4 1  0 0 0  0 0 x—9 11 1       WP Flanagan
```

After bolting to a 9-1 lead behind Mike Flanagan, the Orioles frittered away runs only to hang on in a 9-8 heart-thumper. A shaky performance by Don Stanhouse gave the hometown fans a few anxious moments before the O's nailed down the win.

```
Game 3 at California— October 5              43,199
Baltimore    0 0 0  1 0 1  1 0 0—3 8 3        LP Stanhouse
California    1 0 0  1 0 0  0 0 2—4 9 0        WP Aase
```

The Orioles stood only two outs from sweeping the series when the Angels rallied on a double by Rod Carew, a walk to Brian Downing, an Al Bumbry error on Bobby Grich's line drive and Larry Harlow's game-winning double.

```
Game 4 at California— October 6                    43,199
Baltimore    0 0 2  1 0 0  5 0 0—8 12 1           WP McGregor
California    0 0 0  0 0 0  0 0 0—0  6 0           LP Knapp
```

The Orioles won their first pennant since 1971 as Scott McGregor threw a six-hit shutout over the Angels, 8-0. A key play in the finale came when the Angels had the bases loaded in the fifth inning with a 3-0 Oriole lead. Shortstop Jim Anderson hit a vicious one-hopper down the third base line, but Bird third sacker Doug DeCinces made a brilliant stop to turn it into a rally-killing double play.

Top Oriole hitter— First baseman Eddie Murray, 5 for 12, 1 HR, 5 RBIs, .417
Top Oriole pitcher— Scott McGregor, 1 win, 1 complete game, 0.00 ERA
Top Angel hitter— First baseman Rod Carew, 7 for 17, 10 total bases, 3 doubles, .412
Top Angel pitcher— Nolan Ryan, 7 innings, 8 strikeouts, 1.29 ERA

1979 World Series

The Orioles eagerly entered the 1979 World Series, a rematch with their '71 rivals, the Pittsburgh Pirates. Manager Earl Weaver had proclaimed this '79 squad his best team ever. The Pirates, led by the ever-optimistic Chuck Tanner, were equally confident.

The Bucs had swept the Cincinnati Reds in their league series. Leading the charge for the "Family" was their captain, first baseman Willie Stargell. Hot on his heels for club leadership was right fielder Dave Parker. Both teams boasted top bullpen aces in Don Stanhouse for the O's and Kent Tekulve for the Pirates.

```
Game 1 at Baltimore— October 10                   53,735
Pittsburgh   0 0 0  1 0 2  0 1 0—4 11 3           LP Kison
Baltimore    5 0 0  0 0 0  0 0 x—5  6 3           WP Flanagan
```

After rain and cold postponed the opener for a day, the Series began in weather conditions more suited to a French invasion of Russia. A costly throwing error by second baseman Phil Garner opened the door to a five-run Oriole first inning. Mike Flanagan scattered 11 hits to hang on to a 5-4 win.

```
Game 2 at Baltimore— October 11                   53,739
Pittsburgh   0 2 0  0 0 0  0 0 1—3 11 2           WP D. Robinson
Baltimore    0 1 0  0 0 1  0 0 0—2  6 1           LP Stanhouse
```

The Bucs evened the Series in game two as pinch-hitter Manny Sanguillen delivered a clutch single to score Ed Ott with the lead run. Kent Tekulve nailed down a save with a perfect ninth inning.

```
Game 3 at Pittsburgh— October 12                  50,848
Baltimore    0 0 2  5 0 0  1 0 0—8 13 0           WP McGregor
Pittsburgh   1 2 0  0 0 1  0 0 0—4  9 2           LP Candelaria
```

Despite a rain delay of 67 minutes, game three was played in Pittsburgh, with the Orioles winning 8-4. Shortstop Kiko Garcia banged out four hits, including a bases-loaded triple in the fourth, to lead the O's attack. Scott McGregor scattered nine hits to go the distance for the win.

Game 4 at Pittsburgh— October 13   50,883
Baltimore   0 0 3 0 0 0 0 6 0—9 12 0   WP Stoddard
Pittsburgh   0 4 0 0 1 1 0 0 0—6 17 1   LP Tekulve

After jumping out to a 6-3 lead, the Pirates fell victim to a six-run Oriole eighth-inning rally as pinch-hitters John Lowenstein and Terry Crowley each hit two-run doubles. The loss seemed to take some of the wind out of the Bucs, who had to this point socked 48 hits but gotten only 17 runs.

Game 5 at Pittsburgh— October 14   50,920
Baltimore   0 0 0 0 1 0 0 0 0—1 6 2   LP Flanagan
Pittsburgh   0 0 0 0 0 2 2 3 x—7 13 1   WP Blyleven

Down three games to one, the Pirates bounced back with a 7-1 triumph behind a combined six-hitter by surprise starter Jim Rooker and Bert Blyleven in an unusual relief appearance. Buc third baseman Bill Madlock had four hits to lead the Pirate offense.

Game 6 at Baltimore— October 16   53,739
Pittsburgh   0 0 0 0 0 0 2 2 0—4 10 0   WP Candelaria
Baltimore   0 0 0 0 0 0 0 0 0—0 7 1—   LP Palmer

The Pirates evened the Series at three games as John Candelaria and Kent Tekulve hooked up for a seven-hit, 4-0 shutout of the Birds.

Game 7 at Baltimore— October 17   53,733
Pittsburgh   0 0 0 0 0 2 0 0 2—4 10 0   WP Jackson
Baltimore   0 0 1 0 0 0 0 0 0—1 4 2   LP McGregor

The "Family" completed its amazing comeback from a 3-to-1 deficit in Series games to beat the Orioles for the World's Championship. A two-run homer by Willie Stargell powered the Pirates to a 4-1 win and Kent Tekulve notched his third save of the Series.

Top Oriole hitter— Shortstop Kiko Garcia, 8 for 20, 2 doubles, 6 RBIs, .400
Top Oriole pitcher— Mike Flanagan, 3 games, 1 win, 1 complete game, 3.00 ERA
Top Pirate hitter— First baseman Willie Stargell, 12 for 30, 25 total bases, 4 doubles, 3 HRs, 7 RBIs, .400
Top Pirate pitcher— Kent Tekulve, 5 games, 3 saves, 10 strikeouts, 2.89 ERA
Winning player's share— $28,237
Losing player's share— $22,114

PLAYERS, BY POSITION
(Asterisk indicates player traded during season)

YEAR/FINISH	C	1B	2B	3B	SS	LF	CF	RF	DH/UT	SP	RP	MGR.
1901 8th (Mil.)	Maloney Conner* Donahue	Anderson	Gilbert	Burke* Friel	Conroy Bone	Waldron* Hogriever	Duffy Bruyette	Hallman Jones		Reidy Husting Garvin Sparks	Dowling Hawley	Duffy
1902 2nd (St. L.)	Sugden Kahoe Donahue	Anderson	Padden	McCormick	Wallace	Burkett	Heidrick Maloney*	Hemphill Jones*	Friel	Donahue Powell Harper Sudhoff Reidy	Kane Shields	McAleer
1903 6th	Kahoe Sugden Shannon	Anderson	Friel Padden Bowcock	Hill	Wallace	Burkett	Heidrick Swander	Hemphill Martin	McCormick*	Sudhoff Powell Siever Donahue* Wright	Pelty Evans Reidy Terry Morgan	McAleer
1904 6th	Sugden Kahoe O'Connor	Jones	Padden	Moran Hill*	Wallace	Burkett	Heidrick Huelsman	Hemphill Hynes	Gleason	Glade Pelty Howell Siever Sudhoff	Morgan Hynes Wright	McAleer
1905 8th	Sugden Spencer Roth Weaver	Jones	Rockenfield Moran Padden	Gleason	Wallace	Stone	Koehler	Frisk	Van Zandt Starr	Howell Pelty Sudhoff Glade Powell	Buchanan Morgan Ables	McAleer
1906 5th	Rickey O'Connor Spencer	Jones Nordyke	O'Brien Rockenfield	Hartzell	Wallace	Stone	Hemphill	Niles Koehler		Pelty Howell Glade Powell	Jacobson Smith	McAleer
1907 6th	Spencer Stephens O'Connor Buelow	Jones	Niles Butler	Yeager Delahanty	Wallace	Stone	Hemphill	Pickering	Hartzell	Howell Powell Glade Pelty Jacobson	Dinneen Morgan Bailey McGill	McAleer
1908 4th	Spencer Stephens Smith	Jones	Williams Yeager	Ferris	Wallace	Stone	Hoffman Schweitzer	Hartzell C. Jones	Criss	Waddell Howell Powell Pelty Graham	Dinneen Bailey Criss	McAleer

180

Players, by Position (cont.)

YEAR/FINISH	C	1B	2B	3B	SS	LF	CF	RF	DH/UT	SP	RP	MGR.
1909 7th	Criger Stephens Smith	Jones* Griggs	Williams	Ferris	Wallace	Stone McAleese	Hoffman Schweitzer Shotton	Hartzell Devoy Crompton	Criss	Powell Pelty Waddell Bailey Graham	Dinneen Howell Criss Rose Gilligan	McAleer
1910 8th	Stephens Killefer	Newnam Abstein	Truesdale	Hartzell	Wallace Corriden	Stone	Hoffman Northen	Schweitzer Fisher	Griggs Criss	Lake Bailey Pelty Powell Ray	Waddell Kinsella Nelson Mitchell Criss	O'Connor
1911 8th	Clarke Stephens Krichell	Black Kutina	LaPorte	Austin	Wallace Hallihan	Hogan Murray	Shotton Compton	Schweitzer Meloan	Criss	Lake Powell Pelty Hamilton Mitchell	George Nelson Bailey Hawk Allison	Wallace
1912 7th	Stephens Krichell Alexander	Stovall Kutina	Pratt	Austin	Wallace Hallihan	Hogan	Shotton Jantzen	Compton Williams	LaPorte*	Baumgardner Hamilton Powell Allison E. Brown	C. Brown Mitchell Lake* Adams Weilman	Wallace Stovall
1913 8th	Agnew Alexander McAllester	Stovall Brief Covington	Pratt	Austin	Balenti Wallace Lavan* Walsh	Johnston Compton	Shotton	Williams Walker		Hamilton Mitchell Baumgardner Weilman Leverenz	Stone Allison Taylor Adams	Stovall Austin Rickey
1914 5th	Agnew Crossin Rumler Jenkins	Leary Miller	Pratt	Austin	Lavan Wares Wallace	Walker	Shotton	Williams E. Walker	Howard	Weilman Hamilton James Baumgardner Leverenz	Mitchell Hoch Taylor Manning	Rickey
1915 6th	Agnew Severeid	Leary Sisler Kaufman	Pratt	Austin	Lavan	Shotton Lee	T. Walker Jacobson	Walsh Williams E. Walker	Howard	Weilman Lowdermilk* Hamilton James* Koob	Perryman Sisler Hoch Hoff Baumgardner	Rickey
1916 5th	Severeid Hartley Chapman Rumler	Sisler Burton	Pratt	Austin Deal*	Lavan Johnson	Shotton	Marsans	Miller Tobin	Wallace	Weilman Plank Groom Davenport Koob	Hamilton Park McCabe Fincher Sisler	Jones

Players, by Position (cont.)

YEAR/FINISH	C	1B	2B	3B	SS	LF	CF	RF	DH/UT	SP	RP	MGR.
1917 7th	Severeid Hale	Sisler	Pratt	Austin Magee	Lavan Johnson	Shotton Smith	Sloan Marsans* W. Miller	Jacobson Rumler Demmitt		Davenport Sothoron Groom Koob Plank	Hamilton Rogers Wright Molyneaux Park	Jones
1918 5th	Nunamaker Severeid Hale	Sisler	Gedeon	Maisel	Austin Gerber Johnson	Smith Hendryx	Tobin	Demmitt	Johns	Sothoron Davenport Rogers Wright Gallia	Houck Shocker Lowdermilk Leifield Bennett	Jones Austin Burke
1919 5th (tie)	Severeid Billings Mayer	Sisler	Gedeon	Austin Bronkie Schepner	Gerber	Tobin	Jacobson Sloan	Smith Williams Demmitt		Sothoron Shocker Gallia Weilman Davenport	Koob Wright Leifield Mapel Vangilder	Burke
1920 4th	Severeid Billings Collins	Sisler	Gedeon	Austin Smith Thompson	Gerber Shovlin Lee	Williams Lamb	Jacobson	Tobin Wetzel		Shocker Davis Sothoron Weilman Bayne	Burwell Vangilder De Berry Sanders Lynch	Burke
1921 3rd	Severeid Collins Billings	Sisler	McManus Gleason	Ellerbe Lamb Smith*	Gerber Austin	Williams Wetzel	Jacobson	Tobin	Lee	Shocker Davis Bayne Vangilder Kolp	Burwell Palmero De Berry Boland Sothoron*	Fohl
1922 2nd	Severeid Collins	Sisler	McManus	Ellerbe Foster Bronkie Austin	Gerber	Williams Durst	Jacobson Shorten	Tobin	Robertson	Shocker Vangilder Kolp Davis Wright	Pruett Bayne Danforth Henry Meine	Fohl
1923 5th	Severeid Collins Billings	Schliebner	McManus Foster	Robertson Ezzell Ellerbe	Gerber	Williams Durst	Jacobson Whaley	Tobin		Shocker Vangilder Danforth Kolp Davis	Pruett Root Bayne Wright Grant	Fohl Austin
1924 4th	Severeid Rego Collins	Sisler	McManus	Robertson Rice Ellerbe* Simon	Gerber	Williams Evans Bennett	Jacobson	Tobin	McMillan	Shocker Danforth Wingard Davis Vangilder	Pruett Lyons Grant Bayne Kolp	Sisler
1925 3rd	Dixon Hargrave Severeid*	Sisler	McManus	Robertson	LaMotte Gerber	Williams Bennett	Jacobson Evans	Rice Tobin		Gaston Bush Davis	Vangilder Danforth Stauffer	Sisler

Players, by Position (cont.)

YEAR/FINISH	C	1B	2B	3B	SS	LF	CF	RF	DH/UT	SP	RP	MGR.
1926 7th	Schang Hargrave Dixon	Sisler	Melillo	McManus Robertson	Gerber LaMotte	Williams Durst	Rice Jacobson*	Miller Bennett		Zachary Gaston Ballou Vangilder Giard	Wingard Davis Falk Jonnard Nevers	Sisler
1927 7th	Schang O'Neill Dixon	Sisler	Melillo	O'Rourke	Gerber Miller Kress	Williams Bennett	Miller Schulte	Rice	Adams	Gaston Vangilder Jones Stewart Wingard	Crowder Nevers Ballou Falk Zachary*	Howley
1928 3rd	Schang Manion O'Neill	Blue Sturdy	Brannen Melillo	O'Rourke Bettancourt Sax	Kress	Manush	Schulte	McNeely McGowan		Crowder Gray Ogden Blaeholder Stewart	Coffman Wiltse Strelecki Beck Nevers	Howley
1929 4th	Schang Ferrell Manion	Blue	Melillo Brannan	O'Rourke Dondero	Kress Roetz	Manush	Schulte Badgro	McGowan McNeely		Gray Crowder Blaeholder Collins Stewart	Coffman Kimsey Ogden Strelecki Hopkins	Howley
1930 6th	Ferrell Manion Hungling	Blue	Melillo	O'Rourke Hale	Kress	Goslin Manush*	Schulte Badgro	Gullic Metzler	McNeely	Stewart Blaeholder Coffman Gray Collins	Kimsey Holshouser Stiles Crowder* Stiely	Killefer
1931 5th	Ferrell Bengough Young	Burns	Melillo	Kress Storti Grimes	Levey	Goslin	Schulte Waddey	Jenkins Bettancourt McNeely		Stewart Gray Blaeholder Coffman Collins	Kimsey Stiles Hebert Braxton Cooney	Killefer
1932 6th	Ferrell Bengough	Burns	Melillo	Scharein Storti Grimes	Levey	Goslin Fisher	Schulte Bettancourt	Campbell Garms Jenkins		Stewart Blaeholder Hadley Hebert Fischer*	Gray Kimsey* Cooney Coffman* Polli	Killefer
1933 8th	Shea Ruel Hemsley Ferrell*	Burns	Melillo	Scharein Storti	Levey	Reynolds Garms	West	Campbell	Gullic Hornsby	Hadley Blaeholder Wells Coffman Hebert	Gray Stiles McDonald Knott Braxton	Killefer Sothoron Hornsby

Players, by Position (cont.)

YEAR/FINISH	C	1B	2B	3B	SS	LF	CF	RF	DH/UT	SP	RP	MGR.
1934 6th	Hemsley Grube	Burns	Melillo	Clift	Strange	Pepper Puccinelli	West Clark	Campbell Garms	Bejma Hornsby	Newsom Blaeholder Hadley Coffman Andrews	Knott Wells McAfee Mills Walkup	Hornsby
1935 7th	Hemsley Heath	Burns Mueller	Carey Bejma Melillo*	Clift	Lary Strange*	Solters Pepper	West Mazzera	Coleman Bell	Burnett	Andrews Knott Cain Thomas Walkup	Van Atta Coffman Weiland Hansen Newsom*	Hornsby
1936 7th	Hemsley Giuliani	Bottomley Burns* Hornsby	Carey Bejma	Clift	Lary	Solters Pepper	West	Bell Coleman		Hogsett Thomas Knott Andrews Caldwell	Van Atta Liebhardt Mahaffey Kimberlin Tietje	Hornsby
1937 8th	Hemsley Huffman	Davis Bottomley	Carey Lipscomb Barkley	Clift	Knickerbocker Vosmik		West Allen	Bell Silber	Hornsby	Hildebrand Knott Hogsett Walkup Bonetti	Trotter Koupal Van Atta Blake* Thomas*	Hornsby Bottomley
1938 7th	Sullivan Heath Harshany	McQuinn	Heffner Hughes	Clift	Kress	Mills McQuillan Grace	Almada Mazzera West*	Bell Allen		Newsom Mills Hildebrand Van Atta Walkup	Cole Cox Link Johnson Tietje	Street
1939 8th	Glenn Harshany Spindel	McQuinn	Berardino	Clift	Heffner Christman	Gallagher Grace Solters	Laabs Almada*	Hoag Mazzera	Sullivan	Kramer Kennedy Harris Lawson Mills	Trotter Whitehead Gill Kimberlin Bildilli	Haney
1940 6th	Swift Susce	McQuinn	Heffner Lucadello	Clift	Berardino Strange Lary	Radcliff Grace	Judnich Hoag	Laabs Cullenbine		Auker Kennedy Harris Niggeling Bildilli	Lawson Trotter Coffman Mills Kramer	Haney
1941 6th (tie)	Ferrell Swift Grube	McQuinn Archie	Heffner	Clift	Berardino Strange	Cullenbine Radcliff*	Judnich Estalella	Laabs Grace	Lucadello	Auker Muncrief Harris Galehouse Niggeling	Caster Kramer Trotter Allen* Ostermueller	Haney Sewell

184

YEAR/FINISH	C	1B	2B	3B	SS	LF	CF	RF	DH/UT	SP	RP	MGR.
1942 3rd	Ferrell Hayes Swift*	McQuinn	Gutteridge Heffner	Clift Strange	Stephens	McQuillen Chartak Cullenbine*	Judnich Criscola	Laabs	Berardino	Auker Niggeling Galehouse Hollingsworth Muncrief	Caster Ferens Appleton Sundra Ostermueller	Sewell
1943 6th	Hayes Ferrell Schultz	McQuinn	Gutteridge	Clift Clary	Stephens	Laabs Kreevich	Byrnes Criscola	Chartak Zarilla	Christman	Sundra Muncrief Galehouse Potter Niggeling*	Caster Hollingsworth Fuchs Ostermueller McKain	Sewell
1944 1st	Hayworth Mancuso	McQuinn Chartak	Gutteridge Baker	Christman Clary	Stephens	Kreevich Laabs	Byrnes Demaree	Moore Zarilla		Potter Kramer Muncrief Jakucki Galehouse	Caster Hollingsworth Shirley Zoldak West	Sewell
1945 3rd	Mancuso Hayworth	McQuinn	Gutteridge	Christman Clary	Stephens	Byrnes Finney Laabs	Kreevich* Martin	Moore Gray	Schulte	Potter Hollingsworth Jakucki Kramer Shirley	Zoldak West Muncrief Jones Caster*	Sewell
1946 7th	Mancuso Helf Schultz	Stevens Dahlgren	Berardino	Christman Dillinger	Stephens	Heath Laabs	Judnich Grace*	Zarilla McQuillen	Lucadello	Kramer Galehouse Zoldak Potter Shirley	Ferrick Fannin Kinder Ferens Muncrief	Sewell Taylor
1947 8th	Moss Early	Judnich Witte	Berardino Peters Thompson	Dillinger	Stephens	Heath	Lehner Brown	Zarilla Coleman	Hitchcock	Kramer Kinder Sanford Muncrief Zoldak	Moulder Potter Fannin Brown Galehouse*	Ruel
1948 6th	Moss Partee	Stevens Arft	Priddy Anderson	Dillinger	Pellagrini Dente	Platt Layden	Lehner Lund	Zarilla Kokos		Sanford Fannin Garver Kennedy B. Stephens	Widmar Biscan Ostrowski Drews Shore	Taylor
1949 7th	Lollar Moss	Graham	Priddy Friend	Dillinger	Pellagrini Sullivan Anderson	Sievers Platt	Spence Lehner	Kokos Zarilla* Elder		Garver Fannin Drews Embree Kennedy	Ferrick Papal Ostrowski Starr Shore	Taylor

185

Players, by Position (cont.)

YEAR/ FINISH	C	1B	2B	3B	SS	LF	CF	RF	DH/UT	SP	RP	MGR.
1950 7th	Lollar Moss	Lenhardt Arft	Friend	Sommers Thomas	Upton DeMars	Kokos Sievers	Coleman Delsing	Wood	Stirnweiss	Garver Widmar Overmire Starr Fannin	Marshall Pillette Dorish Johnson Ferrick*	Taylor
1951 8th	Lollar Batts	Arft Long	Young	Marsh Berardino	Jennings Bero Upton	Coleman* Maguire Sievers	Delsing	Wood Mapes		Garver Pillette Byrne Widmar McDonald	Paige Mahoney Suchecki Sleater Hogue	Taylor
1952 7th	Courtney Moss	Kryhoski Goldsberry	Young	Dyck Michaels Thomas*	DeMaestri Marsh Marion	Delsing* Wertz	Rivera* Porter	Nieman Zarilla		Cain Pillette Byrne Garver* Bearden	Paige Harrist Madison* Overmire Stuart	Hornsby Marion
1953 8th	Courtney Moss	Kryhoski Sievers	Young	Dyck Stephens Elliott*	Hunter	Kokos Lenhardt	Groth	Wertz Edwards	Berry*	Larsen Pillette Littlefield Brecheen Cain	Paige Stuart Holloman Blyzka Trucks*	Marion
1954 7th (Balt.)	Courtney Moss Murray	Waitkus Kryhoski	Young Garcia	Stephens Kennedy	Hunter Brideweser	Coan Fridley	Diering Mele*	Abrams Wertz*		Turley Coleman Larsen Pillette Kretlow	Fox Chakales Blyzka Stuart* O'Dell	Dykes
1955 7th	Smith Moss*	Triandos Hale	Marsh Young* Leppert	Causey	Miranda	Philley Coan* Woodling*	Diering Dyck	Abrams Evers* Pope	Cox*	Wilson Palica Wight Moore Rogovin	Dorish Zuverink Johnson Schallock McDonald	Richards
1956 6th	Triandos Smith*	Boyd Hale	Gardner	Kell Causey Adams	Miranda	Nieman Evers	Williams Pyburn Diering	Francona Philley*		Moore Johnson Wight Brown Palica	Zuverink Ferrarese Fornieles Loes Schmitz	Richards
1957 5th	Triandos Ginsberg	Boyd Hale	Gardner	Kell Robinson	Miranda Brideweser	Nieman	Busby Durham	Pilarcik Francona	Goodman Williams*	Johnson Moore Brown Loes Wight	Zuverink Lehman O'Dell Ceccarelli Fornieles*	Richards

186

Players, by Position (cont.)

YEAR/FINISH	C	1B	2B	3B	SS	LF	CF	RF	DH/UT	SP	RP	MGR.
1958 6th	Triandos Ginsberg	Boyd Marshall*	Gardner	Robinson	Miranda Castleman	Woodling Nieman	Busby Green Tasby	Pilarcik Taylor	Williams	Portocarrero O'Dell Harshman Pappas Brown	Zuverink Loes Lehman Beamon Johnson	Richards
1959 6th	Triandos Ginsberg	Boyd Dropo	Gardner	Robinson Finigan	Carrasquel Miranda	Nieman	Tasby Pearson	Woodling Pilarcik	Klaus	Pappas Wilhelm O'Dell Brown Walker	Loes E. Johnson Fisher Portocarrero Hoeft	Richards
1960 2nd	Triandos Courtney	Gentile Dropo Boyd	Breeding	Robinson	Hansen	Woodling Nicholson	Brandt Busby Pearson	Stephens Pilarcik		Estrada Pappas Barber Brown Fisher	Wilhelm Jones Hoeft Stock Walker	Richards
1961 3rd	Triandos Foiles	Gentile Throneberry	Adair Breeding	Robinson	Hansen	Snyder Philley	Brandt E. Robinson Busby	Herzog Williams		Barber Estrada Pappas Fisher Brown	Wilhelm Stock Hall Hoeft Hyde	Richards Harris
1962 7th (tie)	Triandos Lau Landrith	Gentile	Breeding Temple*	Robinson	Adair Hansen	Powell Nicholson	Brandt E. Robinson	Snyder Herzog	Williams	Pappas Roberts Estrada Barber Fisher	Wilhelm Hoeft Hall Stock Brown*	Hitchcock
1963 4th	Orsino Brown Lau*	Gentile	Adair Johnson	Robinson	Aparicio	Powell Gaines Bowens	Brandt Valentine	Snyder Smith	Saverine	Barber Pappas Roberts McNally McCormick	Miller Hall Stock Starrette Brunet	Hitchcock
1964 3rd	Brown Orsino Lau	Siebern	Adair	Robinson	Aparicio Saverine	Powell Kirkland* E. Robinson	Brandt Cimoli	Bowens Snyder	Johnson	Bunker Pappas Roberts McNally Barber	Miller Haddix Hall Estrada Vineyard	Bauer
1965 3rd	Brown Orsino Lau	Powell Siebern	Adair	Robinson D. Johnson	Aparicio	Blefary	Blair Brandt	Snyder Bowens	Johnson	Barber Pappas McNally Bunker J. Miller	Miller Hall Haddix Palmer Larsen	Bauer

Players, by Position (cont.)

YEAR/FINISH	C	1B	2B	3B	SS	LF	CF	RF	DH/UT	SP	RP	MGR.
1966 1st	Etchebarren Roznovsky Haney	Powell	D. Johnson Adair*	Robinson	Aparicio Belanger	Snyder Blefary	Blair Held	F. Robinson Bowens	Johnson	Palmer McNally Bunker J. Miller	Miller E. Fisher Drabowsky Hall Watt	Bauer
1967 6th (tie)	Etchebarren Haney Roznovsky	Powell	D. Johnson	Robinson	Aparicio Belanger	Blefary Snyder Motton	Blair May	F. Robinson Bowens		Phoebus McNally Richert Dillman Hardin	Drabowsky Watt Miller E. Fisher Bunker	Bauer
1968 2nd	Etchebarren Hendricks Haney	Powell	D. Johnson	Robinson	Belanger	Blefary May Rettenmund	Blair Valentine	F. Robinson Motton	Buford	McNally Hardin Phoebus Leonhard Brabender	Watt Drabowsky Richert Nelson Bunker	Bauer Weaver
1969 1st	Hendricks Etchebarren Dalrymple	Powell	D. Johnson Floyd	Robinson	Belanger	Buford Rettenmund	Blair Motton	F. Robinson May	Salmon	Cuellar McNally Palmer Phoebus Hardin	Watt Richert Hall Leonard Lopez	Weaver
1970 1st	Hendricks Etchebarren Dalrymple	Powell	D. Johnson	Robinson	Belanger Grich	Buford Motton	Blair Rettenmund	F. Robinson Crowley	Salmon	Cuellar McNally Palmer Hardin Phoebus	Richert Watt Hall Drabowsky Lopez	Weaver
1971 1st	Hendricks Etchebarren Dalrymple	Powell	D. Johnson Salmon	Robinson	Belanger DaVanon	Buford Shopay	Blair Motton	Rettenmund F. Robinson		McNally Cuellar Dobson Palmer Jackson	Watt Richert Dukes Hall Leonhard	Weaver
1972 3rd	Oates Etchebarren Hendricks	Powell T. Davis	D. Johnson	Robinson	Belanger	Buford Baylor	Blair Shopay	Rettenmund Crowley	Grich	Palmer Cuellar Dobson McNally Alexander	Jackson Watt Harrison Scott Leonard	Weaver
1973 1st	Williams Etchebarren Hendricks	Powell Crowley	Grich	Robinson	Belanger Baker	Baylor Bumbry	Blair	Coggins Rettenmund	T. Davis (1st year for DH)	Palmer Cuellar McNally Alexander Jefferson	Jackson B. Reynolds Watt Hood Pena*	Weaver

188

Players, by Position (cont.)

YEAR/FINISH	C	1B	2B	3B	SS	LF	CF	RF	DH/UT	SP	RP	MGR.
1974 1st	Williams Etchebarren Hendricks	Powell Cabell Oliver	Grich	Robinson	Belanger	Baylor Bumbry	Blair Northrup	Coggins Fuller	T. Davis	Cuellar Grimsley McNally Palmer Alexander	Jackson B. Reynolds Garland Hood Jefferson	Weaver
1975 2nd	Duncan Hendricks	May Muser	Grich	Robinson DeCinces	Belanger Nordbrook	Baylor Northrup	Blair Bumbry	Singleton	T. Davis	Palmer Torrez Cuellar Grimsley Alexander	D. Miller Jackson Garland P. Mitchell Flanagan	Weaver
1976 2nd	Duncan Dempsey	Muser Crowley	Grich	DeCinces Robinson	Belanger	Singleton Mora	Blair Bumbry	Jackson	May Harper	Palmer Garland R. May Grimsley Cuellar	T. Martinez D. Miller Pagan Flanagan Holdsworth	Weaver
1977 2nd	Dempsey Skaggs	May Muser	Smith Dauer	DeCinces Robinson	Belanger Garcia	Kelly Mora	Bumbry Shopay	Singleton Maddox	Murray	Palmer R. May Flanagan Grimsley D. Martinez	T. Martinez Drago Briles McGregor D. Miller*	Weaver
1978 4th	Dempsey Skaggs	Murray Crowley	Dauer Smith	DeCinces	Belanger Garcia	Lopez Kelly Mora	Harlow Bumbry	Singleton Anderson	May	Palmer Flanagan D. Martinez McGregor Briles	Stanhouse T. Martinez Kerrigan Flinn Stoddard	Weaver
1979 1st	Dempsey Skaggs	Murray Crowley	Dauer Smith	DeCinces	Garcia Belanger	Roenicke Lowenstein Ayala	Bumbry	Singleton Kelly	May	Flanagan D. Martinez McGregor Stone Palmer	Stanhouse T. Martinez Stoddard Stewart Ford	Weaver
1980 2nd	Dempsey Graham	Murray	Dauer Sakata	DeCinces	Belanger Garcia	Roenicke Lowenstein Ayala	Bumbry	Singleton Kelly	Crowley May	Stone McGregor Palmer Flanagan D. Martinez	Stoddard T. Martinez Stewart Ford Hartzell	Weaver
1981 2nd	Dempsey Graham	Murray	Dauer	DeCinces	Sakata Belanger	Roenicke Lowenstein	Bumbry	Singleton Ayala	Crowley Dwyer Morales	D. Martinez McGregor Flanagan Palmer Stone	T. Martinez Stoddard Stewart Ford Schneider	Weaver
1982 2nd	Dempsey Nolan	Murray	Dauer Sakata	Gulliver Dauer Raford	Ripken Sakata Bonner	Lowenstein Roenicke Ayala	Bumbry Shelby	Ford Roenicke Dwyer	Singleton Crowley	D. Martinez Flanagan Palmer McGregor	Stoddard Stewart Davis Grimsley T. Martinez	Weaver

189

MEMORABLE BOX SCORES

Earl Hamilton Hurls First No-Hitter in Brown History

August 30, 1912—St. Louis at Detroit

ST. LOUIS

	AB	R	H	O	A
Shotton, CF	4	0	0	4	0
Compton, LF	5	0	2	3	0
Williams, RF	5	0	1	0	0
Pratt, 2B	4	1	1	1	3
Kutina, 1B	4	1	1	16	0
Austin, 3B	3	1	2	1	3
Smoyer, SS	4	0	0	1	3
Alexander, C	3	1	2	0	0
Hamilton, P	1	1	0	1	3
Totals	33	5	9	27	12

DETROIT

	AB	R	H	O	A
Jones, LF	4	0	0	0	0
Bush, SS	4	0	0	5	4
Cobb, CF	2	1	0	2	0
Crawford, RF	4	0	0	0	0
Corriden, 2B	3	0	0	3	5
Moriarty, LF	3	0	0	10	0
Vitt, 3B	3	0	0	2	2
Stanage, C	3	0	0	5	2
Dubuc, P	3	0	0	0	1
Totals	29	1	0	27	14

St. Louis	1 0 2 1 0 0 0 1 0—5	
Detroit	0 0 0 1 0 0 0 0 0—1	

Errors—St. Louis 2, Pratt, Austin; Detroit 3, Corriden 2, Dubuc. Two-base hits—Compton, Williams, Kutina, Alexander. Three-base hit—Austin. Sacrifice fly—Alexander. Sacrifice hit—Hamilton. Stolen bases—Shotton, Austin. Left on bases—St. Louis, 7; Detroit, 3. First base on balls—Off Dubuc, 4; off Hamilton, 2. First base on errors—Detroit, 2; St. Louis, 2. Struck out—By Dubuc, 5. Time—1:35. Umpires—O'Loughlin and Westervelt.

Ernie Koob Baffles the White Sox with a No-Hitter

May 5, 1917—Chicago at St. Louis

CHICAGO

	AB	H	O	A	E
J. Collins, RF	4	0	1	0	0
Weaver, 3B	4	0	0	1	0
E. Collins, 2B	4	0	3	3	0
Jackson, LF	2	0	1	0	0
Felsch, CF	4	0	1	0	0
Gandil, 1B	3	0	7	1	0
Risberg, SS	2	0	3	3	1
Schalk, C	3	0	7	2	0
Cicotte, P	1	0	1	3	0
Totals	27	0	24	13	1

ST. LOUIS

	AB	H	O	A	E
Shotton, LF	4	0	2	0	0
Austin, 3B	4	1	0	3	0
Sisler, 1B	4	1	13	0	0
Severeid, C	3	0	1	0	0
Jacobson, RF	3	0	4	0	0
Marsans, CF	2	1	1	0	0
Johnson, 2B	2	0	3	4	1
Lavan, SS	3	2	3	5	1
Koob, P	2	0	0	3	0
Totals	27	5	27	15	2

Chicago	0 0 0 0 0 0 0 0 0—0
St. Louis	0 0 0 0 0 1 0 0 x—1

Two-base hit—Marsans. Double plays—Koob, Johnson and Sisler; Austin Johnson and Sisler. Bases on balls—Off Koob 5, off Cicotte 2. Struck out—By Koob 2, by Cicotte 3. Umpires—Nallin and Evans.

The Day After Koob's Gem,
Brownie Bob Groom Adds One of His Own

May 6, 1917—Chicago at St. Louis

CHICAGO

	AB	R	H	O	A
Liebold, RF	3	0	0	1	0
Weaver, 3B	2	0	0	3	5
E. Collins, 2B	3	0	0	3	2
Jackson, LF	2	0	0	1	0
Felsch, CF	3	0	0	1	0
Grandil, 1B	3	0	0	10	2
Risberg, SS	2	0	0	1	3
Schalk, C	2	0	0	4	2
Benz, P	2	0	0	0	3
*Murphy	1	0	0	0	0
Totals	23	0	0	24	17

ST. LOUIS

	AB	R	H	O	A
Shotton, LF	4	0	0	1	0
Austin, 3B	4	0	1	1	1
Sisler, 1B	3	2	3	7	2
Jacobson, RF	4	0	2	1	0
Marsans, CF	4	0	0	3	0
Johnson, 2B	3	1	1	2	0
Severeid, C	3	0	0	7	2
Lavan, SS	3	0	1	4	3
Groom, P	2	0	0	1	1
Totals	30	3	8	27	9

* Batted for Benz in 9th inning.

Chicago	0 0 0 0 0 0 0 0 0—0
St. Louis	1 1 0 0 0 0 0 1 x—3

Errors—Chicago, Risberg 2; St. Louis, 0. Two-base hits—Jacobson, Johnson. Stolen bases—Austin, Sisler. Sacrifice hits—Groom, Sisler, Schalk. Double play—Severeid to Lavan to Sisler. Left on bases—Chicago 1, St. Louis 5. First base on errors—St. Louis 2. Bases on balls—Off Groom 3. Hits and earned runs—Off Benz, 8 hits, 3 runs in 8 innings; off Groom, no hits, no runs in 9 innings. Hit by pitcher—By Groom (Weaver). Struck out—By Benz 2, by Groom 4. Umpires—Nallin and Evans. Time—1:21.

Bobo Newsom Hurls 9⅔ Hitless
Innings Only to Lose to Boston in 10

Sept. 18, 1934—Boston at St. Louis

BOSTON

	AB	R	H	O	A	E
Bishop, 2B	3	1	0	1	4	0
Werber, 3B	4	0	0	2	4	1
Almada, CF	5	0	0	2	0	1
Johnson, LF	4	1	1	2	0	0
Graham, RF	4	0	0	2	1	0
R. Ferrell, C	1	0	0	1	0	0
Hinkle, C	3	0	0	4	0	0
Morgan, 1B	2	0	0	15	0	0
Lary, SS	4	0	0	1	2	0
W. Ferrell, P	1	0	0	0	0	0
Walberg, P	3	0	0	0	5	0
Totals	34	2	1	30	16	2

BROWNS

	AB	R	H	O	A	E
Clift, 3B	4	0	1	2	2	0
Garms, LF	4	0	2	4	0	0
Burns, 1B	5	0	1	7	0	0
Pepper, CF	5	0	1	4	0	1
Campbell, RF	4	0	1	1	0	0
Melillo, 2B	4	0	0	1	2	1
Hemsley, C	5	1	2	10	1	0
Strange, SS	2	0	1	0	2	1
Newsom, P	4	0	0	1	3	0
*Bejma	1	0	1	0	0	0
Totals	38	1	10	30	10	3

* Batted for Campbell in tenth inning.

Boston	0 1 0 0 0 0 0 0 0 1	—2
Browns	0 0 0 0 0 1 0 0 0 0	—1

Two-base hits—Garms, Bejma. Runs batted in—Lary, Johnson, Strange. Sacrifice hit—Garms. Stolen bases—Clift, Burns. Passed ball—Hinkle. Base on balls—Off W. Ferrell, 1; off Newsom, 7; off Walberg, 3. Struck out—By W. Ferrell, 1; by Newsom, 9; by Walberg, 4. Pitching record—Off W. Ferrell, no hits, no runs in 1 inning; off Walberg, 10 hits, 1 run in 9 innings. Left on bases—St. Louis, 12, Boston, 9. Umpires—Kolls and Geisel. Winning pitcher—Walberg. Time of game—2:22.

Memorable Box Scores (continued)

The American League Wins the Browns' Lone All-Star Game

July 13, 1948—At Sportsman's Park, St. Louis

NATIONALS

	AB	R	H	PO	A	E
Ashburn (Phillies), CF	4	1	2	1	0	0
Kiner (Pirates), LF	1	0	0	1	0	0
Schoendienst (Cards), 2B	4	0	0	0	1	0
Rigney (Giants), 2B	0	0	0	2	0	0
Musial (Cardinals), LF–CF	4	1	2	3	0	0
Mize (Giants), 1B	4	0	1	4	1	0
Slaughter (Cards), RF	2	0	1	2	0	0
Holmes (Braves), RF	1	0	0	1	0	0
Pafko (Cubs), 3B	2	0	0	0	0	0
Elliott (Braves), 3B	2	0	1	0	0	0
Cooper (Braves), C	2	0	0	3	0	0
Masi (Braves), C	2	0	1	4	0	0
Reese (Dodgers), SS	2	0	0	2	2	0
Kerr (Giants), SS	2	0	0	1	0	0
Branca (Dodgers), P	1	0	0	0	0	0
(b)Gustine (Pirates)	1	0	0	0	0	0
Schmitz (Cubs), P	0	0	0	0	0	0
Sain (Braves), P	0	0	0	0	0	0
(d)Waitkus (Cubs)	0	0	0	0	0	0
Blackwell (Reds), P	0	0	0	0	0	0
(g)Thomson (Giants)	1	0	0	0	0	0
Totals	35	2	8	24	4	0

AMERICANS

	AB	R	H	PO	A	E
Mullin (Tigers), RF	1	0	0	0	0	0
(c)DiMaggio (Yankees)	1	0	0	0	0	0
Zarilla (Browns), RF	2	0	0	2	0	0
Henrich (Yankees), LF	3	0	0	1	0	0
Boudreau (Indians), SS	2	0	0	2	0	0
Stephens (Red Sox), SS	2	0	1	0	0	0
Gordon (Indians), 2B	2	0	0	1	2	0
Doerr (Red Sox), 2B	2	0	0	0	3	0
Evers (Tigers), CF	4	1	1	0	0	0
Keltner (Indians), 3B	3	1	1	1	6	0
McQuinn (Yankees), 1B	4	1	2	14	0	0
Rosar (Athletics), C	1	0	0	1	0	0
Tebbetts (Red Sox), C	1	1	0	5	1	0
Masterson (Senators), P	0	0	0	0	0	0
(a)Vernon (Senators)	0	1	0	0	0	0
Raschi (Yankees), P	1	0	1	0	0	0
(e)Williams (Red Sox)	0	0	0	0	0	0
(f)Newhouser (Tigers)	0	0	0	0	0	0
Coleman (Athletics), P	0	0	0	0	1	0
Totals	29	5	6	27	13	0

| National League | 2 0 0 0 0 0 0 0 0—2 |
| American League | 0 1 1 3 0 0 0 0 x—5 |

Pitching Summary

NATIONAL LEAGUE	IP	H	R	ER	BB	SO
Branca	3	1	2	2	3	3
Schmitz (L)	⅓	3	3	3	1	0
Sain	1⅔	0	0	0	0	3
Blackwell	3	2	0	0	3	1

AMERICAN LEAGUE	IP	H	R	ER	BB	SO
Masterson	3	5	2	2	1	1
Raschi (W)	3	3	0	0	1	3
Coleman	3	0	0	0	2	3

(a)Walked for Masterson in third. (b)Struck out for Branca in fourth. (c)Flied out for Mullin in fourth, scoring Tebbetts from third. (d)Walked for Sain in sixth. (e)Walked for Raschi in sixth. (f)Ran for Williams in sixth. (g)Struck out for Blackwell in ninth. Runs batted in—Musial 2, Evers, Boudreau, Raschi 2, DiMaggio. Home runs—Musial, Evers. Sacrifice hit—Coleman. Stolen bases—Ashburn, Vernon, Mullin, McQuinn. Wild pitch—Masterson. Left on bases—Nationals 10, Americans 8.

Managers: Stanley "Bucky" Harris, New York (AL); Leo Durocher, Brooklyn (NL).

Umpires—Berry and Paparella (AL), Reardon and Stewart (NL). Time—2:27. Attendance—34,009.

Memorable Box Scores (continued)

The Browns' Bobo Holloman Throws a
No-Hitter in His First Major League Start

May 6, 1953—Philadelphia at St. Louis

PHILADELPHIA

	AB	R	H	O	A	E
Joost, SS	3	0	0	3	3	0
Philley, CF	4	0	0	0	0	0
Babe, 3B	3	0	0	1	6	0
Robinson, 1B	4	0	0	8	0	0
Clark, RF	3	0	0	2	0	0
Zernial, LF	3	0	0	1	0	0
Michaels, 2B	3	0	0	5	3	1
Astroth, C	1	0	0	4	2	0
Martin, P	1	0	0	0	0	0
*Hamilton	1	0	0	0	0	0
Scheib, P	0	0	0	0	1	0
†Valo	0	0	0	0	0	0
‡De Maestri	0	0	0	0	0	0
Totals	26	0	0	24	15	1

ST. LOUIS

	AB	R	H	O	A	E
Groth, CF	5	0	2	4	0	0
Hunter, SS	5	1	2	1	4	0
Dyck, LF	3	1	1	1	0	0
Elliott, 3B	4	0	2	1	0	0
Wertz, RF	3	0	1	3	0	0
Moss, C	5	2	2	3	0	0
Sievers, 1B	3	1	1	12	0	0
Young, 2B	2	1	0	1	7	0
Holloman, P	3	0	2	1	1	1
Totals	33	6	13	27	12	1

* Struck out for Martin in sixth.
† Walked for Scheib in ninth.
‡ Ran for Valo in ninth.

Philadelphia	0 0 0 0 0 0 0 0 0—0
St. Louis	0 1 1 0 1 1 0 2 x—6

Pitchers

	IP	H	R	ER	BB	SO
Holloman (W, 1-1)	9	0	0	0	5	3
Martin (L, 1-1)	5	7	3	2	4	2
Scheib	3	6	3	3	3	1

RBI—Holloman 3, Dyck, Wertz, Groth. 2B—Moss 2, Hunter, Wertz, Elliott. SH—Holloman. DP—Young and Sievers; Babe, Michaels and Robinson; Michaels, Joost and Robinson; Young, Hunter and Sievers. LOB—Philadelphia, 4; St. Louis, 12. HP—By Scheib (Young). U—Duffy, Grieve, Passarella and Napp. T—2:09. A—2,473.

Baltimore Hosts an All-Star Win
for the American League as O'Dell Saves the Day

July 8, 1958—At Memorial Stadium, Baltimore

NATIONALS

	AB	R	H	PO	A	E
Mays (Giants), CF	4	2	1	1	0	0
Skinner (Pirates), LF	3	0	1	2	0	0
(g)Walls (Cubs), LF	1	0	0	0	0	0
Musial (Cardinals), 1B	4	1	1	7	0	0
Aaron (Braves), RF	2	0	0	2	0	0
Banks (Cubs), SS	3	0	0	2	3	1
Thomas (Pirates), 3B	3	0	1	1	3	1
Mazeroski (Pirates), 2B	4	0	0	4	5	0
Crandall (Braves), C	4	0	0	5	0	0
Spahn (Braves), P	0	0	0	0	1	0
(a)Blasingame (Cards)	1	0	0	0	0	0
Friend (Pirates), P	0	0	0	0	0	0
Jackson (Cardinals), P	0	0	0	0	0	0
(f)Logan (Braves)	1	0	0	0	0	0
Farrell (Phillies), P	0	0	0	0	0	0
Totals	30	3	4	24	12	2

AMERICANS

	AB	R	H	PO	A	E
Fox (White Sox), 2B	4	1	2	5	3	1
Mantle (Yankees), CF	2	0	1	3	0	0
Jensen (Red Sox), RF	4	0	1	0	0	0
Cerv (Athletics), LF	2	0	0	4	0	0
O'Dell (Orioles), P	0	0	0	0	0	0
Skowron (Yankees), 1B	4	0	0	9	0	0
Malzone (Red Sox), 3B	4	1	1	0	2	0
Triandos (Athletics), C	2	0	1	1	0	1
(c)Berra (Yankees), C	2	0	0	3	0	0
Aparicio (White Sox), SS	2	1	0	1	1	0
(d)Williams (Red Sox), LF	2	0	0	1	0	0
Kaline (Tigers), LF	0	0	0	0	0	0
Turley (Yankees), P	0	0	0	0	0	0
Narleski (Indians), P	1	0	1	0	0	0
(b)Vernon (Indians)	1	1	1	0	0	0
Wynn (White Sox), P	0	0	0	0	0	0
(e)McDougald (Yankees), SS	1	0	1	0	3	0
Totals	31	4	9	27	9	2

National League	2 1 0 0 0 0 0 0 0—3
American League	1 1 0 0 1 1 0 0 0—4

Memorable Box Scores (continued)

Pitching Summary

NATIONAL LEAGUE	IP	H	R	ER	BB	SO
Spahn	3	5	2	1	0	0
Friend (L)	2⅓	4	2	1	2	0
Jackson	⅔	0	0	0	0	0
Farrell	2	0	0	0	1	4

AMERICAN LEAGUE	IP	H	R	ER	BB	SO
Turley	1⅔	3	3	3	2	0
Narleski	3⅓	1	0	0	1	0
Wynn (W)	1	0	0	0	0	0
O'Dell	3	0	0	0	0	2

(a)Flied out for Spahn in fourth. (b)Singled for Narleski in fifth. (c)Popped out for Triandos in sixth. (d)Safe on error for Aparicio in sixth. (e)Singled for Wynn in sixth. (f)Flied out for Jackson in seventh. (g)Grounded out for Skinner in seventh. Runs batted in—Skinner, Aaron, Fox, Jensen, McDougald. Sacrifice hit—O'Dell. Sacrifice fly—Aaron. Stolen base—Mays. Double plays—Thomas, Mazeroski, and Musial; Malzone, Fox, and Skowron; Banks, Mazeroski, and Musial 2. Hit by pitcher—By Turley (Banks). Wild pitch—Turley. Left on bases—Nationals 5, Americans 7.

Managers: Casey Stengel, New York (AL); Fred Haney, Milwaukee (NL).

Umpires—Rommel, McKinley, and Umont (AL), Gorman, Conlan, and Secory (NL). Time—2:13. Attendance—48,829.

Hoyt Wilhelm Pitches the First No-Hitter in Baltimore History

Sept. 20, 1958—New York at Baltimore

NEW YORK

	AB	R	H	TB	PO	A	E
Bauer, RF	4	0	0	0	4	0	0
Lumpe, SS	2	0	0	0	3	2	0
Mantle, CF	3	0	0	0	2	0	0
Skowron, 3B	3	0	0	0	0	1	1
Siebern, LF	3	0	0	0	4	1	0
Howard, C	3	0	0	0	6	0	0
Throneberry, 1B	2	0	0	0	3	0	0
*Berra, 1B	1	0	0	0	1	0	0
Richardson, 2B	2	0	0	0	1	1	0
Larsen, P	2	0	0	0	0	0	0
Shantz, P	0	0	0	0	0	0	0
†Slaughter	1	0	0	0	0	0	0
Totals	26	0	0	0	24	5	1

BALTIMORE

	AB	R	H	TB	PO	A	E
Williams, 3B–LF	4	0	1	2	1	0	0
Boyd, 1B	4	0	1	1	6	0	0
Woodling, RF	2	0	0	0	2	0	0
Busby, CF	1	0	1	1	1	0	0
Nieman, LF	3	0	0	0	2	0	0
Robinson, 3B	1	0	0	0	0	0	0
Triandos, C	3	1	1	4	8	2	0
Tasby, CF–RF	3	0	0	0	4	0	0
Gardner, 2B	3	0	0	0	2	2	0
Castleman, SS	2	0	1	1	1	1	0
Miranda, SS	0	0	0	0	0	0	0
Wilhelm, P	3	0	0	0	0	2	0
Totals	29	1	5	9	27	7	0

* Grounded out for Throneberry in eighth.
† Flied out for Shantz in ninth.

New York	0 0 0 0 0 0 0 0 0—0
Baltimore	0 0 0 0 0 0 1 0 x—1

Run batted in—Triandos. Two-base hit—Williams. Homerun—Triandos. Left on bases—New York 1, Baltimore 6. Bases on balls—Off Wilhelm 2 (Richardson, Lumpe), off Larsen 2 (Castleman, Woodling). Struck out—By Wilhelm 8 (Bauer 2, Howard 2, Lumpe, Mantle, Siebern, Throneberry), by Larsen 2 (Nieman, Tasby), by Shantz 2 (Tasby, Boyd). Hits—Off Larsen 1 in 6 innings, off Shantz 4 in 2 innings. Runs and earned runs—Larsen 0-0, Shantz 1-1. Passed ball—Triandos. Winning pitcher—Wilhelm (3-10). Losing pitcher—Shantz (7-6). Umpires—Paparella, Chylak, Tabacchi and Stewart. Time of game—1:48. Attendance—18,192 (10,941 paid).

199

Barber and Miller Combine for No-Hitter but Still Lose to Tigers

April 30, 1967—Detroit at Baltimore

DETROIT

	AB	R	H	RBI
McAuliffe, 2B	3	0	0	0
Horton, PH	1	0	0	0
Lumpe, 2B	0	0	0	0
Stanley, CF	2	0	0	0
Wert, 2B	3	0	0	0
Kaline, RF	4	0	0	0
Northrup, LF	4	0	0	0
Freehan, C	1	0	0	0
Cash, 1B	1	0	0	0
Tracewski, PH-SS	0	1	0	0
Oyler, SS	2	0	0	0
Wood, PH-1B	0	1	0	0
Wilson, P	3	0	0	0
Gladding, P	0	0	0	0
Totals	24	2	0	0

BALTIMORE

	AB	R	H	RBI
Aparicio, SS	3	0	0	1
Snyder, CF	4	0	0	0
F. Robinson, RF	4	0	1	0
B. Robinson, 3B	3	0	0	0
Epstein, 1B	4	0	0	0
Blefary, LF	2	1	0	0
Held, 2B	2	0	0	0
Haney, C	0	0	0	0
Etchebarren, C	2	0	1	0
Lau, PH	0	0	0	0
Belanger, 2B	0	0	0	0
Barber, P	1	0	0	0
S. Miller, P	0	0	0	0
Totals	25	1	2	1

```
Detroit      0 0 0   0 0 0   0 0 2—2
Baltimore    0 0 0   0 0 0   0 1 0—1
```

DETROIT

	IP	H	R	ER	BB	SO
Wilson (W, 2-2)	8	2	1	1	4	4
Gladding (Save 2)	1	0	0	0	0	1

BALTIMORE

	IP	H	R	ER	BB	SO
Barber (L, 2-1)	8⅔	0	2	1	10	3
S. Miller	⅓	0	0	0	0	0

Memorable Box Scores (continued)

E—Kaline, Belanger, Barber. DP—Detroit 1. Baltimore 1. LOB—Detroit 11, Baltimore 4. SB—Freehan, F. Robinson. SH—Cash, Oyler, Wilson, Barber, Held. SF—Aparicio. HBP—By Barber (McAuliffe, Freehan). WP—Barber. U—Stevens, Stewart, Valentine and Springstead. T—2:38. A—26,884.

Baltimore Native Tom Phoebus No-Hits the Red Sox

April 27, 1968—Boston at Baltimore

BOSTON

	AB	R	H	RBI
Andrews, 2B	2	0	0	0
Jones, 2B	2	0	0	0
Foy, 3B	3	0	0	0
Yastremski, LF	2	0	0	0
Smith, CF	3	0	0	0
Lahoud, RF	3	0	0	0
Scott, 1B	3	0	0	0
Petrocelli SS	3	0	0	0
Howard, C	1	0	0	0
Oliver, C	1	0	0	0
Waslewski, P	1	0	0	0
Tartabull, PH	1	0	0	0
Roggenburk, P	0	0	0	0
Siebern, PH	1	0	0	0
Totals	26	0	0	0

BALTIMORE

	AB	R	H	RBI
Blair, CF	5	1	1	0
Motton, LF	4	1	1	0
Blefary, C	3	1	1	0
B. Robinson, 3B	3	1	1	3
Powell, 1B	3	0	1	0
Johnson, 2B	4	1	3	2
May, RF	4	0	0	0
Belanger, SS	4	0	0	0
Phoebus, P	4	1	2	1
Totals	34	6	10	6

Boston	000 000 000—0
Baltimore	004 010 01x—6

BOSTON

	IP	H	R	ER	BB	SO
Waslewski (L, 2-1)	5	8	5	1	2	3
Roggenburk	3	2	1	1	0	1

BALTIMORE

	IP	H	R	ER	BB	SO
Phoebus (W, 3-1)	9	0	0	0	3	9

E—Scott, Petrocelli. DP—Boston 1. LOB—Boston 2, Baltimore 7. 2B—B. Robinson, Johnson. SH—Blefary. WP—Phoebus, Waslewski 2. U—Honochick, Umont, Valentine and Ashford. T—2:26. A—3,147.

Oriole Ace Jim Palmer No-Hits Oakland in '69 Home Game

August 13, 1969—Oakland at Baltimore

OAKLAND

	AB	R	H	RBI	E
Campaneris, SS	4	0	0	0	0
Tartabull, CF	4	0	0	0	0
Jackson, RF	1	0	0	0	0
Bando, 3B	4	0	0	0	0
Cater, 1B	4	0	0	0	0
Green, 2B	2	0	0	0	0
Reynolds, LF	3	0	0	0	0
Duncan, C	2	0	0	0	0
Kubiak, PH	1	0	0	0	0
Haney, C	1	0	0	0	0
Dobson, P	1	0	0	0	0
Webster, PH	1	0	0	0	0
Blue, P	0	0	0	0	0
Lauzerique, P	0	0	0	0	0
Johnson, PH	1	0	0	0	0
Roland, P	0	0	0	0	0
Totals	29	0	0	0	0

BALTIMORE

	AB	R	H	RBI	E
Buford, 2B	4	2	3	2	0
Blair, CF	4	0	0	1	1
F. Robinson, RF	4	1	1	1	0
Powell, 1B	4	1	1	0	0
B. Robinson, 3B	4	1	1	3	0
Hendricks, C	2	1	1	0	0
Rettenmund, LF	3	1	0	0	0
Floyd, SS	2	0	1	0	1
Palmer, P	3	1	2	1	0
Totals	30	8	10	8	2

Oakland	0 0 0 0 0 0 0 0 0—0
Baltimore	1 0 0 2 0 0 5 0 x—8

OAKLAND

	IP	H	R	ER	BB	SO
Dobson (L, 13-9)	4	6	3	3	4	3
Blue	2⅓	3	4	4	1	3
Lauzerique	⅔	1	1	1	2	0
Roland	1	0	0	0	0	0

BALTIMORE

	IP	H	R	ER	BB	SO
Palmer (W, 11-2)	9	0	0	0	6	3

Double play—Oakland 1. Left on bases—Oakland 8, Baltimore 7. Two-base hit—Palmer. Three-base hit—Buford. Home run—B. Robinson. Stolen base—Buford. Sacrifice hit—Floyd. Sacrifice fly—Blair. Umpires—DiMuro, Neudecker, Chylak and O'Donnell. Time of game—2:22. Attendance—16,826.